Mometrix
TEST PREPARATION

Virginia SOL Grade 7 Secrets Study Guide

I0894334

Dear Future Exam Success Story

First of all, **THANK YOU** for purchasing Mometrix study materials!

Second, congratulations! You are one of the few determined test-takers who are committed to doing whatever it takes to excel on your exam. **You have come to the right place.** We developed these study materials with one goal in mind: to deliver you the information you need in a format that's concise and easy to use.

In addition to optimizing your guide for the content of the test, we've outlined our recommended steps for breaking down the preparation process into small, attainable goals so you can make sure you stay on track.

We've also analyzed the entire test-taking process, identifying the most common pitfalls and showing how you can overcome them and be ready for any curveball the test throws you.

Standardized testing is one of the biggest obstacles on your road to success, which only increases the importance of doing well in the high-pressure, high-stakes environment of test day. Your results on this test could have a significant impact on your future, and this guide provides the information and practical advice to help you achieve your full potential on test day.

Your success is our success

We would love to hear from you! If you would like to share the story of your exam success or if you have any questions or comments in regard to our products, please contact us at **800-673-8175** or **support@mometrix.com**.

Thanks again for your business and we wish you continued success!

Sincerely,
The Mometrix Test Preparation Team

Written and edited by the Mometrix Exam Secrets Test Prep Team
Printed in the United States of America

Table of Contents

Introduction

Thank you for purchasing this resource! You have made the choice to prepare yourself for a test that could have a huge impact on your future, and this guide is designed to help you be fully ready for test day. Obviously, it's important to have a solid understanding of the test material, but you also need to be prepared for the unique environment and stressors of the test, so that you can perform to the best of your abilities.

For this purpose, the first section that appears in this guide is the **Secret Keys**. We've devoted countless hours to meticulously researching what works and what doesn't, and we've boiled down our findings to the five most impactful steps you can take to improve your performance on the test. We start at the beginning with study planning and move through the preparation process, all the way to the testing strategies that will help you get the most out of what you know when you're finally sitting in front of the test.

We recommend that you start preparing for your test as far in advance as possible. However, if you've bought this guide as a last-minute study resource and only have a few days before your test, we recommend that you skip over the first two Secret Keys since they address a long-term study plan.

If you struggle with **test anxiety**, we strongly encourage you to check out our recommendations for how you can overcome it. Test anxiety is a formidable foe, but it can be beaten, and we want to make sure you have the tools you need to defeat it.

Secret Key #1 – Plan Big, Study Small

There's a lot riding on your performance. If you want to ace this test, you're going to need to keep your skills sharp and the material fresh in your mind. You need a plan that lets you review everything you need to know while still fitting in your schedule. We'll break this strategy down into three categories.

Information Organization

Start with the information you already have: the official test outline. From this, you can make a complete list of all the concepts you need to cover before the test. Organize these concepts into groups that can be studied together, and create a list of any related vocabulary you need to learn so you can brush up on any difficult terms. You'll want to keep this vocabulary list handy once you actually start studying since you may need to add to it along the way.

Time Management

Once you have your set of study concepts, decide how to spread them out over the time you have left before the test. Break your study plan into small, clear goals so you have a manageable task for each day and know exactly what you're doing. Then just focus on one small step at a time. When you manage your time this way, you don't need to spend hours at a time studying. Studying a small block of content for a short period each day helps you retain information better and avoid stressing over how much you have left to do. You can relax knowing that you have a plan to cover everything in time. In order for this strategy to be effective though, you have to start studying early and stick to your schedule. Avoid the exhaustion and futility that comes from last-minute cramming!

Study Environment

The environment you study in has a big impact on your learning. Studying in a coffee shop, while probably more enjoyable, is not likely to be as fruitful as studying in a quiet room. It's important to keep distractions to a minimum. You're only planning to study for a short block of time, so make the most of it. Don't pause to check your phone or get up to find a snack. It's also important to **avoid multitasking**. Research has consistently shown that multitasking will make your studying dramatically less effective. Your study area should also be comfortable and well-lit so you don't have the distraction of straining your eyes or sitting on an uncomfortable chair.

The time of day you study is also important. You want to be rested and alert. Don't wait until just before bedtime. Study when you'll be most likely to comprehend and remember. Even better, if you know what time of day your test will be, set that time aside for study. That way your brain will be used to working on that subject at that specific time and you'll have a better chance of recalling information.

Finally, it can be helpful to team up with others who are studying for the same test. Your actual studying should be done in as isolated an environment as possible, but the work of organizing the information and setting up the study plan can be divided up. In between study sessions, you can discuss with your teammates the concepts that you're all studying and quiz each other on the details. Just be sure that your teammates are as serious about the test as you are. If you find that your study time is being replaced with social time, you might need to find a new team.

Secret Key #2 – Make Your Studying Count

You're devoting a lot of time and effort to preparing for this test, so you want to be absolutely certain it will pay off. This means doing more than just reading the content and hoping you can remember it on test day. It's important to make every minute of study count. There are two main areas you can focus on to make your studying count.

Retention

It doesn't matter how much time you study if you can't remember the material. You need to make sure you are retaining the concepts. To check your retention of the information you're learning, try recalling it at later times with minimal prompting. Try carrying around flashcards and glance at one or two from time to time or ask a friend who's also studying for the test to quiz you.

To enhance your retention, look for ways to put the information into practice so that you can apply it rather than simply recalling it. If you're using the information in practical ways, it will be much easier to remember. Similarly, it helps to solidify a concept in your mind if you're not only reading it to yourself but also explaining it to someone else. Ask a friend to let you teach them about a concept you're a little shaky on (or speak aloud to an imaginary audience if necessary). As you try to summarize, define, give examples, and answer your friend's questions, you'll understand the concepts better and they will stay with you longer. Finally, step back for a big picture view and ask yourself how each piece of information fits with the whole subject. When you link the different concepts together and see them working together as a whole, it's easier to remember the individual components.

Finally, practice showing your work on any multi-step problems, even if you're just studying. Writing out each step you take to solve a problem will help solidify the process in your mind, and you'll be more likely to remember it during the test.

Modality

Modality simply refers to the means or method by which you study. Choosing a study modality that fits your own individual learning style is crucial. No two people learn best in exactly the same way, so it's important to know your strengths and use them to your advantage.

For example, if you learn best by visualization, focus on visualizing a concept in your mind and draw an image or a diagram. Try color-coding your notes, illustrating them, or creating symbols that will trigger your mind to recall a learned concept. If you learn best by hearing or discussing information, find a study partner who learns the same way or read aloud to yourself. Think about how to put the information in your own words. Imagine that you are giving a lecture on the topic and record yourself so you can listen to it later.

For any learning style, flashcards can be helpful. Organize the information so you can take advantage of spare moments to review. Underline key words or phrases. Use different colors for different categories. Mnemonic devices (such as creating a short list in which every item starts with the same letter) can also help with retention. Find what works best for you and use it to store the information in your mind most effectively and easily.

Secret Key #3 – Practice the Right Way

Your success on test day depends not only on how many hours you put into preparing, but also on whether you prepared the right way. It's good to check along the way to see if your studying is paying off. One of the most effective ways to do this is by taking practice tests to evaluate your progress. Practice tests are useful because they show exactly where you need to improve. Every time you take a practice test, pay special attention to these three groups of questions:

- The questions you got wrong
- The questions you had to guess on, even if you guessed right
- The questions you found difficult or slow to work through

This will show you exactly what your weak areas are, and where you need to devote more study time. Ask yourself why each of these questions gave you trouble. Was it because you didn't understand the material? Was it because you didn't remember the vocabulary? Do you need more repetitions on this type of question to build speed and confidence? Dig into those questions and figure out how you can strengthen your weak areas as you go back to review the material.

Additionally, many practice tests have a section explaining the answer choices. It can be tempting to read the explanation and think that you now have a good understanding of the concept. However, an explanation likely only covers part of the question's broader context. Even if the explanation makes perfect sense, **go back and investigate** every concept related to the question until you're positive you have a thorough understanding.

As you go along, keep in mind that the practice test is just that: practice. Memorizing these questions and answers will not be very helpful on the actual test because it is unlikely to have any of the same exact questions. If you only know the right answers to the sample questions, you won't be prepared for the real thing. **Study the concepts** until you understand them fully, and then you'll be able to answer any question that shows up on the test.

It's important to wait on the practice tests until you're ready. If you take a test on your first day of study, you may be overwhelmed by the amount of material covered and how much you need to learn. Work up to it gradually.

On test day, you'll need to be prepared for answering questions, managing your time, and using the test-taking strategies you've learned. It's a lot to balance, like a mental marathon that will have a big impact on your future. Like training for a marathon, you'll need to start slowly and work your way up. When test day arrives, you'll be ready.

Start with the strategies you've read in the first two Secret Keys—plan your course and study in the way that works best for you. If you have time, consider using multiple study resources to get different approaches to the same concepts. It can be helpful to see difficult concepts from more than one angle. Then find a good source for practice tests. Many times, the test website will suggest potential study resources or provide sample tests.

Practice Test Strategy

If you're able to find at least three practice tests, we recommend this strategy:

Untimed and Open-Book Practice

Take the first test with no time constraints and with your notes and study guide handy. Take your time and focus on applying the strategies you've learned.

TIMED AND OPEN-BOOK PRACTICE

Take the second practice test open-book as well, but set a timer and practice pacing yourself to finish in time.

TIMED AND CLOSED-BOOK PRACTICE

Take any other practice tests as if it were test day. Set a timer and put away your study materials. Sit at a table or desk in a quiet room, imagine yourself at the testing center, and answer questions as quickly and accurately as possible.

Keep repeating timed and closed-book tests on a regular basis until you run out of practice tests or it's time for the actual test. Your mind will be ready for the schedule and stress of test day, and you'll be able to focus on recalling the material you've learned.

Secret Key #4 – Pace Yourself

Once you're fully prepared for the material on the test, your biggest challenge on test day will be managing your time. Just knowing that the clock is ticking can make you panic even if you have plenty of time left. Work on pacing yourself so you can build confidence against the time constraints of the exam. Pacing is a difficult skill to master, especially in a high-pressure environment, so **practice is vital**.

Set time expectations for your pace based on how much time is available. For example, if a section has 60 questions and the time limit is 30 minutes, you know you have to average 30 seconds or less per question in order to answer them all. Although 30 seconds is the hard limit, set 25 seconds per question as your goal, so you reserve extra time to spend on harder questions. When you budget extra time for the harder questions, you no longer have any reason to stress when those questions take longer to answer.

Don't let this time expectation distract you from working through the test at a calm, steady pace, but keep it in mind so you don't spend too much time on any one question. Recognize that taking extra time on one question you don't understand may keep you from answering two that you do understand later in the test. If your time limit for a question is up and you're still not sure of the answer, mark it and move on, and come back to it later if the time and the test format allow. If the testing format doesn't allow you to return to earlier questions, just make an educated guess; then put it out of your mind and move on.

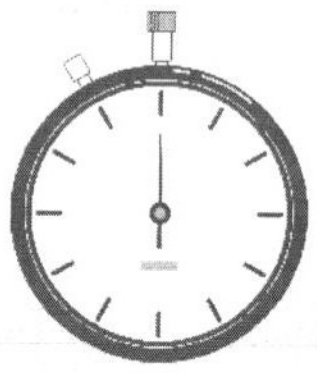

On the easier questions, be careful not to rush. It may seem wise to hurry through them so you have more time for the challenging ones, but it's not worth missing one if you know the concept and just didn't take the time to read the question fully. Work efficiently but make sure you understand the question and have looked at all of the answer choices, since more than one may seem right at first.

Even if you're paying attention to the time, you may find yourself a little behind at some point. You should speed up to get back on track, but do so wisely. Don't panic; just take a few seconds less on each question until you're caught up. Don't guess without thinking, but do look through the answer choices and eliminate any you know are wrong. If you can get down to two choices, it is often worthwhile to guess from those. Once you've chosen an answer, move on and don't dwell on any that you skipped or had to hurry through. If a question was taking too long, chances are it was one of the harder ones, so you weren't as likely to get it right anyway.

On the other hand, if you find yourself getting ahead of schedule, it may be beneficial to slow down a little. The more quickly you work, the more likely you are to make a careless mistake that will affect your score. You've budgeted time for each question, so don't be afraid to spend that time. Practice an efficient but careful pace to get the most out of the time you have.

Secret Key #5 – Have a Plan for Guessing

When you're taking the test, you may find yourself stuck on a question. Some of the answer choices seem better than others, but you don't see the one answer choice that is obviously correct. What do you do?

The scenario described above is very common, yet most test takers have not effectively prepared for it. Developing and practicing a plan for guessing may be one of the single most effective uses of your time as you get ready for the exam.

In developing your plan for guessing, there are three questions to address:

- When should you start the guessing process?
- How should you narrow down the choices?
- Which answer should you choose?

When to Start the Guessing Process

Unless your plan for guessing is to select C every time (which, despite its merits, is not what we recommend), you need to leave yourself enough time to apply your answer elimination strategies. Since you have a limited amount of time for each question, that means that if you're going to give yourself the best shot at guessing correctly, you have to decide quickly whether or not you will guess.

Of course, the best-case scenario is that you don't have to guess at all, so first, see if you can answer the question based on your knowledge of the subject and basic reasoning skills. Focus on the key words in the question and try to jog your memory of related topics. Give yourself a chance to bring the knowledge to mind, but once you realize that you don't have (or you can't access) the knowledge you need to answer the question, it's time to start the guessing process.

It's almost always better to start the guessing process too early than too late. It only takes a few seconds to remember something and answer the question from knowledge. Carefully eliminating wrong answer choices takes longer. Plus, going through the process of eliminating answer choices can actually help jog your memory.

Summary: Start the guessing process as soon as you decide that you can't answer the question based on your knowledge.

How to Narrow Down the Choices

The next chapter in this book (**Test-Taking Strategies**) includes a wide range of strategies for how to approach questions and how to look for answer choices to eliminate. You will definitely want to read those carefully, practice them, and figure out which ones work best for you. Here though, we're going to address a mindset rather than a particular strategy.

Your odds of guessing an answer correctly depend on how many options you are choosing from.

Number of options left	5	4	3	2	1
Odds of guessing correctly	20%	25%	33%	50%	100%

You can see from this chart just how valuable it is to be able to eliminate incorrect answers and make an educated guess, but there are two things that many test takers do that cause them to miss out on the benefits of guessing:

- Accidentally eliminating the correct answer
- Selecting an answer based on an impression

We'll look at the first one here, and the second one in the next section.

To avoid accidentally eliminating the correct answer, we recommend a thought exercise called **the $5 challenge**. In this challenge, you only eliminate an answer choice from contention if you are willing to bet $5 on it being wrong. Why $5? Five dollars is a small but not insignificant amount of money. It's an amount you could afford to lose but wouldn't want to throw away. And while losing $5 once might not hurt too much, doing it twenty times will set you back $100. In the same way, each small decision you make—eliminating a choice here, guessing on a question there—won't by itself impact your score very much, but when you put them all together, they can make a big difference. By holding each answer choice elimination decision to a higher standard, you can reduce the risk of accidentally eliminating the correct answer.

The $5 challenge can also be applied in a positive sense: If you are willing to bet $5 that an answer choice *is* correct, go ahead and mark it as correct.

Summary: Only eliminate an answer choice if you are willing to bet $5 that it is wrong.

Which Answer to Choose

You're taking the test. You've run into a hard question and decided you'll have to guess. You've eliminated all the answer choices you're willing to bet $5 on. Now you have to pick an answer. Why do we even need to talk about this? Why can't you just pick whichever one you feel like when the time comes?

The answer to these questions is that if you don't come into the test with a plan, you'll rely on your impression to select an answer choice, and if you do that, you risk falling into a trap. The test writers know that everyone who takes their test will be guessing on some of the questions, so they intentionally write wrong answer choices to seem plausible. You still have to pick an answer though, and if the wrong answer choices are designed to look right, how can you ever be sure that you're not falling for their trap? The best solution we've found to this dilemma is to take the decision out of your hands entirely. Here is the process we recommend:

Once you've eliminated any choices that you are confident (willing to bet $5) are wrong, select the first remaining choice as your answer.

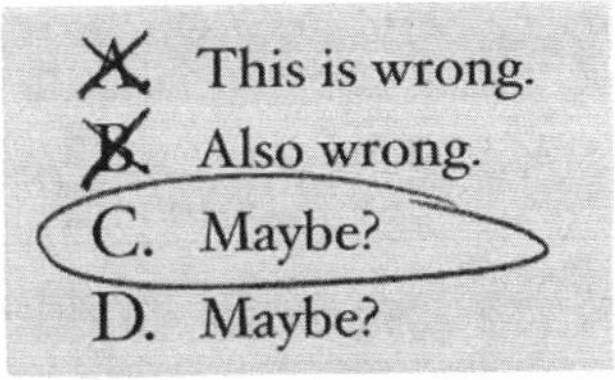

Whether you choose to select the first remaining choice, the second, or the last, the important thing is that you use some preselected standard. Using this approach guarantees that you will not be enticed into selecting an answer choice that looks right, because you are not basing your decision on how the answer choices look.

This is not meant to make you question your knowledge. Instead, it is to help you recognize the difference between your knowledge and your impressions. There's a huge difference between thinking an answer is right because of what you know, and thinking an answer is right because it looks or sounds like it should be right.

Summary: To ensure that your selection is appropriately random, make a predetermined selection from among all answer choices you have not eliminated.

Test-Taking Strategies

This section contains a list of test-taking strategies that you may find helpful as you work through the test. By taking what you know and applying logical thought, you can maximize your chances of answering any question correctly!

It is very important to realize that every question is different and every person is different: no single strategy will work on every question, and no single strategy will work for every person. That's why we've included all of them here, so you can try them out and determine which ones work best for different types of questions and which ones work best for you.

Question Strategies

⊘ Read Carefully

Read the question and the answer choices carefully. Don't miss the question because you misread the terms. You have plenty of time to read each question thoroughly and make sure you understand what is being asked. Yet a happy medium must be attained, so don't waste too much time. You must read carefully and efficiently.

⊘ Contextual Clues

Look for contextual clues. If the question includes a word you are not familiar with, look at the immediate context for some indication of what the word might mean. Contextual clues can often give you all the information you need to decipher the meaning of an unfamiliar word. Even if you can't determine the meaning, you may be able to narrow down the possibilities enough to make a solid guess at the answer to the question.

⊘ Prefixes

If you're having trouble with a word in the question or answer choices, try dissecting it. Take advantage of every clue that the word might include. Prefixes can be a huge help. Usually, they allow you to determine a basic meaning. *Pre-* means before, *post-* means after, *pro-* is positive, *de-* is negative. From prefixes, you can get an idea of the general meaning of the word and try to put it into context.

⊘ Hedge Words

Watch out for critical hedge words, such as *likely, may, can, often, almost, mostly, usually, generally, rarely*, and *sometimes*. Question writers insert these hedge phrases to cover every possibility. Often an answer choice will be wrong simply because it leaves no room for exception. Be on guard for answer choices that have definitive words such as *exactly* and *always*.

⊘ Switchback Words

Stay alert for *switchbacks*. These are the words and phrases frequently used to alert you to shifts in thought. The most common switchback words are *but, although*, and *however*. Others include *nevertheless, on the other hand, even though, while, in spite of, despite*, and *regardless of*. Switchback words are important to catch because they can change the direction of the question or an answer choice.

⊘ Face Value

When in doubt, use common sense. Accept the situation in the problem at face value. Don't read too much into it. These problems will not require you to make wild assumptions. If you have to go beyond creativity and warp time or space in order to have an answer choice fit the question, then you should move on and consider the other answer choices. These are normal problems rooted in reality. The applicable relationship or explanation may not be readily apparent, but it is there for you to figure out. Use your common sense to interpret anything that isn't clear.

Answer Choice Strategies

⊘ Answer Selection

The most thorough way to pick an answer choice is to identify and eliminate wrong answers until only one is left, then confirm it is the correct answer. Sometimes an answer choice may immediately seem right, but be careful. The test writers will usually put more than one reasonable answer choice on each question, so take a second to read all of them and make sure that the other choices are not equally obvious. As long as you have time left, it is better to read every answer choice than to pick the first one that looks right without checking the others.

⊘ Answer Choice Families

An answer choice family consists of two (in rare cases, three) answer choices that are very similar in construction and cannot all be true at the same time. If you see two answer choices that are direct opposites or parallels, one of them is usually the correct answer. For instance, if one answer choice says that quantity x increases and another either says that quantity x decreases (opposite) or says that quantity y increases (parallel), then those answer choices would fall into the same family. An answer choice that doesn't match the construction of the answer choice family is more likely to be incorrect. Most questions will not have answer choice families, but when they do appear, you should be prepared to recognize them.

⊘ Eliminate Answers

Eliminate answer choices as soon as you realize they are wrong, but make sure you consider all possibilities. If you are eliminating answer choices and realize that the last one you are left with is also wrong, don't panic. Start over and consider each choice again. There may be something you missed the first time that you will realize on the second pass.

⊘ Avoid Fact Traps

Don't be distracted by an answer choice that is factually true but doesn't answer the question. You are looking for the choice that answers the question. Stay focused on what the question is asking for so you don't accidentally pick an answer that is true but incorrect. Always go back to the question and make sure the answer choice you've selected actually answers the question and is not merely a true statement.

⊘ Extreme Statements

In general, you should avoid answers that put forth extreme actions as standard practice or proclaim controversial ideas as established fact. An answer choice that states the "process should be used in certain situations, if..." is much more likely to be correct than one that states the "process should be discontinued completely." The first is a calm rational statement and doesn't even make a definitive, uncompromising stance, using a hedge word *if* to provide wiggle room, whereas the second choice is far more extreme.

⊘ Benchmark

As you read through the answer choices and you come across one that seems to answer the question well, mentally select that answer choice. This is not your final answer, but it's the one that will help you evaluate the other answer choices. The one that you selected is your benchmark or standard for judging each of the other answer choices. Every other answer choice must be compared to your benchmark. That choice is correct until proven otherwise by another answer choice beating it. If you find a better answer, then that one becomes your new benchmark. Once you've decided that no other choice answers the question as well as your benchmark, you have your final answer.

⊘ Predict the Answer

Before you even start looking at the answer choices, it is often best to try to predict the answer. When you come up with the answer on your own, it is easier to avoid distractions and traps because you will know exactly what to look for. The right answer choice is unlikely to be word-for-word what you came up with, but it should be a close match. Even if you are confident that you have the right answer, you should still take the time to read each option before moving on.

General Strategies

☑ Tough Questions

If you are stumped on a problem or it appears too hard or too difficult, don't waste time. Move on! Remember though, if you can quickly check for obviously incorrect answer choices, your chances of guessing correctly are greatly improved. Before you completely give up, at least try to knock out a couple of possible answers. Eliminate what you can and then guess at the remaining answer choices before moving on.

☑ Check Your Work

Since you will probably not know every term listed and the answer to every question, it is important that you get credit for the ones that you do know. Don't miss any questions through careless mistakes. If at all possible, try to take a second to look back over your answer selection and make sure you've selected the correct answer choice and haven't made a costly careless mistake (such as marking an answer choice that you didn't mean to mark). This quick double check should more than pay for itself in caught mistakes for the time it costs.

☑ Pace Yourself

It's easy to be overwhelmed when you're looking at a page full of questions; your mind is confused and full of random thoughts, and the clock is ticking down faster than you would like. Calm down and maintain the pace that you have set for yourself. Especially as you get down to the last few minutes of the test, don't let the small numbers on the clock make you panic. As long as you are on track by monitoring your pace, you are guaranteed to have time for each question.

☑ Don't Rush

It is very easy to make errors when you are in a hurry. Maintaining a fast pace in answering questions is pointless if it makes you miss questions that you would have gotten right otherwise. Test writers like to include distracting information and wrong answers that seem right. Taking a little extra time to avoid careless mistakes can make all the difference in your test score. Find a pace that allows you to be confident in the answers that you select.

☑ Keep Moving

Panicking will not help you pass the test, so do your best to stay calm and keep moving. Taking deep breaths and going through the answer elimination steps you practiced can help to break through a stress barrier and keep your pace.

Final Notes

The combination of a solid foundation of content knowledge and the confidence that comes from practicing your plan for applying that knowledge is the key to maximizing your performance on test day. As your foundation of content knowledge is built up and strengthened, you'll find that the strategies included in this chapter become more and more effective in helping you quickly sift through the distractions and traps of the test to isolate the correct answer.

Now that you're preparing to move forward into the test content chapters of this book, be sure to keep your goal in mind. As you read, think about how you will be able to apply this information on the test. If you've already seen sample questions for the test and you have an idea of the question format and style, try to come up with questions of your own that you can answer based on what you're reading. This will give you valuable practice applying your knowledge in the same ways you can expect to on test day.

Good luck and good studying!

Mathematics

Number, Number Sense, Computation, and Estimation

Rational Numbers

Rational numbers are all numbers that can be written as a fraction. **Rational numbers** include positive numbers, negative numbers, fractions, improper fractions, most decimals, and some repeating decimals. If it can be written as a fraction, it is rational. An example is 6, which can be written as $\frac{6}{1}$. Another example is 0.75, which can be written as $\frac{3}{4}$. A number that is not rational is called an irrational number. An example of an **irrational number** is π, or 3.1415963..., because it is a decimal that continues without a pattern and cannot be written as a fraction.

Rational numbers, integers, whole numbers, and **natural numbers** are four categories used to classify numbers. Rational numbers include all numbers that can be written as a fraction, and these numbers form the broadest category of the four. All integers, whole numbers, and natural numbers can be described as rational numbers.

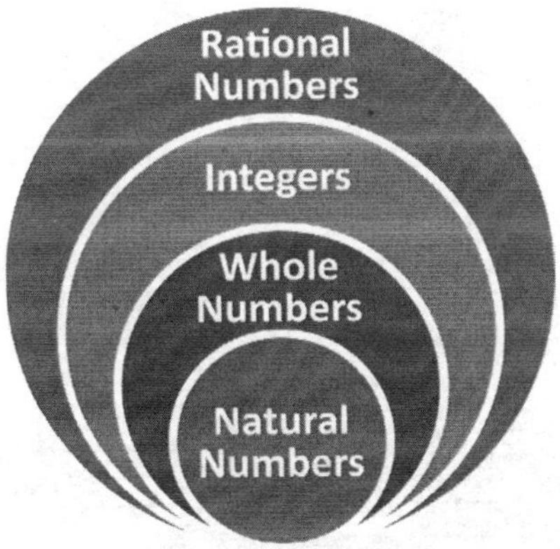

Review Video: Rational and Irrational Numbers
Visit mometrix.com/academy and enter code: 280645

Integers

Integers are a subset of rational numbers, and they include all positive and negative numbers that can be written without a fraction or decimal. Some examples include 7 and –56. All integers are rational numbers, as they can be written as a fraction.

Whole Numbers

Whole numbers are a subset of integers that include all the positive numbers that can be written without a fraction or decimal. 0, 1, 2, 3... to infinity are all whole numbers. All whole numbers can also be described as integers or rational numbers.

NATURAL NUMBERS

Natural numbers are a subset of whole numbers that include all whole numbers greater than zero. This means that zero is a whole number, but not a natural number. All natural numbers can also be described as whole numbers, integers, and rational numbers. Natural numbers form the most specific subset of the number categories.

> **Review Video: Classification of Numbers**
> Visit mometrix.com/academy and enter code: 461071
>
> **Review Video: Ordering Rational Numbers**
> Visit mometrix.com/academy and enter code: 419578

ABSOLUTE VALUE

A precursor to working with negative numbers is understanding what **absolute values** are. A number's absolute value is simply the distance away from zero a number is on the number line. The absolute value of a number is always positive and is written $|x|$. For example, the absolute value of 3, written as $|3|$, is 3 because the distance between 0 and 3 on a number line is three units. Likewise, the absolute value of -3, written as $|-3|$, is 3 because the distance between 0 and -3 on a number line is three units. So $|3| = |-3|$.

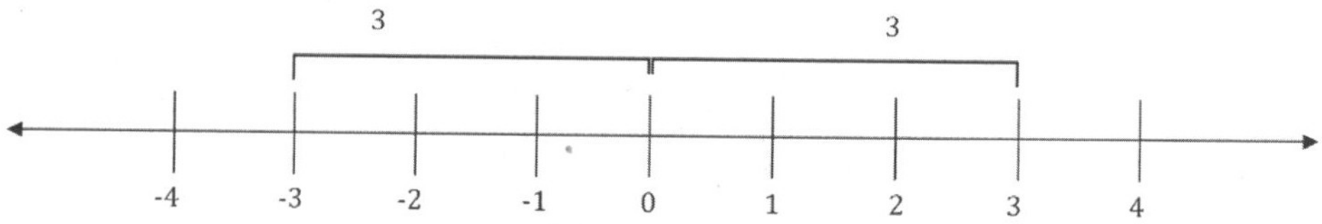

The same is true for negative rational numbers. The absolute value of $-\frac{2}{3}$ is written as $|-\frac{2}{3}|$. Since the distance away from zero on a number line is $\frac{2}{3}$, the $\left|-\frac{2}{3}\right| = \frac{2}{3}$.

> **Review Video: Absolute Value**
> Visit mometrix.com/academy and enter code: 314669

THE FOUR OPERATIONS

It is important to be able to add, subtract, multiply, and divide rational numbers quickly and easily. This includes operations with whole numbers, integers, and rational numbers, including fractions and decimals. When you are solving operations with integers, a common way to get a question wrong is to mix up your signs. There are a few rules that you should remember and practice frequently so you can avoid sign errors.

ADDITION

When you add two positive numbers, your answer will be positive.

$$7 + 32 = 39$$

When you add two negative numbers, your answer will be negative.

$$-7 + (-32) = -39$$

When you add a negative number to a positive number, the total value will be less than the positive number. Adding a negative number is the same as subtracting the positive version of that negative number.

$$\begin{aligned} &= 25 + (-5) \\ &= 25 - 5 \\ &= 20 \end{aligned}$$

When you add a positive number to a negative number, the total value will be greater than the negative number. When adding a positive number to a negative number, use subtraction.

$$
\begin{aligned}
&= -6 + 36 \\
&= 36 + -6 \\
&= 36 - 6 \\
&= 30
\end{aligned}
$$

Subtraction

When you subtract two positive numbers, and the first number is larger, your answer will be positive.

$$24 - 3 = 21$$

When you subtract two positive numbers, and the first number is smaller, your answer will be negative.

$$3 - 24 = -21$$

When you subtract two negative numbers, your answer will be greater than the starting value. Subtracting a negative number is equivalent to adding the number.

$$
\begin{aligned}
-16 - (-4) &= -16 + 4 = -12 \\
-4 - (-16) &= -4 + 16 = 12
\end{aligned}
$$

Example

What is the value of the expression $5\frac{1}{4} + (-12.42)$?

This problem focuses on adding and subtracting rational numbers. To solve this problem, we need to understand operations with positive and negative rational numbers and converting the given values to the same form.

In this problem, you could convert these values to fraction form or decimal form. Decimal form would give numbers that are easier to work with, so converting to decimals would be the best option.

$$5\frac{1}{4} + (-12.42) = 5.25 + (-12.42)$$

Adding a negative number is the same as subtracting its opposite.

$$5.25 + (-12.42) = 5.25 - 12.42$$

The final step is to subtract.

$$5.25 - 12.42 = -7.17$$

The correct answer is -7.17.

Multiplication and Division

When multiplying and dividing positive and negative rational numbers, it is important to remember and practice the rules for integer multiplication and division. Whether the answer will be negative or positive depends on the number of negative numbers in your problem. If the total number of negative signs is even, your answer will be positive. If you have an odd number of negative numbers, your answer will be negative.

When multiplying and dividing two positive numbers, the answer will be positive.

$$5 \cdot 6 = 30$$

$$72 \div 9 = 8$$

When multiplying and dividing two negative numbers, the answer will be positive.

$$-7 \cdot (-3) = 21$$
$$-16 \div (-4) = 4$$

When multiplying or dividing a negative number and a positive number, the answer will be negative.

$$-2 \cdot 8 = -16$$
$$-24 \div 6 = -4$$

Review Video: Mathematical Operations
Visit mometrix.com/academy and enter code: 208095

EXAMPLE

What is the value of the expression $\left(-2\frac{3}{4}\right)(30.2)$?

This problem focuses on multiplying rational numbers. To solve this problem, the first step is to convert these values so they are written in the same form. You may choose to convert these values to fractions or decimals. Your choice depends on which form you feel most comfortable working with.

Strategy 1:

If you choose to convert the values to fractions, converting values to improper fractions makes the numbers easier to multiply. To convert a mixed number to an improper fraction, begin by multiplying the whole number by the denominator of the fraction. Next, add the product to the numerator of the fraction. This value becomes the numerator for the improper fraction. The denominator used in the mixed number will be the denominator used in the improper fraction.

$$-2\frac{3}{4} = -\frac{11}{4}$$

$$30.2 = 30\frac{2}{10} = 30\frac{1}{5} = \frac{151}{5}$$

When multiplying fractions, multiply numerator by the other numerator and the denominator by the other denominator. That is, multiply straight across.

$$-\frac{11}{4} \times \frac{151}{5} = \frac{(-11 \times 151)}{(4 \times 5)} = \frac{-1{,}661}{20}$$

This can also be expressed as the mixed number $-83\frac{1}{20}$.

Strategy 2:

If you choose to convert the values to decimals, the expression $\left(-2\frac{3}{4}\right)(30.2)$ can be converted to $-2.75(30.2)$.

Now you can use multiplication to solve.

$$-2.75 \times 30.2 = -83.05$$

The correct answer is -83.05.

Example

What is the value of the expression $36.75 \div \left(-7\frac{1}{2}\right)$?

This problem focuses on dividing rational numbers. To solve this problem, each value should be converted so they are written in the same form. You may choose to convert these values to fractions or decimals.

Strategy 1:

If you choose to convert the values to fractions, the conversion should be to improper fractions to make the numbers easier to divide.

$$36.75 = 36\frac{3}{4} = \frac{147}{4}$$

$$-7\frac{1}{2} = -\frac{15}{2}$$

When dividing fractions, find the reciprocal of the divisor and multiply.

$$\frac{147}{4} \div \left(-\frac{15}{2}\right) = \frac{147}{4} \times \left(-\frac{2}{15}\right) = \frac{(147 \times (-2))}{(4 \times 15)} = \frac{-294}{60} = -\frac{49}{10}$$

This can also be expressed as a mixed number: $-4\frac{9}{10}$.

Strategy 2:

If you choose to convert the values to decimals, the expression $36.75 \div \left(-7\frac{1}{2}\right)$ can be converted to $36.75 \div (-7.5)$.

Now you can use division to solve.

$$36.75 \div (-7.5) = -4.9$$

The correct answer is –4.9.

Word Problems and the Four Operations

Solving problems using all operations might include answering word problems that involve more than one step or operation. When you encounter a problem that describes a situation, the best way to approach these problems is to identify the information that is known, identify the information that is unknown, and draw a picture.

Example

Theresa is planning a family trip to an amusement park. The total cost of admission is $88.25. There are 3 adults and 7 children going to the amusement park. Children's tickets cost $7.25 each. What is the price of 1 adult ticket?

The first step to solve this problem is by identifying the known and the unknowns. Let's start with what is known. We know that there are 3 adults and 7 children going to the amusement park, we know that children's tickets cost $7.25 each, and we know that the total cost is $88.25.

Now, what is the unknown? In this problem, the unknown is the price of 1 adult's ticket. This is what we need to find. We do not have all the information needed to quickly determine the cost of adult tickets, so there might be a "hidden" unknown.

A picture can be helpful to find out other missing pieces.

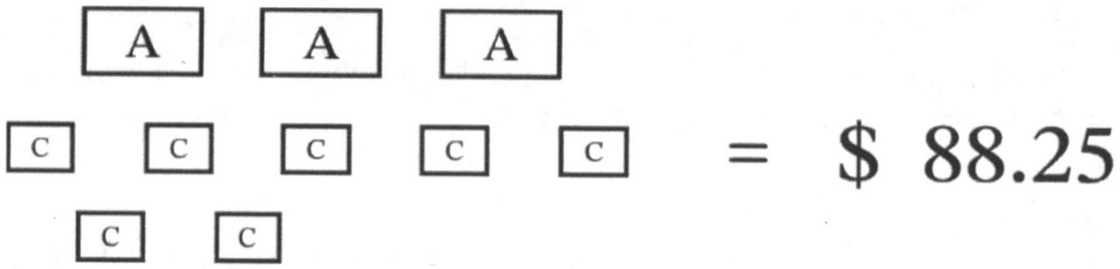

Now, we can see that there are two parts that make the total cost: the total cost of adults' tickets and the total cost of children's tickets. If we can find the total cost of children tickets, we can find the total cost of adult tickets. The total cost of children's tickets is the "hidden" unknown. We have the information to find this value. We know that there are 7 children going and that each child's ticket costs \$7.25 and we can use multiplication to find the total cost.

$$\$7.25 \times 7 = \$50.75$$

If the children's tickets cost a total of \$50.75, then we can use this value to find the total cost of adult's tickets. The total cost of adult's tickets is the difference between the total ticket cost and the total children's ticket cost.

$$\$88.25 - \$50.75 = \$37.50$$

Now we know that the total cost of adult's tickets is \$37.50, but we need to find the cost of 1 adult's ticket. We now have all the information we need. We know the total cost of adult's tickets is \$37.50 and there are 3 adults going to the amusement park. We can use division to solve.

$$\$37.50 \div 3 = \$12.50$$

The cost of 1 adult's ticket is \$12.50.

This problem took multiple steps to complete, but by starting with the knowns and unknowns and drawing a picture, we were able to work through the problem using logical steps.

EXAMPLE

The middle school student council sold cupcakes to raise money. They sold 345 cupcakes.

- $\frac{2}{5}$ of the cupcakes sold were chocolate.
- $\frac{1}{3}$ of the cupcakes sold were red velvet.
- The rest of the cupcakes sold were vanilla.
- Cupcakes were sold for \$3.

How much money did the student council collect by selling vanilla cupcakes?

To solve this problem, we will start with identifying the knowns, identifying the unknowns, and making a table.

We know the total number of cupcakes, we know the fraction of cupcakes that were chocolate and the fraction that were red velvet, and we know that cupcakes were sold for \$3. We want to know how much money was collected from vanilla cupcakes.

$\frac{2}{5}$ chocolate	$\frac{1}{3}$ red velvet	? vanilla

From the table we can see that the hidden unknowns are the number of cupcakes of each flavor that were sold.

There are a couple of ways to approach this problem. One way would be to start by identifying the number of cupcakes in each flavor.

To find the number of chocolate cupcakes, we can multiply the fraction by the total.

$$345 \times \frac{2}{5} = \frac{345}{1} \times \frac{2}{5} = \frac{690}{5} = 690 \div 5 = 138$$

There were 138 chocolate cupcakes sold.

We can use the same strategy to find the number of red velvet cupcakes sold.

$$345 \times \frac{1}{3} = \frac{345}{1} \times \frac{1}{3} = \frac{345}{3} = 115$$

There were 115 red velvet cupcakes sold.

To find the number of vanilla cupcakes sold, we can subtract the number of chocolate and red velvet cupcakes sold from the total number of cupcakes sold.

$$138 + 115 = 253$$

$$345 - 253 = 92$$

There were 92 vanilla cupcakes sold.

Now, we can multiply this value by \$3 to find the total amount of money collected from selling vanilla cupcakes.

$$92 \times \$3 = \$276$$

The middle school student council collected \$276 selling vanilla cupcakes.

EXPONENTS

An **exponent** is a superscript number placed next to another number at the top right. It indicates how many times the base number is to be multiplied by itself. Exponents provide a shorthand way to write what would be a longer mathematical expression, Example: $2^4 = 2 \times 2 \times 2 \times 2$. A number with an exponent of 2 is said to be "squared," while a number with an exponent of 3 is said to be "cubed." The value of a number raised to an exponent is called its power. So 8^4 is read as "8 to the 4th power," or "8 raised to the power of 4."

Review Video: Exponents
Visit mometrix.com/academy and enter code: 600998

A **root**, such as a square root, is another way of writing a fractional exponent. Instead of using a superscript, roots use the radical symbol ($\sqrt{\ }$) to indicate the operation. Nearly all of the roots you encounter will be square roots. A square root is the same as a number raised to the one-half power. When we say that a is the square root of b ($a = \sqrt{b}$), we mean that a multiplied by itself equals b: ($a \times a = b$). A **perfect square** is a number that has an integer for its square root. There are 10 perfect squares from 1 to 100: 1, 4, 9, 16, 25, 36, 49, 64, 81, 100 (the squares of integers 1 through 10).

Review Video: Perfect Squares and Square Roots
Visit mometrix.com/academy and enter code: 648063

Properties of Exponents

The properties of exponents are as follows:

Property	Description
$a^1 = a$	Any number to the power of 1 is equal to itself
$1^n = 1$	The number 1 raised to any power is equal to 1
$a^0 = 1$	Any number raised to the power of 0 is equal to 1
$a^n \times a^m = a^{n+m}$	Add exponents to multiply powers of the same base number
$a^n \div a^m = a^{n-m}$	Subtract exponents to divide powers of the same base number
$(a^n)^m = a^{n \times m}$	When a power is raised to a power, the exponents are multiplied
$(a \times b)^n = a^n \times b^n$ $(a \div b)^n = a^n \div b^n$	Multiplication and division operations inside parentheses can be raised to a power. This is the same as each term being raised to that power.
$a^{-n} = \frac{1}{a^n}$	A negative exponent is the same as the reciprocal of a positive exponent

Note that exponents do not have to be integers. Fractional or decimal exponents follow all the rules above as well. Example: $5^{\frac{1}{4}} \times 5^{\frac{3}{4}} = 5^{\frac{1}{4}+\frac{3}{4}} = 5^1 = 5$.

Review Video: Properties of Exponents
Visit mometrix.com/academy and enter code: 532558

Scientific Notation

Scientific notation is a way of writing large numbers in a shorter form. The form $a \times 10^n$ is used in scientific notation, where a is greater than or equal to 1 but less than 10, and n is the number of places the decimal must move to get from the original number to a. Example: The number 230,400,000 is cumbersome to write. To write the value in scientific notation, place a decimal point between the first and second numbers, and include all digits through the last non-zero digit ($a = 2.304$). To find the appropriate power of 10, count the number of places the decimal point had to move ($n = 8$). The number is positive if the decimal moved to the left, and negative if it moved to the right. We can then write 230,400,000 as 2.304×10^8. If we look instead at the number 0.00002304, we have the same value for a, but this time the decimal moved 5 places to the right ($n = -5$). Thus, 0.00002304 can be written as 2.304×10^{-5}. Using this notation makes it simple to compare very large or very small numbers. By comparing exponents, it is easy to see that 3.28×10^4 is smaller than 1.51×10^5, because 4 is less than 5.

Review Video: Scientific Notation
Visit mometrix.com/academy and enter code: 976454

Converting Between Percentages, Fractions, and Decimals

Converting decimals to percentages and percentages to decimals is as simple as moving the decimal point. To *convert from a decimal to a percentage*, move the decimal point **two places to the right**. To *convert from a percentage to a decimal*, move it **two places to the left**. It may be helpful to remember that the percentage number will always be larger than the equivalent decimal number. Example:

$$0.23 = 23\% \qquad 5.34 = 534\% \qquad 0.007 = 0.7\%$$
$$700\% = 7.00 \qquad 86\% = 0.86 \qquad 0.15\% = 0.0015$$

To convert a fraction to a decimal, simply divide the numerator by the denominator in the fraction. To convert a decimal to a fraction, put the decimal in the numerator with 1 in the denominator. Multiply the numerator and denominator by tens until there are no more decimal places. Then simplify the fraction to lowest terms. For example, converting 0.24 to a fraction:

$$0.24 = \frac{0.24}{1} = \frac{0.24 \times 100}{1 \times 100} = \frac{24}{100} = \frac{6}{25}$$

Fractions can be converted to a percentage by finding equivalent fractions with a denominator of 100. Example:

$$\frac{7}{10} = \frac{70}{100} = 70\% \quad \frac{1}{4} = \frac{25}{100} = 25\%$$

To convert a percentage to a fraction, divide the percentage number by 100 and reduce the fraction to its simplest possible terms. Example:

$$60\% = \frac{60}{100} = \frac{3}{5} \quad 96\% = \frac{96}{100} = \frac{24}{25}$$

Review Video: Converting Fractions to Percentages and Decimals
Visit mometrix.com/academy and enter code: 306233

Review Video: Converting Percentages to Decimals and Fractions
Visit mometrix.com/academy and enter code: 287297

Review Video: Converting Decimals to Fractions and Percentages
Visit mometrix.com/academy and enter code: 986765

Review Video: Converting Decimals, Improper Fractions, and Mixed Numbers
Visit mometrix.com/academy and enter code: 696924

Rates and Ratios

Rates and ratios are a way to express the relationship between units.

A **ratio** expresses the relationship between two values, often with similar units. A **rate** also expresses the relationship between two values, but usually these values have unlike units. Rates also describe the relationship between a dependent unit and an independent unit. Rates use the word "per" to compare the values. In a ratio, there is not one independent unit and one dependent unit. A few examples of ratios include comparing green paint to white paint, dogs to cats, or flour to sugar. Some common examples of rates include dollars per hour, miles per hour, and beats per second.

Rates and ratios are commonly expressed through words, symbols, and quotients.

Let's say that for every 2 cups of sugar, we need to add 3 cups of flour to a recipe. This is a comparison between sugar and flour for this recipe. You could say that the ratio of sugar to flour is 2 to 3, or the relationship between sugar and flour is $\frac{2}{3}$.

Review Video: Ratios
Visit mometrix.com/academy and enter code: 996914

PROPORTIONS

We can use proportions to solve problems with ratios and rates. A **proportion** is an equation with two equivalent comparisons. We use proportions to compare ratios and to solve ratio and rate problems.

For example, we can calculate that for every 4 cups of sugar, we would add 6 cups of flour because these ratios are equivalent. This can be described by the proportion.

$$\frac{\text{sugar}}{\text{flour}} = \frac{2}{3} = \frac{4}{6}$$

Each ratio is equivalent, so the relationship between sugar and flour remains proportional.

Review Video: Proportions
Visit mometrix.com/academy and enter code: 505355

EXAMPLE

We are making cookies. The ratio of sugar to flour is 2 cups of sugar to every 3 cups of flour. We are increasing the recipe and using 8 cups of sugar. How many cups of flour will we need for the recipe?

We can use proportions to help us solve this problem where x is the number of cups of flour needed. Since the ratio of sugar to flour does not change, the proportion in the original recipe is equal to the proportion in the adjusted recipe.

$$\frac{2}{3} = \frac{8}{x}$$

Now, we can solve the proportion for the number of cups of flour needed for 8 cups of sugar by using cross multiplication.

$$\frac{2}{3} = \frac{8}{x}$$
$$2 \times x = 8 \times 3$$

$$2x = 24$$
$$\frac{2x}{2} = \frac{24}{2}$$
$$12 = x$$

So, if we are using 8 cups of sugar, we need 12 cups of flour.

$$\frac{2}{3} = \frac{8}{12}$$

These are equivalent ratios. Their equivalent values show that the comparison of flour to sugar remains proportional.

REPRESENTING RATES

TABLES

Rates can be expressed through tables. If you make $12 per hour, you can create a table to express how much you would make after a certain number of hours.

Hours (x)	Dollars (y)
1	12
2	24
10	120
20	240

This table expresses the relationship, or comparison, of dollars and hours. For each hour, the value of dollars increases at a rate of 12.

EQUATIONS

Rates can be expressed algebraically using the equation $y = kx$, where k is the rate of change. If you make $12 per hour, the rate of pay could be described as $y = 12x$. This equation can also be determined from the table provided where x represents the number of hours and y represents the number of dollars. The rate of change is 12, so the value of dollars, y, is determined by the number of hours, x, multiplied by 12.

GRAPHS

Finally, rates can be expressed graphically. Combining the data found on the table and the given equation, $y = 12x$, the rate of $12 per hour can be expressed using a graph where the x values align with the number of hours and the y values align with the number of dollars.

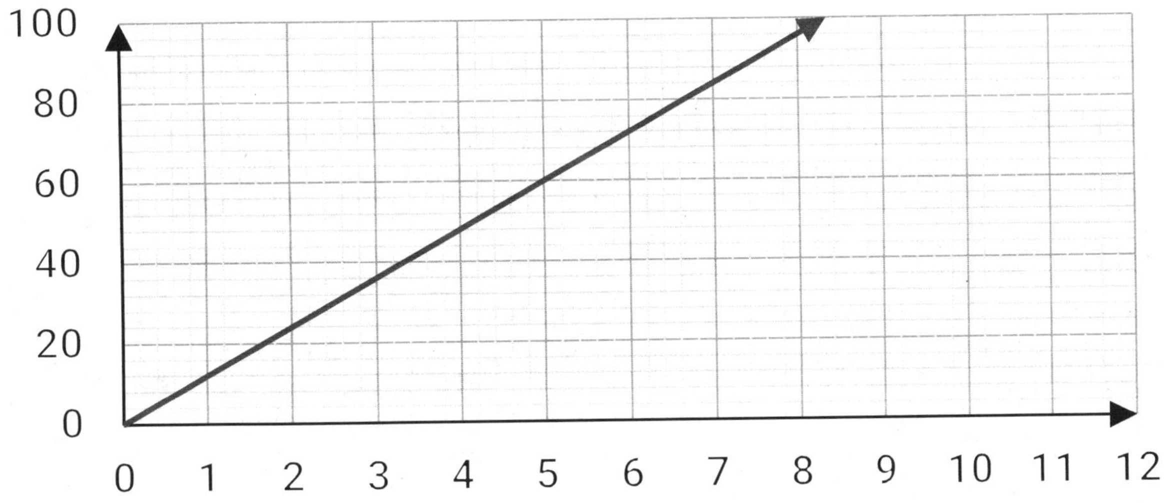

This graph represents the rate of pay if you make $12 per hour and represents the equation $y = 12x$. To verify that a graph represents the rate, we can identify a point on the line and compare its x value and its y value. If the relationship between those values matches the rate, then we can reasonably conclude that the graph represents the rate. On the graph, a point on the line is (5,60), where $x = 5$ and $y = 60$. We know that $\frac{60}{5} = 12$, or the rate of $\frac{60 \text{ dollars}}{5 \text{ hours}} = \frac{12 \text{ dollars}}{1 \text{ hour}}$. The graph should also have a y-intercept of 0. This graph crosses the y-axis at (0,0), so it has a y-intercept of 0.

EXAMPLE

Apples cost $1.30 per pound at the grocery store. Which equation represents the relationship between d, dollars, and p, pounds?

a. $p = 1.3d$
b. $p = d + 1.3$
c. $d = 1.3p$
d. $d = p + 1.3$

This problem focuses on representing rates using equations. The given rate is that apples cost $1.30 per pound. We want to identify the equation that appropriately represents the relationship between d, dollars, and p, pounds.

If the rate of the cost of apples, or the relationship between dollars and pounds, is $1.30 per pound, this means that the number of dollars the apples cost depends on the number of pounds of apples purchased. To find the number of dollars, you can take the number of pounds and multiply that value by 1.3. This can also be stated as dollars is equal to the number of pounds times 1.3, or $d = p \times 1.3$, which can also be written as $d = 1.3p$.

The correct answer is C.

EXAMPLE

Kim types at a rate of 45 words each minute. Which graph can be used to represent the relationship between w, words and m, minutes?

a. 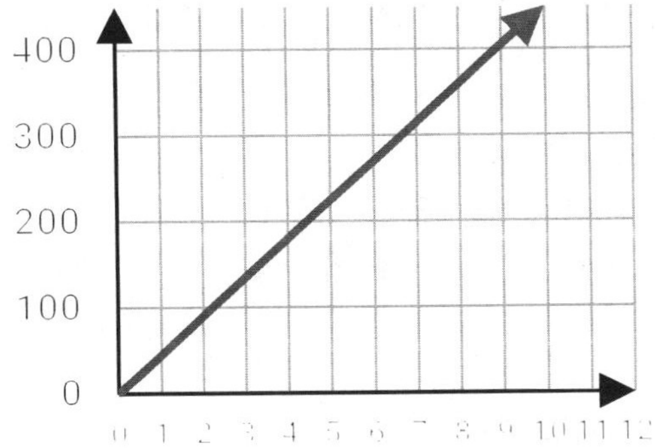

$(y = 45x)$

b. 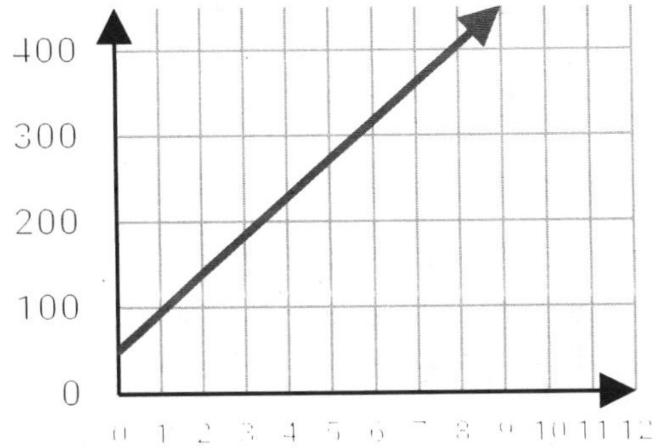

$(y = 45x + 45)$

c. 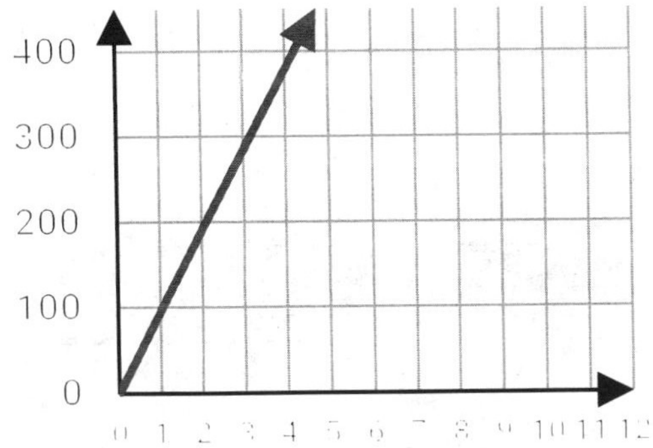

$(y = 90x)$

d. 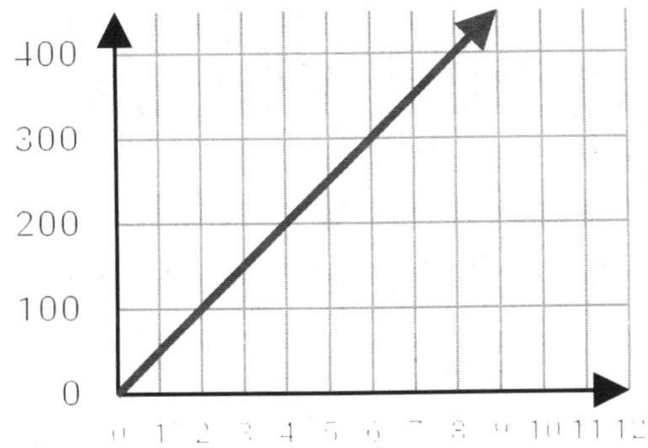

$(y = 50x)$

The given rate is that Kim types 45 words per minute. We want to identify the graph that appropriately represents the relationship between w, words, and m, minutes.

If Kim types at a rate of 45 words per minute, then the number of words typed is dependent on the number of minutes spent typing. For example, after 1 minute, Kim will type 45 words, and after 10 minutes, Kim will type 450 words. This information can be described in a table.

Minutes	1	2	5	10
Words	45	90	225	450

We can see that the value of words is 45 times the value of minutes, so we can say that the number of words is 45 times the number of minutes, $w = 45m$.

This information can be expressed graphically using x and y values. If the number of words is dependent on the number of minutes, words is going to be our y value, and minutes will be our x value. This means that $w = 45m$ can be graphed using the equation $y = 45x$. To express this rate graphically, we will need to find at least two points. The table can be used to find our points. The graphed line that represents the rate 45 words per minute will include the points (0,0) and (1,45).

The correct answer is A.

UNIT RATES

A rate describes the relationship between units. A **unit rate** is a rate written in simplest form, where one of the two units is one. Let's say you work as a dog trainer for 4 hours and make $50. You are paid at a rate of $50 per 4 hours. The unit rate would describe how much you make in 1 hour.

To find the unit rate, this rate can be written as a fraction, $\frac{50}{4}$ dollars per hour. By simplifying the fraction, we find the unit rate.

$$\frac{50}{4} = \frac{12.5}{1} = 12.5$$

So, you work for $12.50 per hour.

Review Video: Rates and Unit Rates
Visit mometrix.com/academy and enter code: 185363

EXPRESSING UNIT RATES

Rates can be expressed in two ways. For example, we can find the rate of dollars to 1 hour, and we can also find the rate of hours to 1 dollar.

If you work as dog trainer and earn $50 for 4 hours of work, you make $12.50 per hour. But how many hours do you have to work to make 1 dollar? We can use the same strategies as before to express the relationship between hours and dollars.

$$4 \text{ hours per } \$50 = \frac{4 \text{ hours}}{50 \text{ dollars}} = \frac{4}{50} \text{ hours per dollar}$$

Simplify the fraction and convert it to a decimal to find the unit rate.

$$= \frac{4}{50}$$
$$= \frac{1}{12.5}$$

$$= 0.08$$

You work 0.08 hours to make 1 dollar.

We can also use a table.

Hours	Dollars
4	50
	1

We can find the unit rate of hours to dollars by dividing each value by 50 to find the rate of 0.08 hours per dollar, which means that you will make $1 for every 0.08 hours of work.

When working as a dog trainer, you made 12.5 dollars per hour and worked $\frac{1}{12.5}$ hours per dollar.

Hours	Dollars	$\frac{\text{hours}}{\text{dollars}}$	$\frac{\text{dollars}}{\text{hours}}$
4	50	$\frac{4}{50}$	$\frac{50}{4}$
1	12.5	$\frac{1}{12.5}$	$\frac{12.5}{1}$

<u>EXAMPLE</u>

Trevor read 150 pages in 8 hours. At this rate, how many pages does Trevor read each hour? Write your answer in decimal form.

This problem focuses on finding the unit rate of pages to 1 hour. If Trevor read 150 pages in 8 hours, then how many pages did he read in 1 hour? To solve this problem, we can use equivalent fractions. Since the number of pages Trevor reads in 1 hour is unknown, we can represent it using the variable x.

$$\frac{150 \text{ pages}}{8 \text{ hours}} = \frac{x \text{ pages}}{1 \text{ hours}}$$

When solving for a variable using equivalent fractions, which may also be called a **proportion**, it is helpful to convert the fractions to non-fraction values. Remember that in an equation, if you multiply one side by a value, you must do the same to the other side. When you multiply a fraction by its denominator, the product will be equal to the numerator.

$$\frac{150}{8} \times 8 = 150$$

However, when we know that the denominator of both fractions will be canceled out by multiplying each numerator by the other fraction's denominator, we can skip these steps and rewrite the equation. One side of the new equation will show the numerator of one fraction multiplied by the denominator of the second fraction. This will be equal to the numerator of the second fraction multiplied by the denominator of the first fraction. This strategy is called **cross multiplication**.

$$8x = 150 \times 1$$

Then, solve for the variable by dividing both sides by 8.

$$8x = 150 \times 1$$
$$8x = 150$$
$$\frac{8x}{8} = \frac{150}{8}$$
$$x = 18.75$$

Trevor read at a rate of 18.75 pages per hour.

Constant Rates

A **rate** is a comparison of two values with different units. A **constant rate** means that the relationship between units remains the same. Some common examples are the comparison of dollars to hour, miles to hours, and beats to seconds. Rates can be expressed in a variety of ways, including using language, as quotients, using equivalent rates, algebraically, using tables, or graphically.

Rates can be expressed through language. Let's say you get your first job working at a store making $12 for every hour of work. This is a rate, a comparison between two unlike units, dollars and hours. This rate can be expressed through words. We use the word *per* when expressing rates. You could say that you make 12 dollars per hour.

Rates can be expressed as a fraction, or division. If you make 12 dollars per hour, you could express that as $12/hour. You could express the rate as $\frac{12 \text{ dollars}}{1 \text{ hour}}$. You could even say that the rate of dollars per hour is $\frac{12}{1}$.

Rates can be expressed using equivalent rates. $12/hour can be expressed as $24/2 hours. Or, if you work 20 hours per week, you could say you make $240/week. Regardless of the number of hours worked, the number of dollars made per hour remains constant, or the same.

Constant of Proportionality

A rate or unit rate describes the relationship between units. If the relationship between units is constant, then the relationship is proportional. If a car is traveling at a constant rate of 60 miles per hour, then it will travel 120 miles in 2 hours, and 180 miles in 3 hours.

Hours (x)	1	2	3	4	5
Miles (y)	60	120	180	240	300

Regardless of the value of hours or miles, the relationship between miles, y, and hours, x, remains constant. The relationship between miles and hours in this case is that miles is 60 times the number of hours. This can be described using the equation $y = 60x$.

When there is a constant relationship between units, the rate can be described algebraically using the equation $y = kx$, where k represents the **constant of proportionality,** or the value of the relationship between x and y.

Example

A donut shop sells sets of donuts for a constant rate. The table below shows the cost for different amounts of donuts.

Number of Donuts	Cost
6	$4.50
12	$9.00
24	$18

Number of Donuts	Cost
50	$37.50

What is the constant of proportionality that relates the number of donuts, x, and the cost of the donuts, y?

This problem focuses on identifying the constant of proportionality from a situation. We know that the constant of proportionality is the value of the relationship between x and y, and this relationship can be modeled using the equation $y = kx$, where k represents the constant of proportionality.

Use the equation $k = \frac{y}{x}$ to solve for the constant of proportionality, k.

The y value is the cost of the donuts, and the x value is the number of donuts. We can choose any of the given pairs of x and y values.

$$k = \frac{y}{x}$$
$$k = \frac{4.5}{6}$$
$$k = 0.75$$

The constant of proportionality is 0.75.

Measurement and Geometry

VOLUME

Volume is the measure of how much **space** is contained within a **three-dimensional figure**. Calculating volume is a real-world skill with many applications. For example, volume calculations are involved when determining how much water can be added to a swimming pool, how much lemonade can be contained in a pitcher, or how much soup is contained within a can. There are formulas that make volume calculations efficient and straightforward. We use **cubic units**, which can be thought of as cubed units, to describe volume because volume is the number of unit cubes it takes to fill a space.

VOLUME OF A RECTANGULAR PRISM

A **rectangular prism** is a three-dimensional shape that has 6 rectangular faces.

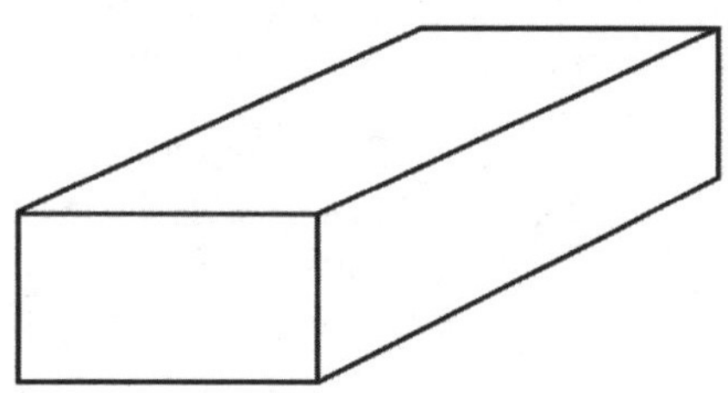

If we have a rectangular prism with side lengths that are measured in centimeters, the volume of the rectangular prism is the total number of cubic centimeters that it would take to fill the inside space.

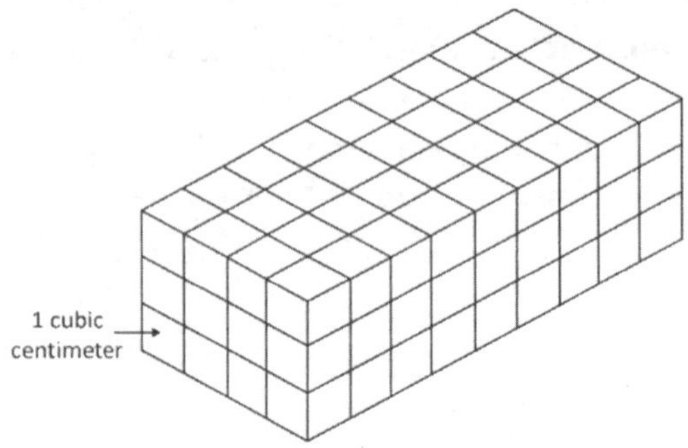

We can fill a physical rectangular prism with smaller unit cubes to find the total volume. We can count the number of cubes in each "layer" and add them up to find the total volume, but the most efficient way to find the volume of a rectangular prism is by using the volume formula.

To find the volume of a rectangular prism, we find the area of a face and multiply that by the height of the prism. In other words, we find the volume of the first layer, and multiply that by how many layers make up the prism.

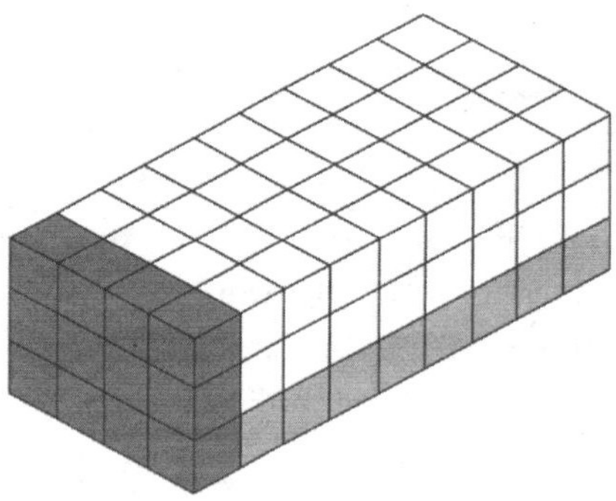

More simply put, the volume of a rectangular prism is the length times the width times the height, or $V = l \cdot w \cdot h$.

If we have a rectangular prism with a length of 9 cm, a width of 4 cm, and a height of 3 cm, we will multiply these values to find the volume in cubic centimeters.

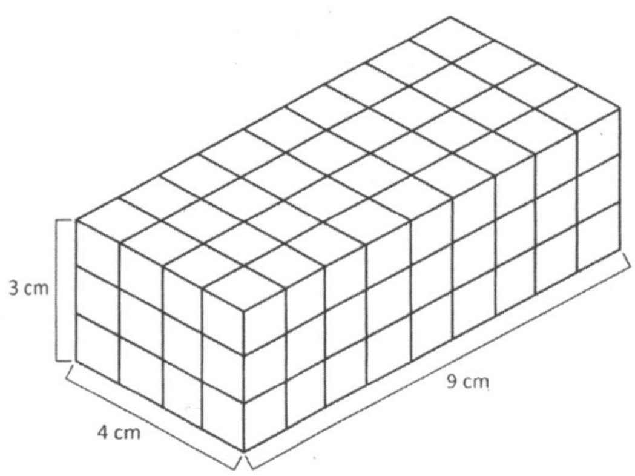

$$V = l \times w \times h$$
$$V = 9 \times 4 \times 3$$

$$V = 9 \times 12$$
$$V = 108 \text{ cubic centimeters}$$

EXAMPLE

A rectangular prism is shown below.

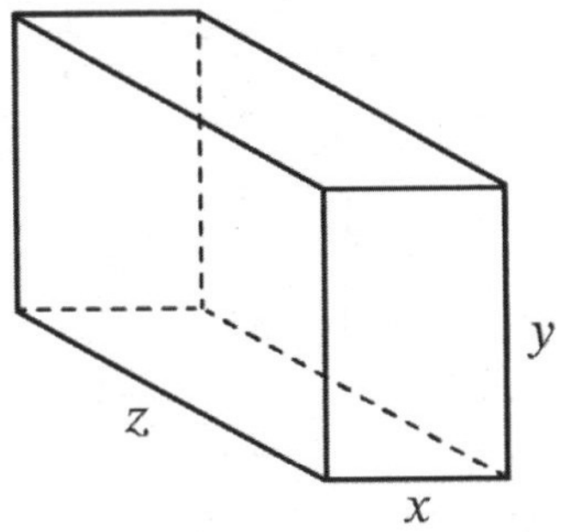

What equation can be used to calculate the volume of the rectangular prism?

a. $V = x + y + z$
b. $V = x \cdot y \cdot z$
c. $V = (x \cdot y) + z$
d. $V = (x + y) \cdot z$

In this problem, we are given a rectangular prism with the dimensions labeled by variables, and we need to determine which equation can be used to calculate the volume of the prism.

The formula for volume of a rectangular prism is $V = l \cdot w \cdot h$.

Because of the associative property, it does not matter the order that we multiply these values, so the actual labels of length, width, and height do not matter and depend on how the prism is placed. Instead, we need to know that we need to multiply all three values.

In the diagram, we see that the length, width, and height of the rectangular prism are labeled using the variables x, y, and z. So, to find the volume of the prism, we need to multiply all side lengths, or multiply x, y, and z.

$$V = x \cdot y \cdot z$$

Because of the associative property and the fact that you can multiply values in any order, there are many equations that can be used to find the volume of this figure, but only one of the answer choices above will work. The correct answer is B.

CYLINDER

A **cylinder** consists of two circular base shapes and a curved rectangular side shape.

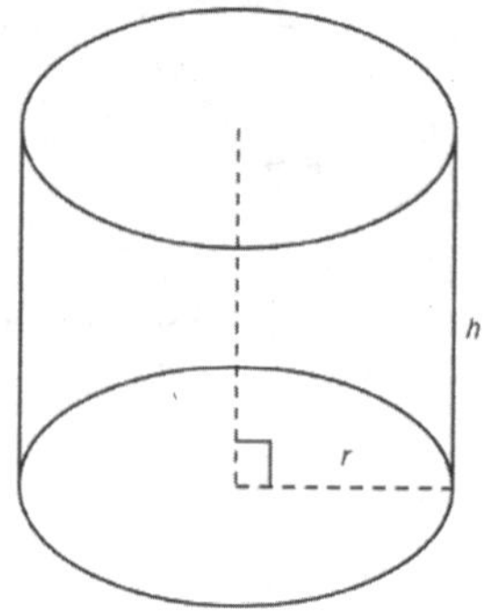

The volume formula for of a cylinder is calculated as $V = \pi r^2 h$, where V represents volume, π is approximated as 3.14, r represents radius, and h represents height.

Calculate the volume of a can of soup with a height of 20 centimeters and a radius of 5 centimeters. Use 3.14 as an approximation for pi.

$$V = \pi r^2 h$$
$$V = (3.14)(5)^2(20)$$
$$V = 1{,}570$$

The volume of the cylinder is 1,570 cubic centimeters.

EXAMPLE

A cylinder has a height of 7 feet and a radius of 5 feet. Calculate the volume of the cylinder. Use 3.14 as an approximation for π.

$$V = \pi r^2 h$$
$$V = (3.14)(5)^2(7)$$
$$V = 549.5$$

The volume of the cylinder is 549.5 cubic feet.

$$V = 549.5 \text{ ft}^3$$

SURFACE AREA

The **surface area** of a three-dimensional figure is the total two-dimensional area of the surface of the figure. We can find the surface area of a three-dimensional figure by adding the area of each face of the figure.

Lateral surface area refers to the surface area of a figure minus the **bases**. For example, the lateral area of a cylinder is just the rectangular side that wraps around the two circular base shapes.

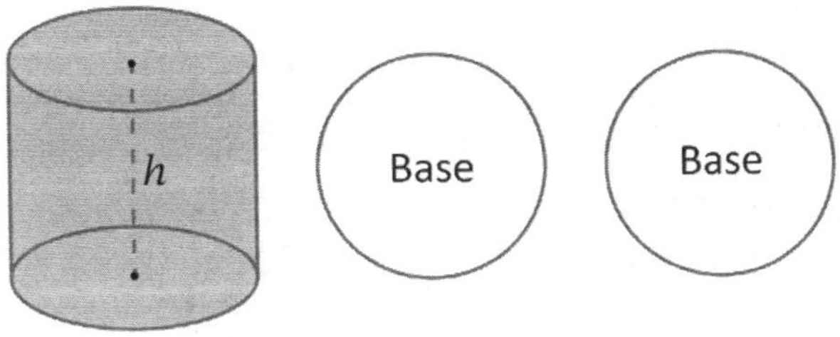

Lateral Surfaces

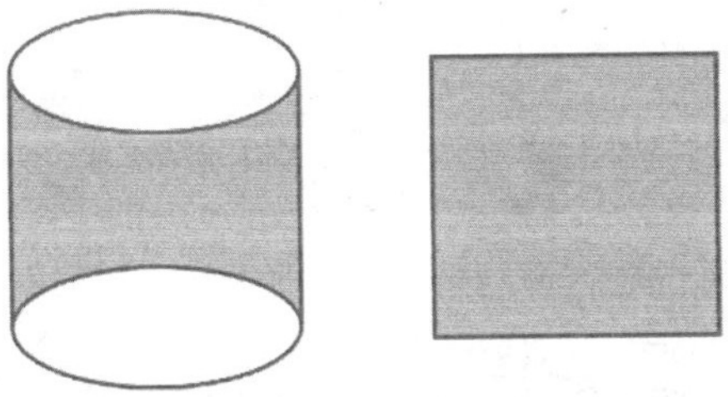

The ends of a prism are always parallel. The bases are connected by the **lateral faces** which are always parallelograms. For example, in a cylinder, the base shapes are circular.

Total surface area refers to the lateral surface area plus the surface area of the base shapes.

A **net** is an "unfolded" version of a three-dimensional figure. It is as if the figure is opened and laid flat. The net of a three-dimensional figure accurately identifies the polygon faces that make a three-dimensional figure.

RECTANGULAR PRISMS

The net of a rectangular prism consists of 4 rectangular lateral faces and 2 rectangular bases. The total surface area of a rectangular prism is calculated by adding the surface area of the four sides, the lateral surface area, to the surface area of the base shapes.

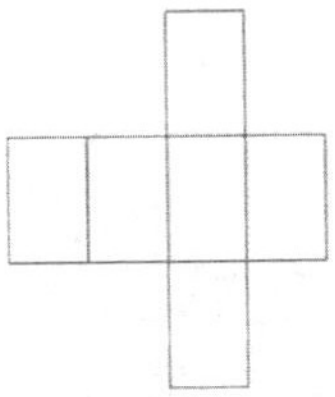

Lateral surface area: Calculate the area of all the faces except for the bases, the two smallest rectangles.

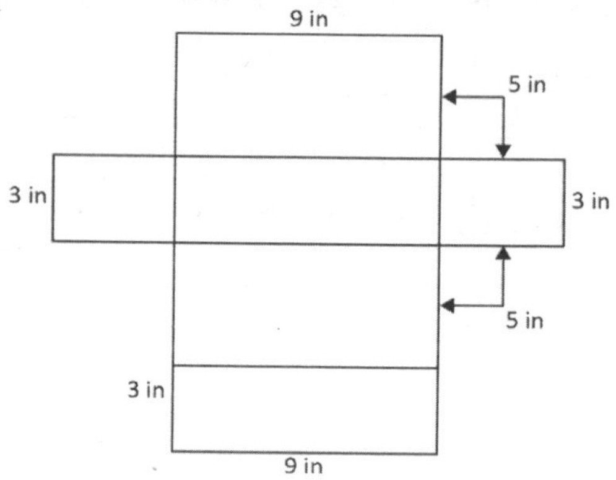

In this case, the lateral surface area consists of two 9×5 inch rectangles and two 9×3 rectangles.

$$2(9 \times 5) + 2(9 \times 3) = 144$$

The lateral surface area is 144 square inches.

Area of the bases: The base shapes consist of two 3×5 inch rectangles.

$$2(3 \times 5) = 30$$

The area of the base shapes is 30 square inches.

Total surface area: Combine the lateral surface area with the surface area of the base shapes.

$$30 + 144 = 174$$

The total surface area of the rectangular prism is 174 square inches.

Review Video: Volume and Surface Area of a Rectangular Prism
Visit mometrix.com/academy and enter code: 282814

EXAMPLE

The net of a rectangular prism is shown.

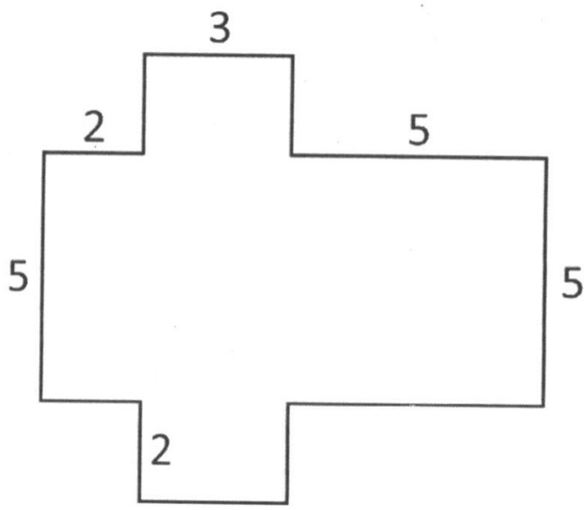

The total surface area of the rectangular prism can be found by finding the sum of the areas of each polygon in the figure. All "pieces" of the surface area of a rectangular prism are rectangles, so we can use the rectangle area formula to find the area of each rectangle.

There are many ways to divide the net of a rectangular prism into smaller rectangles. In this example, the net can be divided into one large rectangle, a small rectangle, and a square. It could also be divided into one large rectangle and two small rectangles, or it could be divided into five rectangles. The surface area is the same for every way it is divided.

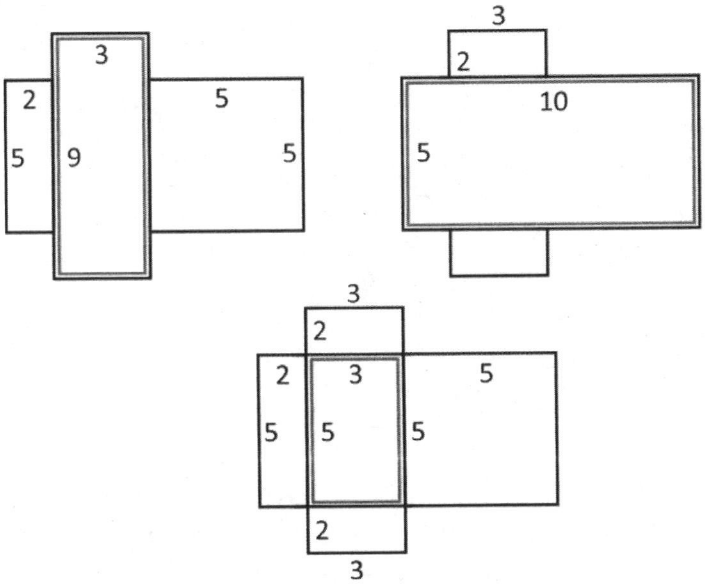

We will divide the net into one large rectangle and two small rectangles. The surface area of the rectangular prism is the sum of the areas of each rectangle. The areas of each rectangle can be found by multiplying the base and the height.

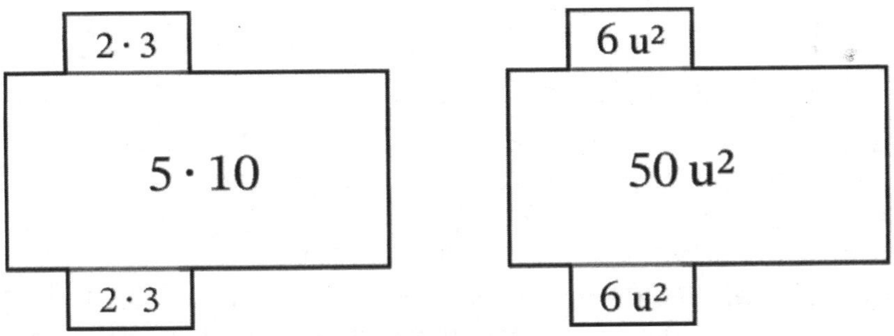

The surface area of the rectangular prism is the sum of the areas of each rectangle.

$$6 + 6 + 50 = 62$$

The surface area of the rectangular prism is 62 square units.

CYLINDERS

The net of a cylinder consists of 1 rectangular lateral face and 2 circular bases.

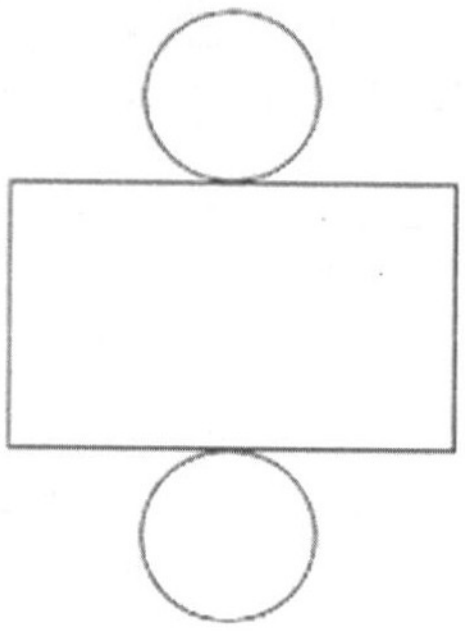

Lateral surface area: Calculate the area of all the faces except for the bases.

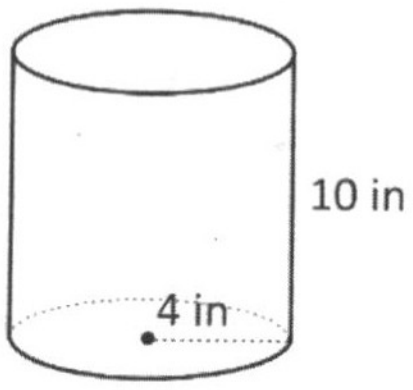

In this case, the lateral surface area consists of one rectangle. The area of rectangle is calculated as $A = bh$, where b represents base and h represents height. The height of the rectangle is 10 inches. The base of the rectangle is best visualized by drawing a net of the cylinder.

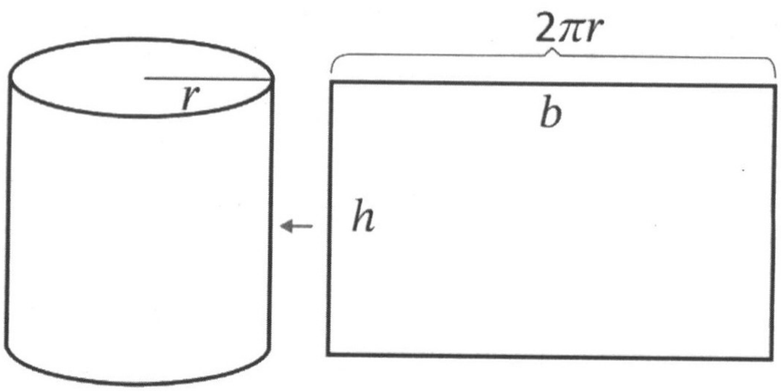

The base of the rectangle is $2\pi r$ which is the formula for the circumference of a circle. Notice how the base of the rectangle is the circumference for the circular base that it wraps around. So, the area of the rectangular lateral face of the cylinder is found using the formula

$A = bh$ or more specifically $A = (2\pi r)(h)$. When 3.14 is used as an approximation for π, the formula becomes $A = 2(3.14)(4)(10)$, which simplifies to 251.2. The lateral surface area is 251.2 square inches.

Area of the bases: The base shapes consist of two circles. The formula $A = \pi r^2$ can be used to determine the area of each circle. When 3.14 is used as an approximation for π, $A = \pi r^2$ becomes $A = (3.14)(4)^2$, which simplifies to 50.24. The total area of the base shapes is $2 \times 50.24 = 100.48$, or 100.48 square inches.

Total surface area: Combine the lateral surface area with the surface area of the base shapes.

$$251.2 + 100.48 = 351.68$$

The total surface area of the cylinder is 351.68 square inches.

EXAMPLE

Calculate the total surface area of a cylinder that has a radius of 2 ft and a height of 6 ft.

The lateral surface area consists of one rectangle. The area of a rectangle is calculated by multiplying the base by the height. In this case, the base of the rectangle is equivalent to the circumference of the circular base. The formula for circumference is $C = 2\pi r$. This means that the base of the rectangular lateral face is $2\pi r$. $A = bh$ becomes $A = 2\pi rh$.

$$A = 2\pi rh$$
$$A = 2(3.14)(2)(6)$$
$$A = 75.36$$

The lateral surface area is 75.36 square feet.

There are two circular base shapes. Use the formula $A = \pi r^2$ to determine the surface area of each circle.

$$A = \pi r^2$$
$$A = (3.14)(2)^2$$
$$A = 12.56$$
$$2 \times 12.56 = 25.12$$

The total area of the base shapes is 25.12 square feet.

Combine the lateral area and the base areas.

$$75.36 + 25.12 = 100.48$$

The total surface area of the cylinder is 100.48 square feet.

100.48 square feet

SIMILAR FIGURES

Similar figures are figures that have the same shape, but are different sizes. Similar figures have the same number of sides and angles. Their corresponding angles are congruent, and their sides are proportional.

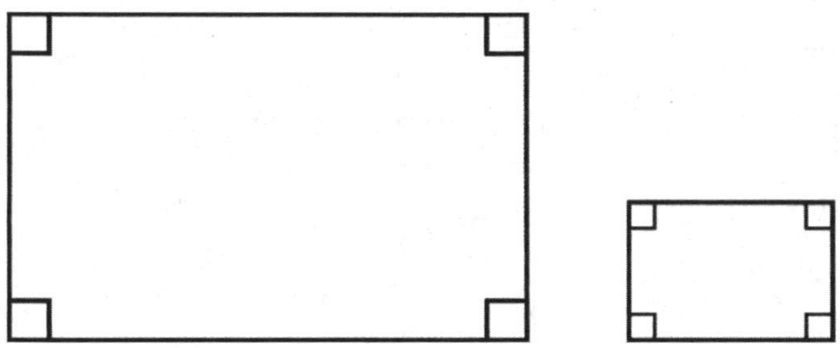

These two figures are rectangles. We know they are both rectangles because they each have four right angles and two sets of parallel sides. These rectangles are the same shape but are different sizes, which means these figures are similar.

The side lengths of similar figures are proportional. That means that when we compare the side lengths of these rectangles, the relationship will be constant.

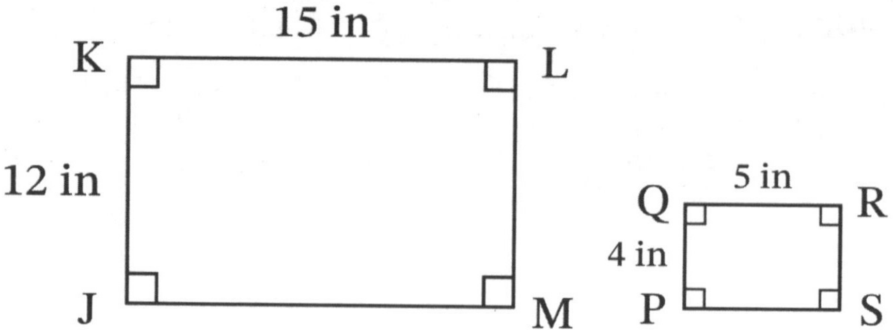

$$\frac{x}{y} = \frac{QP}{KJ} = \frac{4 \text{ in}}{12 \text{ in}} = \frac{1}{3}$$
$$\frac{x}{y} = \frac{QR}{KL} = \frac{5 \text{ in}}{15 \text{ in}} = \frac{1}{3}$$

The relationship between figure x and figure y is $\frac{1}{3}$.

This also means that $\frac{QP}{KJ} = \frac{QR}{KL}$. We can use cross multiplication to confirm.

$$\frac{4}{12} = \frac{5}{15}$$
$$4 \cdot 15 = 12 \cdot 5$$
$$60 = 60$$

This is also true if you compare the smaller rectangle to the larger rectangle.

$$\frac{y}{x} = \frac{KJ}{QP} = \frac{12 \text{ in}}{4 \text{ in}} = \frac{3}{1} = 3$$

$$\frac{y}{x} = \frac{KL}{QR} = \frac{15 \text{ in}}{5 \text{ in}} = \frac{3}{1} = 3$$

The relationship between figure y and figure x is 3.

This also means that $\frac{KJ}{QP} = \frac{KL}{QR}$. We can use cross multiplication to confirm.

$$\frac{12}{4} = \frac{15}{5}$$
$$12 \cdot 5 = 15 \cdot 4$$
$$60 = 60$$

Example

We can use proportional relationships in similar figures to solve for missing side lengths.

Let's say we are given two triangles and told that these triangles are similar. This means that their side lengths are proportional.

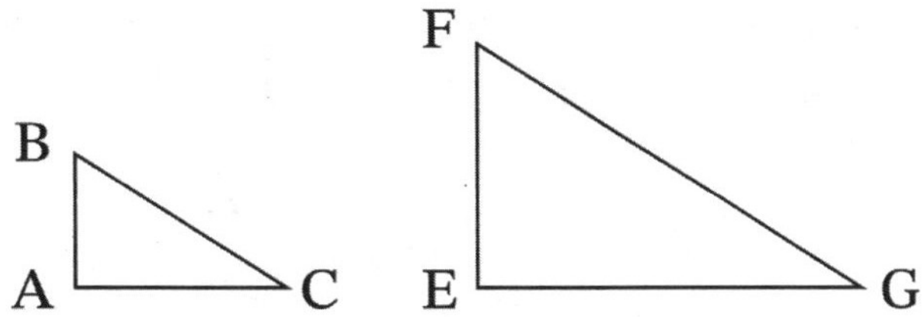

Since triangle ABC is similar to triangle EFG, their side lengths are proportional. Here are some true statements about these similar triangles.

$$\frac{AB}{EF} = \frac{AC}{EG}$$

$$\frac{BC}{FG} = \frac{AB}{EF}$$

$$\frac{AC}{EG} = \frac{BC}{FG}$$

Because these statements are true, we can use this information to find a missing side length. Since these triangles are similar, we can use proportions to solve for missing side lengths.

Triangle ABC and triangle EFG are pictured, but triangle EFG has a missing side length. What is the value of the missing side length?

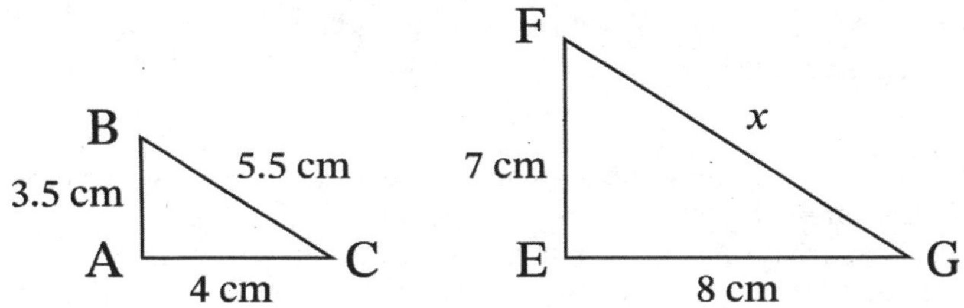

To find the value of the missing side length, we can use what we know about similar shapes. For example, we know that $\frac{AB}{EF} = \frac{BC}{FG}$. We can use this to solve for FG.

$$\frac{AB}{EF} = \frac{BC}{FG}$$
$$\frac{3.5}{7} = \frac{5.5}{x}$$
$$3.5x = 5.5 \times 7$$
$$\frac{3.5x}{3.5} = \frac{38.5}{3.5}$$
$$x = 11$$

The length of $\overline{FG}$ is 11 centimeters.

SCALE FACTOR

Similar figures are the same shapes but different sizes. The change between similar figures can be described as a scale factor. The **scale factor** is the ratio between corresponding side lengths.

Let's say that we start with the smaller figure and increase the size to create the larger figure.

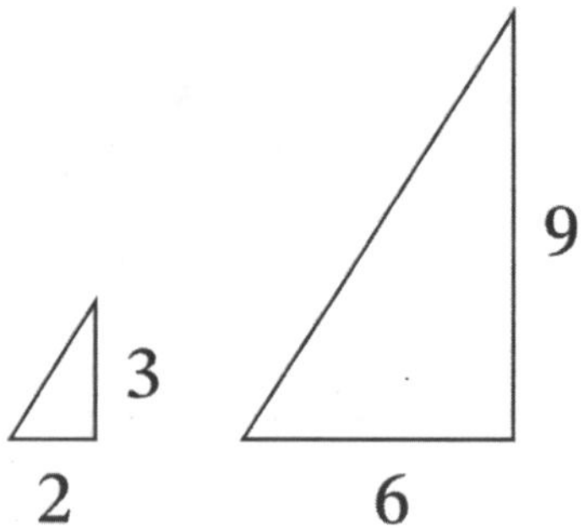

We can see that the ratio between side lengths is proportional and can identify the scale factor by identifying the value of the ratio of the new figure (the larger figure) to the original figure (the smaller figure).

$$\frac{\text{new figure}}{\text{original figure}} = \frac{6}{2} = 3$$
$$\frac{\text{new figure}}{\text{original figure}} = \frac{9}{3} = 3$$

When we compare the new figure side length to the original figure side length, we can see that the side lengths are proportional because the ratios are equivalent. We can also see that the change from figure 1 to figure 2 is an increase by a scale factor of 3.

Review Video: Proportional Change of Dimensions
Visit mometrix.com/academy and enter code: 186545

SCALE DRAWINGS

A **scale drawing** is a drawing used to represent similar figures. A map is an example of a scale drawing. Maps represent distances and measurements that are much too large to fit on a wall or sheet of paper, and the distance between locations on a map is proportional to the distance between those locations on earth. A scale drawing is a proportional representation, which means that the real measurements are proportional to the drawn measurements. A scale is used to define this proportional relationship.

The **scale** in a scale drawing is included in the key and shows the relationship between the original item and the scale drawing. The scale includes a measurement from the scale drawing and gives an equivalent measurement from the original item. An example of a scale is 1 inch = 100 miles. This means that in the scale drawing, 1 inch is equivalent to 100 miles in the original.

EXAMPLE

Let's say you are building a bird house. You may encounter a scale drawing in the directions to represent the size of the real-life bird house you will make. A realistic sized drawing of a bird house cannot fit on a small sheet of paper, so scale drawings are used to represent the dimensions of the bird house.

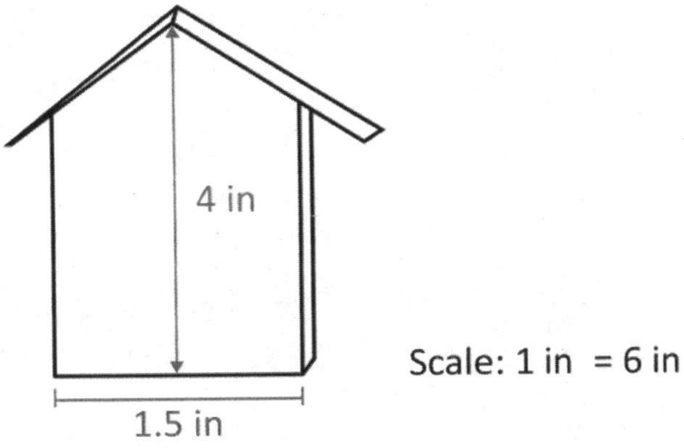

This scale drawing has the same proportions of the real-life bird house. There is a scale included with the scale drawing that says that 1 inch is equivalent to 6 inches. This means that in the scale drawing, 1 inch is equivalent to 6 inches in the real-life bird house.

In the drawing, the length of the bottom of the bird house measures 1.5 inches. This means that the length of the bottom of the real-life bird house will be $1.5 \times 6 = 9$ inches. The height of the bird house is 4 inches in the scale drawing. If the scale is 1 inch = 6 inches, the real-life bird house will be $4 \times 6 = 24$ inches tall.

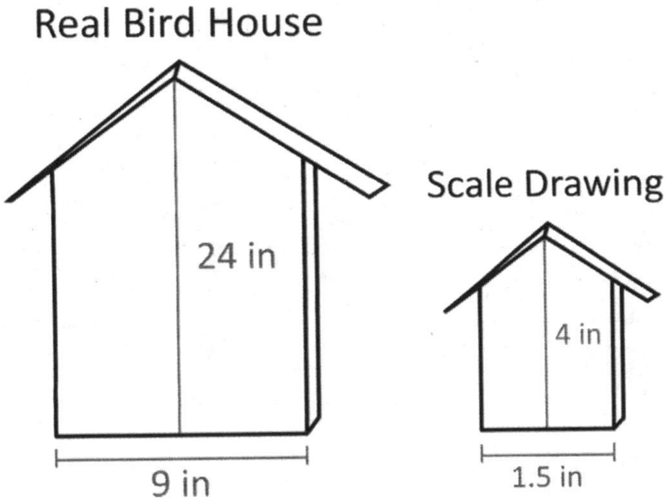

QUADRILATERALS

A **quadrilateral** is a closed two-dimensional geometric figure that has four straight sides. The sum of the interior angles of any quadrilateral is 360°.

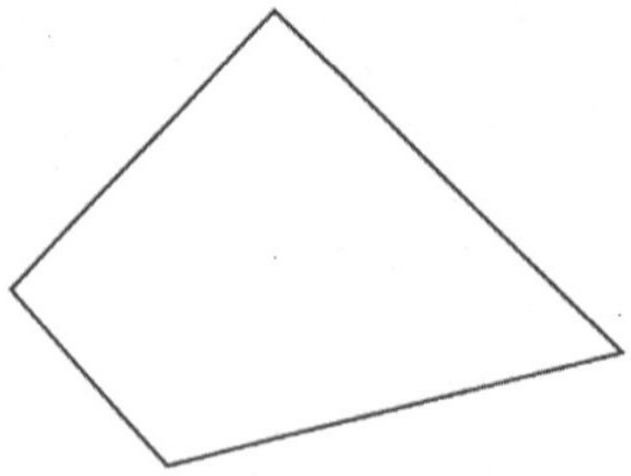

Review Video: Diagonals of Parallelograms, Rectangles, and Rhombi
Visit mometrix.com/academy and enter code: 320040

KITE

A **kite** is a quadrilateral with two pairs of adjacent sides that are congruent. A result of this is perpendicular diagonals. A kite can be concave or convex and has one line of symmetry.

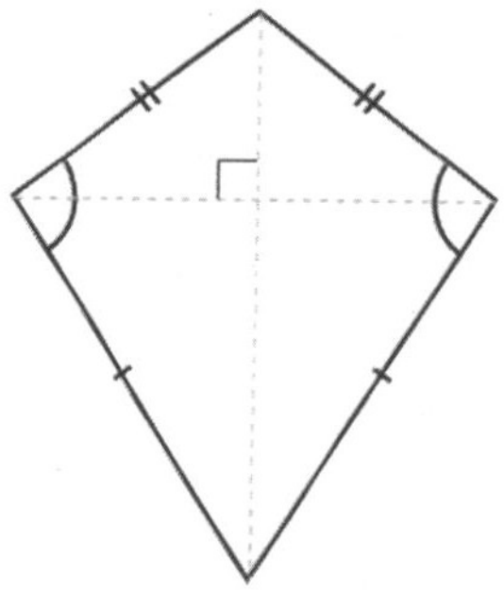

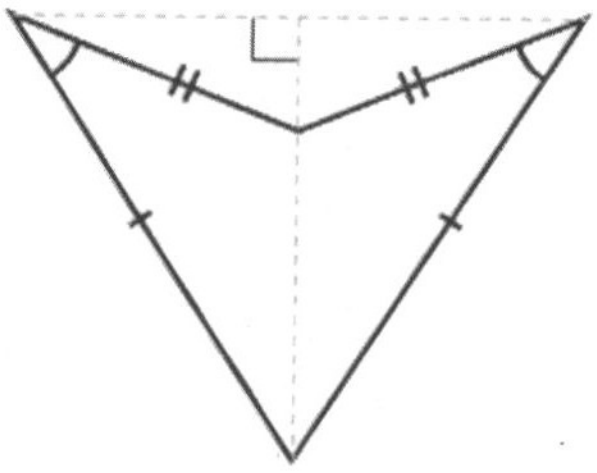

TRAPEZOID

Trapezoid: A trapezoid is defined as a quadrilateral that has at least one pair of parallel sides. There are no rules for the second pair of sides. So, there are no rules for the diagonals and no lines of symmetry for a trapezoid.

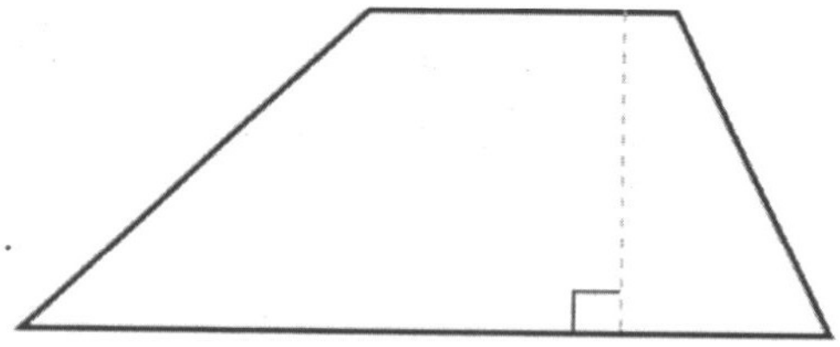

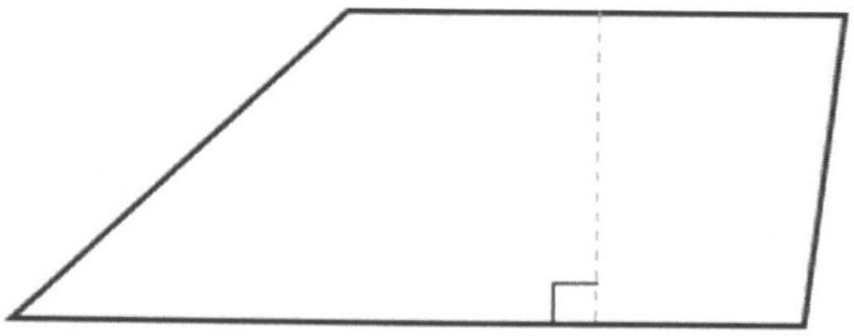

The **area of a trapezoid** is found by the formula $A = \frac{1}{2}h(b_1 + b_2)$, where h is the height (segment joining and perpendicular to the parallel bases), and b_1 and b_2 are the two parallel sides (bases). Do not use one of the other two sides as the height unless that side is also perpendicular to the parallel bases.

The **perimeter of a trapezoid** is found by the formula $P = a + b_1 + c + b_2$, where a, b_1, c, and b_2 are the four sides of the trapezoid.

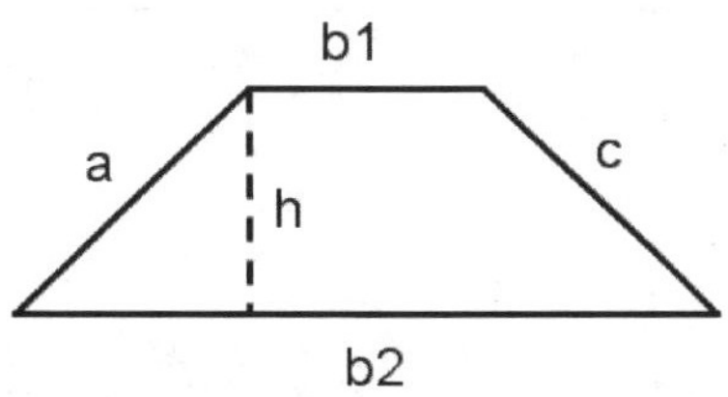

Review Video: Area and Perimeter of a Trapezoid
Visit mometrix.com/academy and enter code: 587523

Isosceles trapezoid: A trapezoid with equal base angles. This gives rise to other properties including: the two nonparallel sides have the same length, the two non-base angles are also equal, and there is one line of symmetry through the midpoints of the parallel sides.

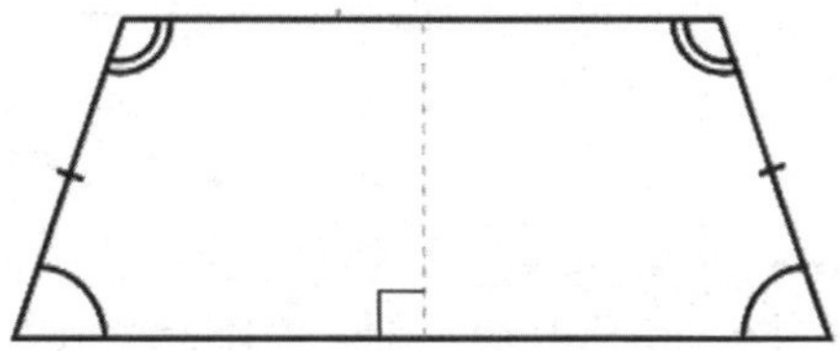

PARALLELOGRAM

A **parallelogram** is a quadrilateral that has two pairs of opposite parallel sides. As such it is a special type of trapezoid. The sides that are parallel are also congruent. The opposite interior angles are always congruent, and the consecutive interior angles are supplementary. The diagonals of a parallelogram divide each other. Each diagonal divides the parallelogram into two congruent triangles. A parallelogram has no line of symmetry, but does have 180-degree rotational symmetry about the midpoint.

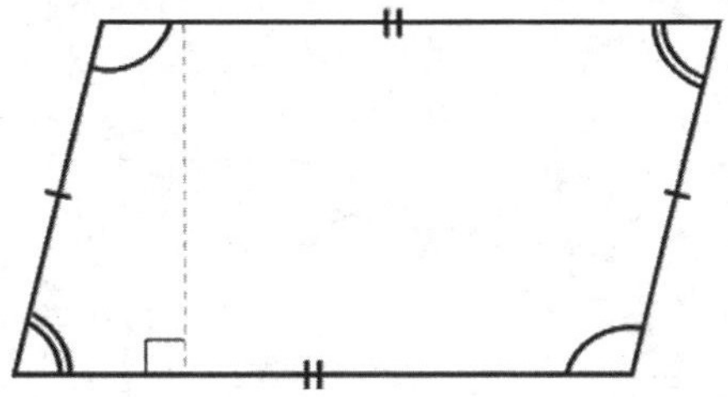

The **area of a parallelogram** is found by the formula $A = bh$, where b is the length of the base, and h is the height. Note that the base and height correspond to the length and width in a rectangle, so this formula would apply to rectangles as well. Do not confuse the height of a parallelogram with the length of the second side. The two are only the same measure in the case of a rectangle.

The **perimeter of a parallelogram** is found by the formula $P = 2a + 2b$ or $P = 2(a + b)$, where a and b are the lengths of the two sides.

Review Video: Area and Perimeter of a Parallelogram
Visit mometrix.com/academy and enter code: 718313

RECTANGLE

A **rectangle** is a quadrilateral with four right angles. All rectangles are parallelograms and trapezoids, but not all parallelograms or trapezoids are rectangles. The diagonals of a rectangle are congruent. Rectangles have two lines of symmetry (through each pair of opposing midpoints) and 180-degree rotational symmetry about the midpoint.

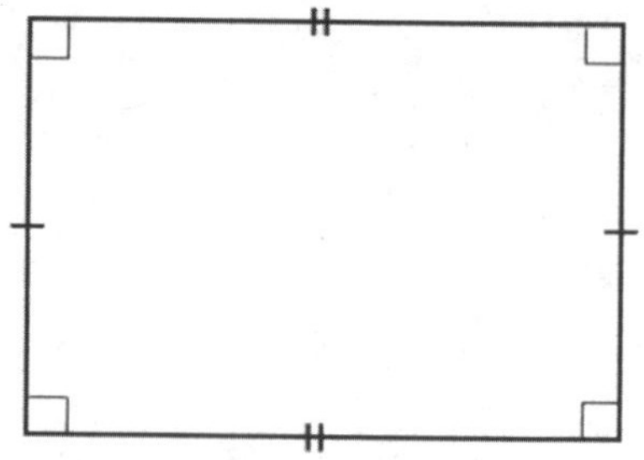

The **area of a rectangle** is found by the formula $A = lw$, where A is the area of the rectangle, l is the length (usually considered to be the longer side) and w is the width (usually considered to be the shorter side). The numbers for l and w are interchangeable.

The **perimeter of a rectangle** is found by the formula $P = 2l + 2w$ or $P = 2(l + w)$, where l is the length, and w is the width. It may be easier to add the length and width first and then double the result, as in the second formula.

RHOMBUS

A **rhombus** is a quadrilateral with four congruent sides. All rhombuses are parallelograms and kites; thus, they inherit all the properties of both types of quadrilaterals. The diagonals of a rhombus are perpendicular to each other. Rhombi have two lines of symmetry (along each of the diagonals) and 180° rotational symmetry. The **area of a rhombus** is half the product of the diagonals: $A = \frac{d_1 d_2}{2}$ and the perimeter of a rhombus is: $P = 2\sqrt{(d_1)^2 + (d_2)^2}$.

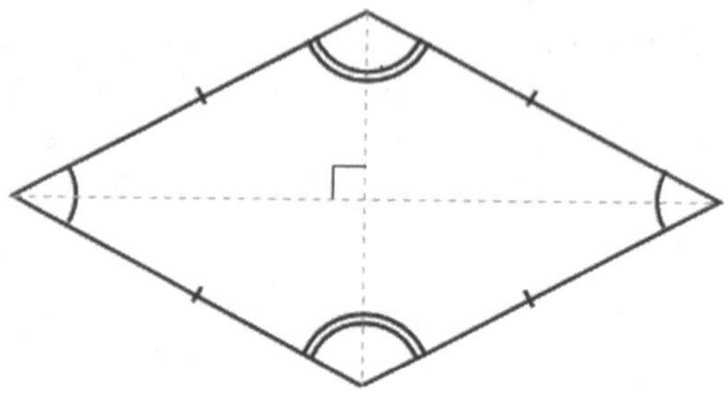

SQUARE

A **square** is a quadrilateral with four right angles and four congruent sides. Squares satisfy the criteria of all other types of quadrilaterals. The diagonals of a square are congruent and perpendicular to each other. Squares have four lines of symmetry (through each pair of opposing midpoints and along each of the diagonals) as well as 90° rotational symmetry about the midpoint.

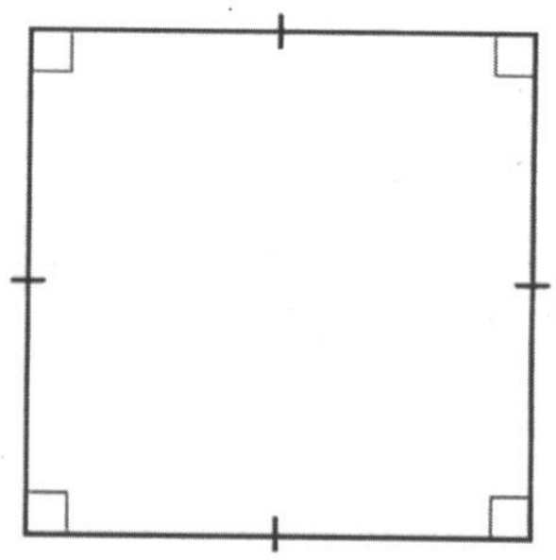

The **area of a square** is found by using the formula $A = s^2$, where s is the length of one side. The **perimeter of a square** is found by using the formula $P = 4s$, where s is the length of one side. Because all four sides are equal in a square, it is faster to multiply the length of one side by 4 than to add the same number four times. You could use the formulas for rectangles and get the same answer.

Review Video: Area and Perimeter of Rectangles and Squares
Visit mometrix.com/academy and enter code: 428109

HIERARCHY OF QUADRILATERALS

The hierarchy of quadrilaterals is as follows:

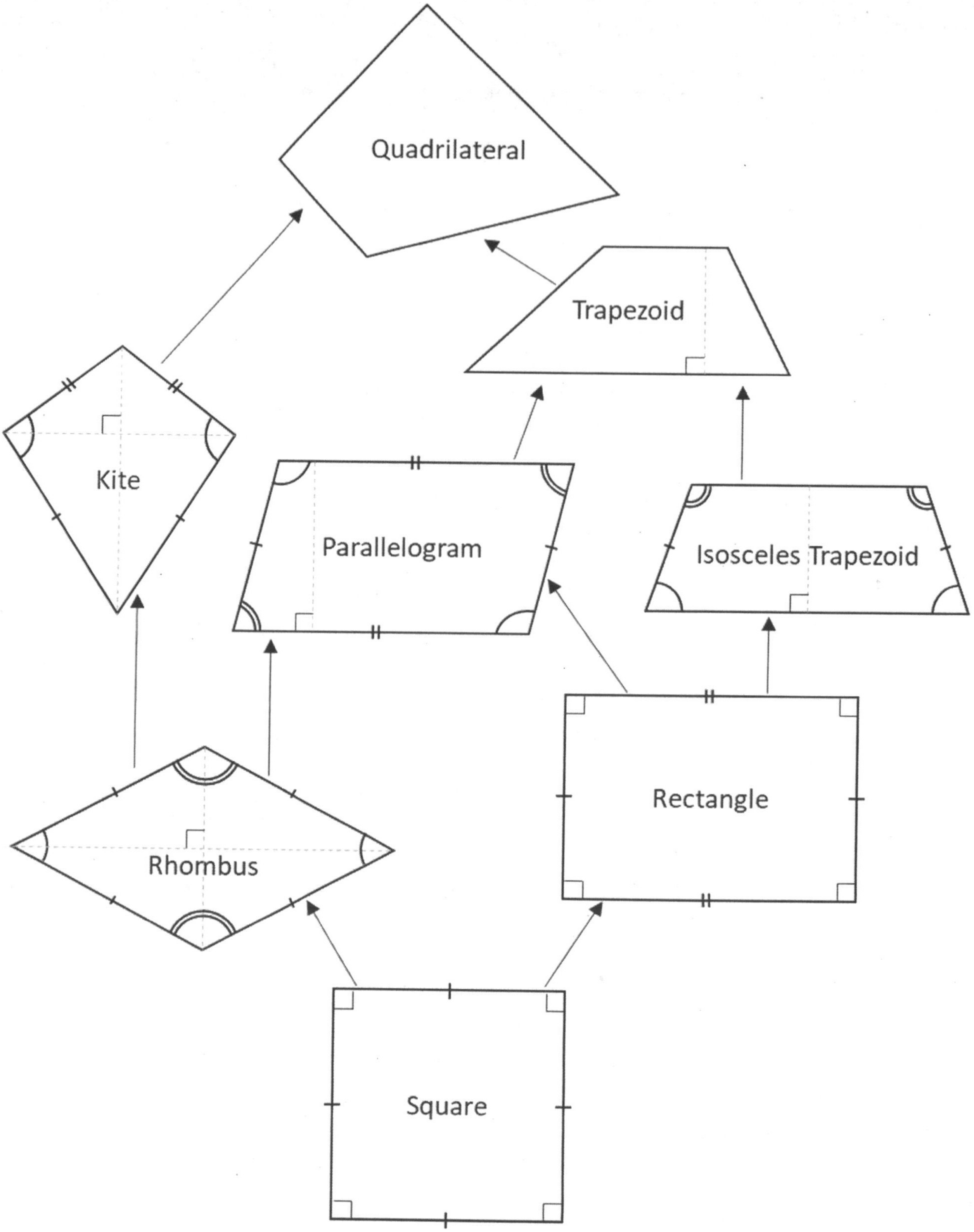

ANGLES

ANGLES AND VERTICES

An **angle** is formed when two lines or line segments meet at a common point. It may be a common starting point for a pair of segments or rays, or it may be the intersection of lines. Angles are represented by the symbol $\angle$.

The **vertex** is the point at which two segments or rays meet to form an angle. If the angle is formed by intersecting rays, lines, and/or line segments, the vertex is the point at which four angles are formed. The pairs of angles opposite one another are called vertical angles, and their measures are equal.

- An **acute** angle is an angle with a degree measure less than 90°.
- A **right** angle is an angle with a degree measure of exactly 90°.
- An **obtuse** angle is an angle with a degree measure greater than 90° but less than 180°.
- A **straight angle** is an angle with a degree measure of exactly 180°. This is also a semicircle.
- A **reflex angle** is an angle with a degree measure greater than 180° but less than 360°.
- A **full angle** is an angle with a degree measure of exactly 360°. This is also a circle.

Review Video: Angles
Visit mometrix.com/academy and enter code: 264624

RELATIONSHIPS BETWEEN ANGLES

Two angles whose sum is exactly 90° are said to be **complementary**. The two angles may or may not be adjacent. In a right triangle, the two acute angles are complementary.

Two angles whose sum is exactly 180° are said to be **supplementary**. The two angles may or may not be adjacent. Two intersecting lines always form two pairs of supplementary angles. Adjacent supplementary angles will always form a straight line.

Two angles that have the same vertex and share a side are said to be **adjacent**. Vertical angles are not adjacent because they share a vertex but no common side.

Review Video: Adjacent Angles
Visit mometrix.com/academy and enter code: 100375

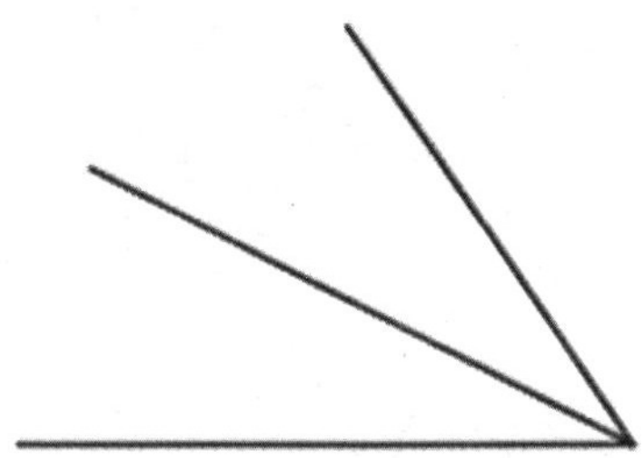

Adjacent
Share vertex and side

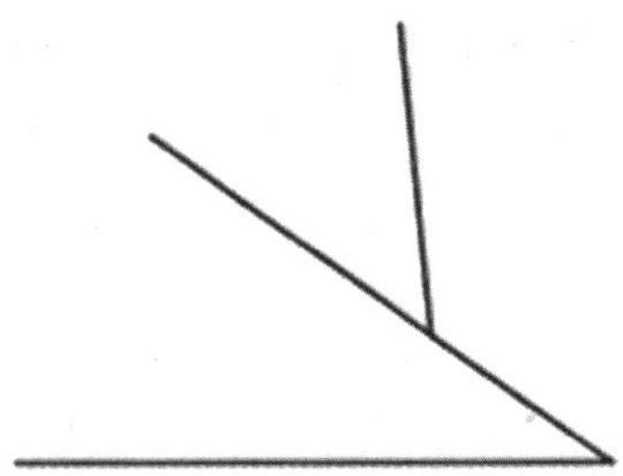

Not adjacent
Share part of a side, but not vertex

Solving for Unknown Angle Measurements

When an unknown angle is formed from a **benchmark angle**, such as 180° or 90°, **subtraction** can be used to determine the missing angle. For example, the angle below shows a 90° angle formed by two adjacent angles. The sum of the 40° angle and the unknown angle need to combine to form a 90° angle.

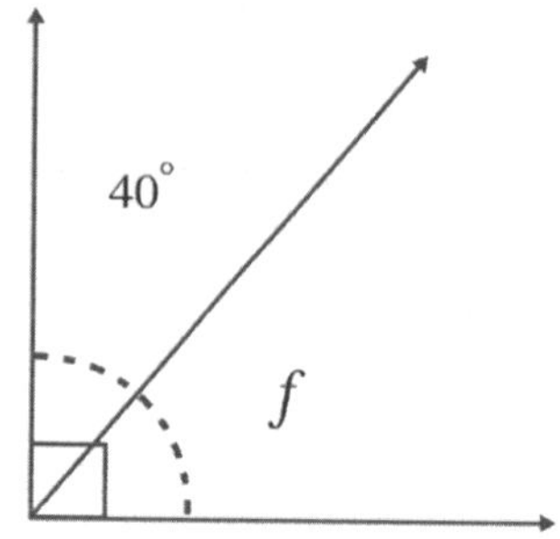

$$f = 90° - 40° = 50°$$

Adjacent angles won't always combine to form benchmark angles. For example, the adjacent angles below don't combine to form a benchmark angle. However, both angles combine to 120°. This means that angle $\angle a + \angle b = 120°$. $\angle a$ is 62°, so an addition equation can be set up.

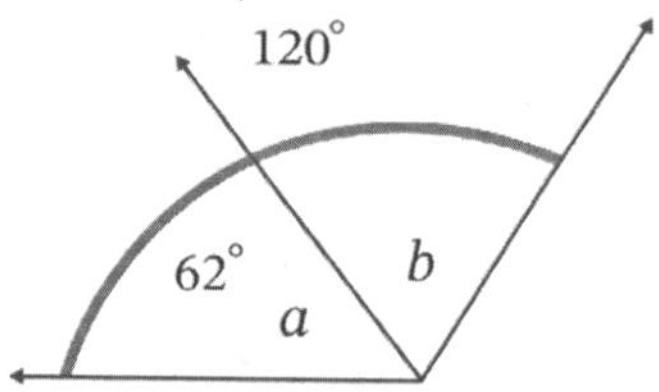

$$b = 120° - 62°$$
$$b = 58°$$

Writing and Solving Equations Involving Angle Measurements

Equations with variables can be used to find missing measurements in geometric figures. By using what we know about geometry, we can create and solve equations to find these measurements.

Triangles have three interior angles. The sum of the three interior angles of a triangle is always 180°.

Let's use this information to solve a missing angle problem. Below, we are given a triangle whose angle measures are 35°, $(3x + 15)°$, and 85° and are directed to solve for the value of x.

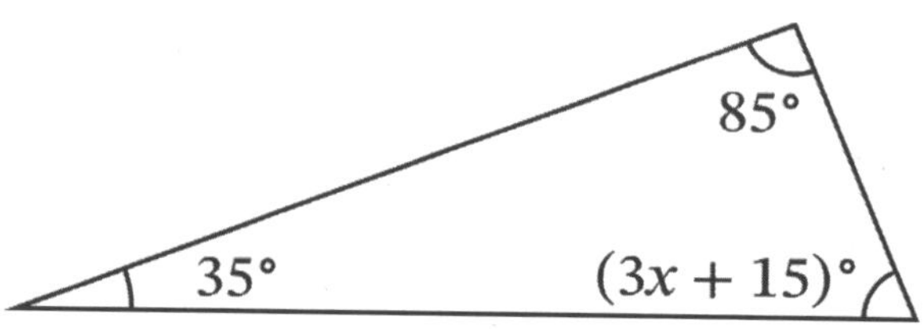

We can use an equation to solve for x and find the missing angle value.

First, we know that the sum of all angles in a triangle is 180°, so we can find the measurement of the angle that is equal to $3x + 15$ by isolating x.

$$3x = 45$$
$$\frac{3x}{3} = \frac{45}{3}$$
$$x = 15$$

Now we can solve for the missing angle measurement. Since we now know that $x = 15$, and the missing angle measurement is equal to $3x + 15$, we can plug x into the expression to find the angle measurement.

$$3(15) + 15$$

$$45 + 15$$

$$60$$

The missing angle measurement is 60°.

EXAMPLE

The angle measures of a triangle are shown in the diagram.

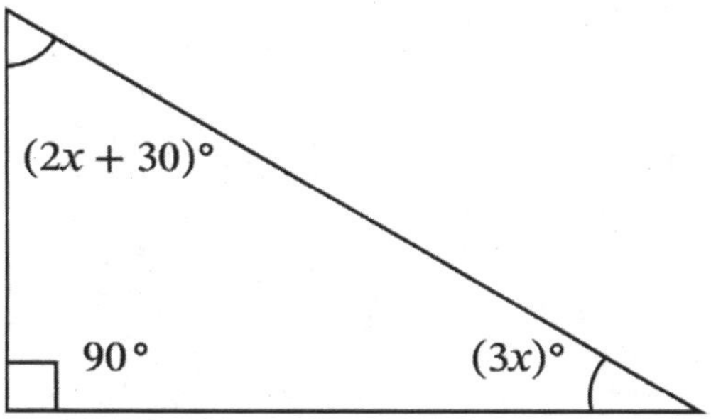

What is the value of x?

This triangle shows two angles with missing angle measures and one angle with a measure of 90°.

If we know that the sum of all angles of a triangle is 180°, then we can use subtraction to find the sum of the two missing angles.

$$180° - 90° = 90°$$

The sum of the two missing angles is 90°. This means that the sum of $3x$ and $2x + 30$ is 90°. Write and solve an equation that shows this.

$$3x + (2x + 30) = 90$$

Because the expressions on the left side of the equation are being added together, there is no need for parentheses.

$$3x + 2x + 30 = 90$$

Combine like terms.

$$5x + 30 = 90$$

Now, solve for x.

$$5x + 30 - 30 = 90 - 30$$
$$5x = 60$$

$$\frac{5x}{5} = \frac{60}{5}$$
$$x = 12$$

The value of x is 12.

We can check to see if this makes sense with the given triangle by using $x = 12$ to find the measurements of each angle.

$$3x = 3(12) = 36°$$

$$2x + 30 = 2(12) + 30 = 24 + 30 = 54°$$

The missing angle measures are 36° and 54°. If that were true, the sum of all angle measures would be 180°.

$$36 + 54 + 90 = 180$$
$$90 + 90 = 180$$
$$180 = 180$$

This is true, so we have confirmed the value of x is 12.

TRANSFORMATIONS

Transformations move, flip, or change a figure in order to create a new figure. Two of the common **transformations** are reflections and translations.

REFLECTIONS

A **reflection** can be visualized as a "flip."

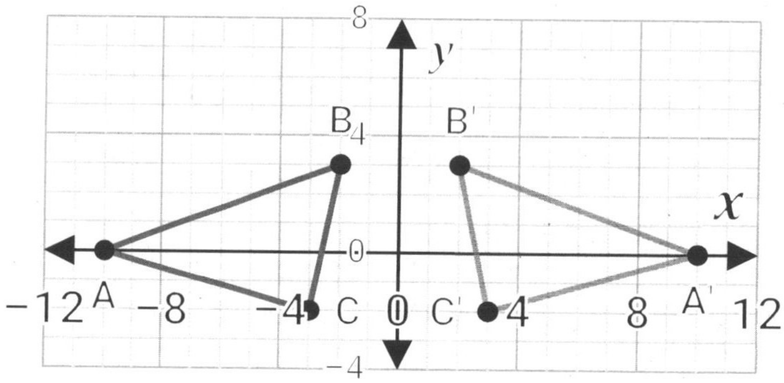

When a figure is mirrored across a line or a plane, the figure has been reflected. The line that an image is reflected across is referred to as the mirror line. Mirror lines can be in any direction. Each point on the reflected figure will be the same distance from the mirror line as the point on the original figure. A reflected image will remain the same size as the original image.

Review Video: Reflection
Visit mometrix.com/academy and enter code: 955068

TRANSLATIONS

A **translation** can be visualized as a "slide."

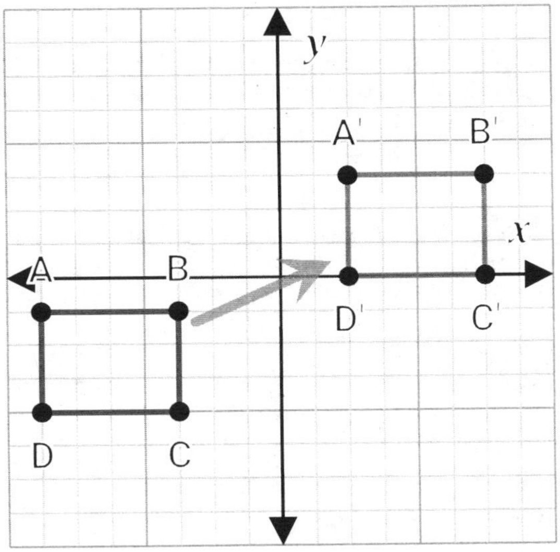

In a translation, every point of the figure must be moved the same distance, in the same direction. For example, all points on the original rectangle *ABCD* have moved 9 units to the right and 4 units up in order to form the new rectangle. The new and original figures remain congruent when translated.

Review Video: Translation
Visit mometrix.com/academy and enter code: 718628

PRESERVING CONGRUENCE IN TRANSFORMATIONS

When a transformation is applied to a figure, a new figure is created. Two of the common transformations include reflections and translations.

When reflections and translations occur the new figure is the same shape and size as the original figure, which means it is **congruent** to the original figure. The new shape has a new orientation on the coordinate plane.

Consider the reflection and translation in the graphics. Notice how the original and new shapes are congruent despite having a new orientation on the coordinate plane.

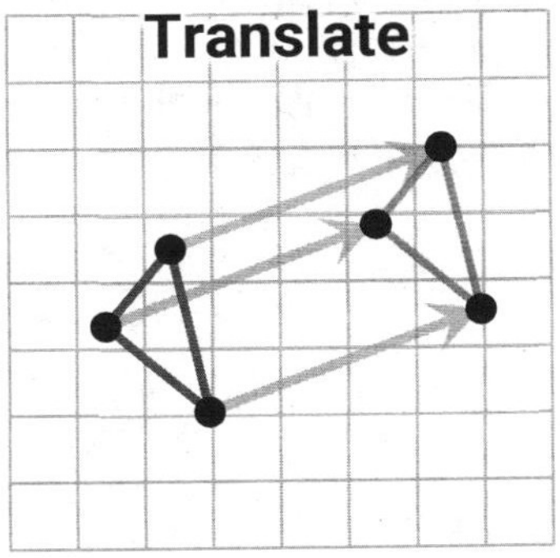

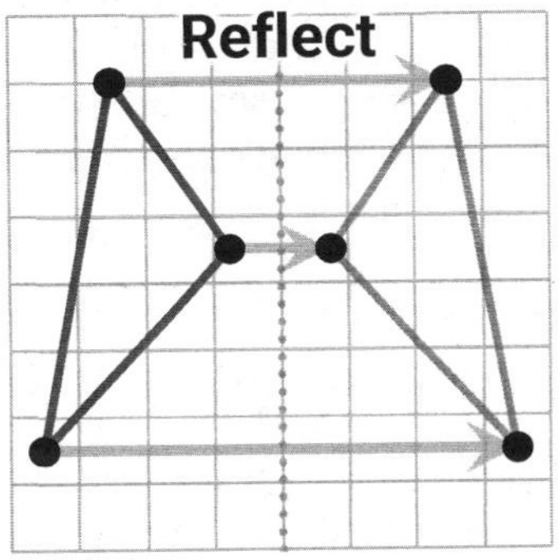

A translation "slides" and a reflection "flips". Regardless of the new orientation of the shape on the coordinate plane, the new shapes are all the same shape and size as the originals. This means that when a shape is translated or reflected it will maintain congruency.

REPRESENTING TRANSFORMATIONS

Translations, reflections, and rotations are all examples of **transformations**. In general, reflections occur over the x-axis or y-axis, and rotations are limited to 90°, 180°, 270°, and 360° with the origin as the center of rotation. Transformations can be expressed verbally or algebraically.

TRANSLATIONS

A translation is a type of transformation. **Translations** move or **slide** a figure from one location to another. When a translation occurs, the new figure is congruent to the original figure. The size and shape do not change, just the location on the coordinate grid.

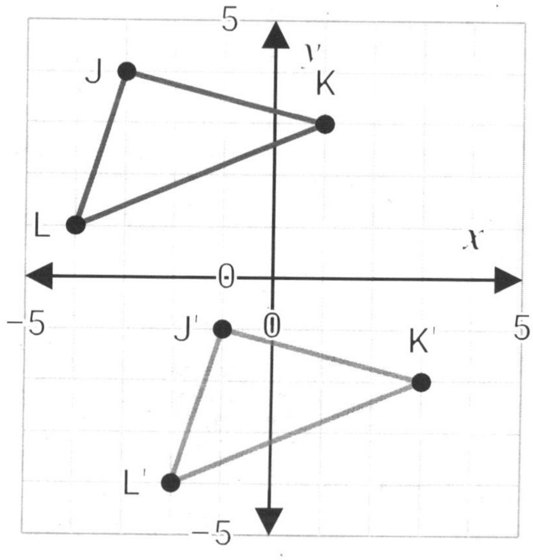

Triangle JKL has been translated. The original triangle contained the points $J(-3,4)$, $K(1,3)$, and $L(-4,1)$. The new triangle contains the points $J'(-1,-1)$, $K'(3,-2)$ and $L'(-2,-4)$. This can be described as a translation of 2 units to the right and 5 units down. This can be tested by counting the movements of each point. Notice how each point, J, K, and L, move 2 units to the right and 5 units down.

A translation can be described using an algebraic representation. In the translation above, each point, J, K, and L have moved 2 units to the right and 5 units down. Algebraically, "2 units to the right" is equivalent to the x-coordinate moving 2 units in the positive direction, or +2. "5 units down" is equivalent to the y-coordinate moving 5 units in the negative direction, or –5. The original points (x, y) now become $(x + 2, y - 5)$. An arrow is used to indicate how the original points are translated into the new points. The transformation is expressed as $(x, y) \rightarrow (x + 2, y - 5)$ algebraically.

REFLECTIONS

A **reflection** is a transformation that can be visualized as a **flip**. Shapes are reflected over a line of reflection, which is usually the x- or y-axis. When a shape is reflected over the x- or y-axis, each point maintains the same distance from the line of reflection.

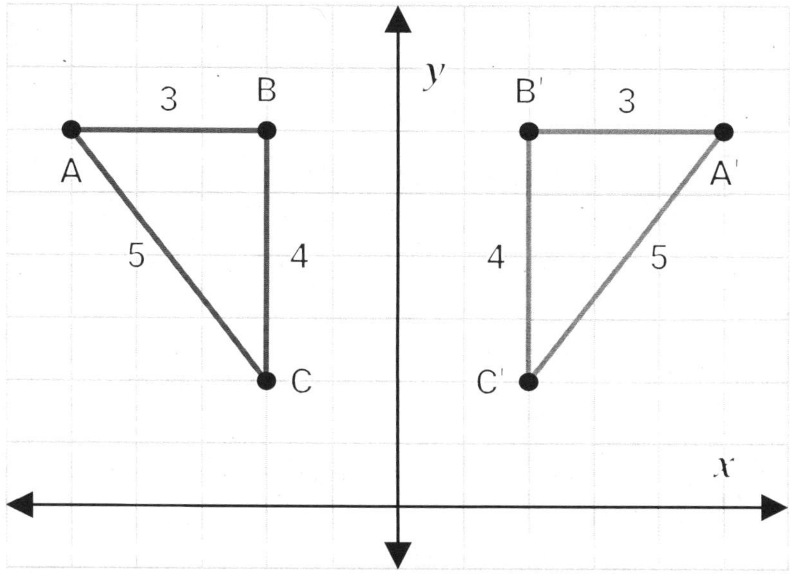

For example, triangle ABC is reflected over the y-axis to form the triangle $A'B'C'$. Point A is 5 units from the y-axis, and point A' is also 5 units from the y-axis. Point B is 2 units from the y-axis, and point B' is also 2 units from the y-axis. Point C is 2 units from the y-axis, and point C' is also 2 units from the y-axis. When a reflection occurs over the y-axis, the y-coordinates stay the same. When a reflection occurs over the x-axis, the x-coordinates stay the same.

When an (x, y) point is reflected over the x-axis, the x-value will remain the same, but the sign associated with the y-value will change. Similarly, when an (x, y) point is reflected over the y-axis, the y-value will remain the same, but the sign associated with the x-value will change.

For example, in triangle ABC shown above, point A was located at $(-5,6)$. This is reflected over the y-axis, so the y-value will remain the same, but the sign associated with the x-value will change so that the point $(-5,6)$ becomes $(5,6)$.

Point A: $(-5,6)$ becomes $(5,6)$

Point B: $(-2,6)$ becomes $(2,6)$

Point C: $(-2,2)$ becomes $(2,2)$

The table below summarizes the changes that occur to the x- and y-values when a reflection takes place over the x- or y-axis.

Type of Reflection	Point of the pre-image (before reflection)	Point of the image (after reflection)
Reflection about the $\boldsymbol{x}$-axis	(x, y)	$(x, -y)$
Reflection about the $\boldsymbol{y}$-axis	(x, y)	$(-x, y)$

Probability, Statistics, Patterns, Functions, and Algebra

Probability

Simple and Compound Events

Lists and tree diagrams can be used to represent sample spaces for simple and compound events. A **simple event** is an event where there is one trial. For example, a coin flip is a simple event, since it has one trial that has one outcome. A **compound event** is an event with multiple, separate trials. For example, flipping two coins would have two trials: one for the first coin and another for the second coin. Flipping one coin twice would also be a compound event, since a different trial occurs each time the coin is flipped.

Review Video: Intro to Probability
Visit mometrix.com/academy and enter code: 212374

Experimental Probability

Predictions can be made about the outcomes of simple and compound events based on experimental data. A prediction based on experimental data is called **experimental probability**. Experimental data is the data that is collected by observing an experiment. The experimental probability can be found by reviewing experimental data then setting up and solving a proportion.

Let's say that an experiment is performed where a spinner is spun 100 times. One spin has three possible outcomes. The spinner could land on A, B, or C.

This table shows the experimental data.

Spin Outcome	Frequency
A	42
B	22
C	36

The table includes the three possible outcomes from a spin and the frequency that the spinner landed in each section. With this information, we can determine the experimental probability that the spinner could land on each section. Let's find the experimental probability that the spinner will land on section A.

The experimental probability is a comparison between the frequency of an outcome and the total number of outcomes; usually written as a fraction. In this example, the spinner landed on section A 42 times, so the frequency of the outcome is 42. The total number of outcomes is the total number of spins, which in this case is 100.

In this example, the experimental probability the spinner will land on A is $\frac{42}{100}$.

$$\frac{\text{frequency}}{\text{total}} = \frac{\text{number of times the spinner landed on A}}{\text{number of times the spinner was spun}} = \frac{42}{100}$$

Review Video: Empirical Probability
Visit mometrix.com/academy and enter code: 513468

Example

We can make predictions using experimental data.

The table shows the experimental data of a spinner landing in section A, B, or C.

Spin Outcome	Frequency
A	42
B	22
C	36

Using this data, we can make reasonable predictions about future spins. We can predict the number of times the spinner will land on a certain section when it is spun in the future based on the experimental probability.

Let's explore how many times the spinner will land on section B in the next 50 spins.

The spinner landed on B 22 times out of 100 spins, which means that the experimental probability the spinner will land on B is $\frac{22}{100}$.

To predict the number of times the spinner will land on B in the next 50 spins, we can use a proportion.

$$\frac{22}{100} = \frac{x}{50}$$
$$22 \cdot 50 = 100x$$

$$1{,}100 = 100x$$
$$\frac{1{,}100}{100} = \frac{100x}{100}$$
$$11 = x$$

This means that the experimental probability that the spinner will land on B in 50 spins is $\frac{11}{50}$. Based on the experimental data, we can expect the spinner to land on B 11 times in the next 50 spins.

Theoretical Probability

The theoretical probability of an outcome differs from the experimental probability. An experimental probability represents the probability of an outcome after reviewing experimental data. This means that an experiment has been completed, there is experimental data, and you can make predictions about future events based on what happened already. **Theoretical probability** represents the probability of an outcome before an experiment, based on formulas. This means the experiment hasn't happened yet, but we can make predications based on calculated likelihood. The theoretical probability of an outcome can be described as the comparison between the number of desired outcomes and the number of possible outcomes.

Let's say a coin will be flipped. This is a simple event with two outcomes: heads or tails. Because there are only two options, the theoretical probability that the coin will land on heads in one flip is $\frac{1}{2}$.

$$\frac{\text{outcome of heads}}{\text{total possible outcomes}} = \frac{1}{2}$$

Now let's say we are rolling a six-sided dice. This is a simple event with six possible outcomes: 1, 2, 3, 4, 5, or 6. The theoretical probability that the dice will land on 5 in one roll is $\frac{1}{6}$.

$$\frac{\text{outcome of 5}}{\text{total possible outcomes}} = \frac{1}{6}$$

Or we can find the theoretical probability that the dice will land on an even number. Out of the total possible outcomes, there are three even numbers: 2, 4, and 6. And there are six possible outcomes.

$$\frac{\text{outcome of an even number}}{\text{total possible outcomes}} = \frac{3}{6}$$

This fraction can be reduced.

$$\frac{3}{6} = \frac{1}{2}$$

The theoretical probability that the dice will land on an even number is $\frac{1}{2}$.

By identifying the theoretical probability within experiments, we can make predictions about the frequency of outcomes using proportions.

<u>EXAMPLE</u>

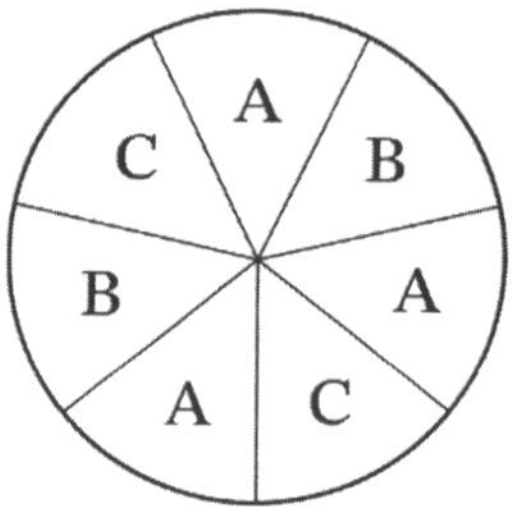

The spinner has seven congruent sections and is spun 35 times. What is a reasonable prediction for the number of times the spinner will land on B?

To solve this problem, we will find the theoretical probability and use a proportion.

The spinner shows seven congruent sections. Out of the seven sections, two are labeled with a B. There are seven possible outcomes for each spin, and two of them are B, so the theoretical probability that the spinner will land on B is $\frac{2}{7}$.

$$\frac{\text{outcome}}{\text{total possible outcomes}} = \frac{\text{sections labeled B}}{\text{total sections}} = \frac{2}{7}$$

Now, we need to calculate a reasonable prediction for the number of times the spinner will land on B when the spinner is spun 35 times. We can set up a proportion to solve this problem.

$$\begin{aligned} \frac{2}{7} &= \frac{x}{35} \\ 2 \cdot 35 &= 7x \\ 70 &= 7x \\ \frac{70}{7} &= \frac{7x}{7} \\ 10 &= x \end{aligned}$$

A reasonable prediction for the number of times the spinner will land on B when the spinner is spun 35 times is 10 times.

Probabilities and Complements of a Simple Event

The **probability** of an outcome describes the comparison between a proposed outcome and the total possible outcomes of an event. The **complement** of a probability is the probability that a proposed outcome will not happen.

If the probability that something will happen is 100%, then there is a 0% probability that it will not happen. This shows that a probability and its complement, when expressed as percentages, must add up to 100%.

When performing calculations involving probability, these percentages are usually expressed as decimals or fractions. In this form, the probability and its complement should add up to 1. This means that the formula $1 - P = C$, where P is the original probability and C is its complement, can be used to find the complement of a probability.

For instance, a six-sided dice is rolled. The probability that the dice will land on the number 1 is $\frac{1}{6}$ because there is one side that reads 1 and there are six total sides.

The complement of this probability is the probability that the dice will not land on the number 1. There are five sides on the dice that are not the number 1, out of a total of six sides, so the probability that the dice will not land on the number 1 is $\frac{5}{6}$. This means that the complement of the probability that the dice will land on the number 1 is $\frac{5}{6}$.

Example

A student selects a bead out of the bag at random. There are 16 red beads, 14 green beads, 24 blue beads, and 18 yellow beads. Which statement is true?

a. The probability of selecting a blue bead is $\frac{1}{4}$, and the probability of selecting a bead that is not blue is $\frac{3}{4}$.
b. The probability of selecting a blue bead is $\frac{3}{4}$, and the probability of selecting a bead that is not blue is $\frac{1}{4}$.
c. The probability of selecting a blue bead is $\frac{1}{3}$, and the probability of selecting a bead that is not blue is $\frac{2}{3}$.
d. The probability of selecting a blue bead is $\frac{2}{3}$, and the probability of selecting a bead that is not blue is $\frac{1}{3}$.

This problem focuses on identifying the probability of an outcome and its complement. To identify the true statement, we will identify the probability of selecting a blue bead and probability of NOT selecting a blue bead.

There are 24 blue beads in the bag and a total of $16 + 14 + 24 + 18 = 72$ beads in the bag. The probability of selecting a blue bead is $\frac{24}{72}$. This can be simplified by dividing the numerator and denominator by the greatest common factor, 24.

$$\frac{24 \div 24}{72 \div 24} = \frac{1}{3}$$

The probability that a blue bead will be selected is $\frac{1}{3}$.

The probability of selecting a bead that is not blue can be determined by finding the complement of this probability. The formula $1 - P = C$ can be used to find the complement.

$$1 - \frac{1}{3} = C$$
$$\frac{3}{3} - \frac{1}{3} = C$$

$$\frac{2}{3} = C$$

$$\frac{48 \div 24}{72 \div 24} = \frac{2}{3}$$

The probability of selecting a bead that is not blue is $\frac{2}{3}$.

The correct answer is C.

REPRESENTING DATA

FREQUENCY TABLES

Categorical data is data that is divided into qualitative categories. You get categorical data if you are taking a survey of favorite foods, or when a company collects data about the sizes of t-shirts they sold. This type of data is categorical data because the data can be divided into categories. One way to describe categorical data is through frequency tables. A **frequency table** is a table that visually divides this categorical data into categories and shows how frequently a category shows up in the data. For example, let's say a food truck is keeping track of how often each menu item is ordered to see which is their most popular item. The food truck sells tacos, sandwiches, salads, and burgers. A frequency table can be created to keep track of this data throughout the day.

Menu Item	Number Sold
Tacos	
Sandwiches	
Salads	
Burgers	

As items are sold, tallies or marks can be made on the frequency table to keep track of information. Let's say the food truck sold 13 taco plates, 10 sandwiches, 9 salads, and 18 burgers. These frequency tables display the data from the food truck.

Menu Item	Number Sold
Tacos	𝍸 𝍸 |||
Sandwiches	𝍸 𝍸
Salads	𝍸 ||||
Burgers	𝍸 𝍸 𝍸 |||

Menu Item	Number Sold
Tacos	13
Sandwiches	10
Salads	9
Burgers	18

HISTOGRAMS

Data can be represented visually in many ways including bar graphs, histograms, dot plots, and circle graphs.

A **histogram** organizes data by showing the frequency of data in certain ranges. A histogram contains a vertical and horizontal axis. Typically, the frequency is listed vertically. Histograms can illustrate many types of data sets.

Review Video: Data Interpretation of Graphs
Visit mometrix.com/academy and enter code: 200439

EXAMPLE

The table shows the number of likes some promotional videos each received on a social media platform.

953	1,634	1,348	450	2,349	879
1,334	2,145	587	994	1,045	950
2,231	1,287	1,898	1,934	2,150	2,476

Which histogram displays the data in the table accurately?

a.

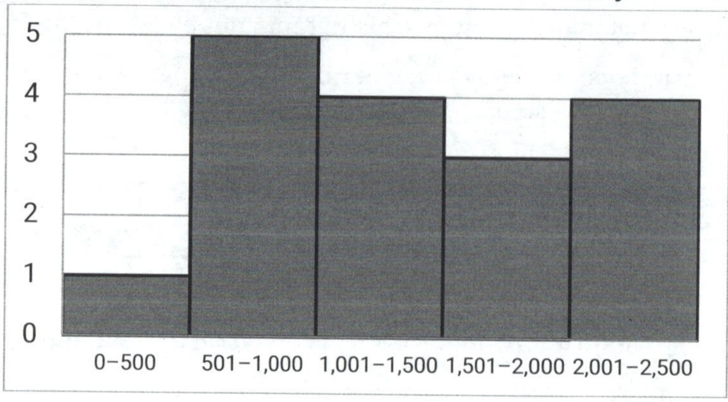

b.

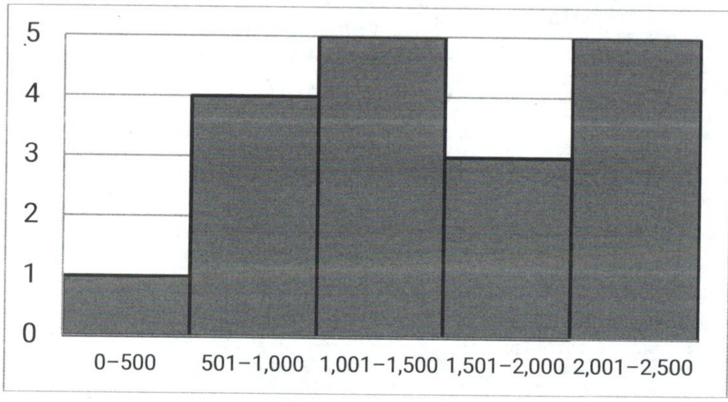

c.

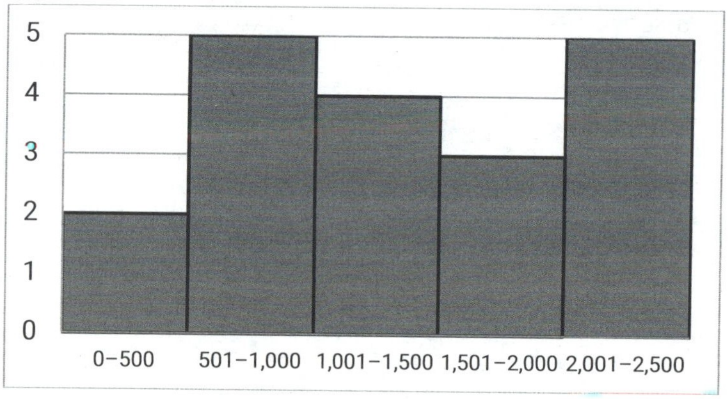

d.

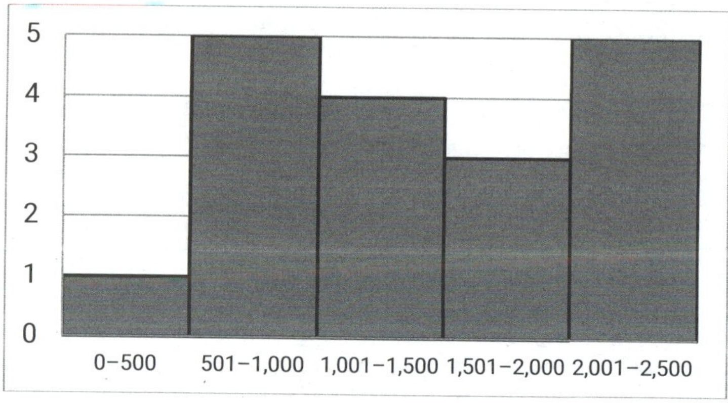

In this problem, we are given a table of values. Each value represents the number of likes a promotional video got. We need to choose the histogram that accurately displays the data.

To solve this problem, we need to first understand the data in the table, and the data on the graphs. As you can see, each graph option has the same horizontal and vertical values. Each number along the left of the histogram represents the number of videos, or the frequency, and increases by 1. Along the bottom, the values are divided by 500s. We have five categories: 0-500, 500-1,000, 1,000-1,500, 1,500-2,000, and 2,000-2,500. Each bar on the graph will show how many videos got a number of likes within these ranges.

First, we need to identify how many videos got the number of likes in each category.

By going through the list, we can see that 1 video got between 0 and 500 likes. It got 450.

5 videos had between 500 and 1,000 likes.

4 videos had between 1,000 and 1,500 likes.

3 videos had between 1,500 and 2,000 likes.

5 videos had between 2,000 and 2,500 likes.

Now that we have this information, we can compare the given choices.

Choice A shows accurate data in every column except the last one. Instead of 5 videos between 2,000 and 2,500 likes, it shows only 4. This is not the correct graph.

Choice B switches the data in the second and third columns. Instead of 5 videos between 500 and 1,000 likes and 4 videos between 1,000 and 1,500 likes, it shows 4 videos and 5 videos. This is not the correct graph.

Choice C shows accurate information in every column except the first column. Instead of showing 1 video with 0-500 likes, this graph shows that 2 videos had between 0 and 500 likes. This is not the correct graph.

Choice D shows all accurate information.

The correct answer is D.

Dot Plots

Data can be represented graphically, or visually, in many ways. We have seen data represented using a coordinate plane. Data may also be represented through dot plots, stem-and-leaf plots, histograms, and box plots.

A **dot plot**, also referred to as a line plot, is a type of graph where values are lined up vertically, like a number line, and dots or x's are used to show the frequency of each value, or how many times that value appears in the data. Dot plots are used to show how often something happens. Dot plots are mostly used when gathering data from multiple trials or surveys. Using a dot plot is a way to represent these types of results in an organized way.

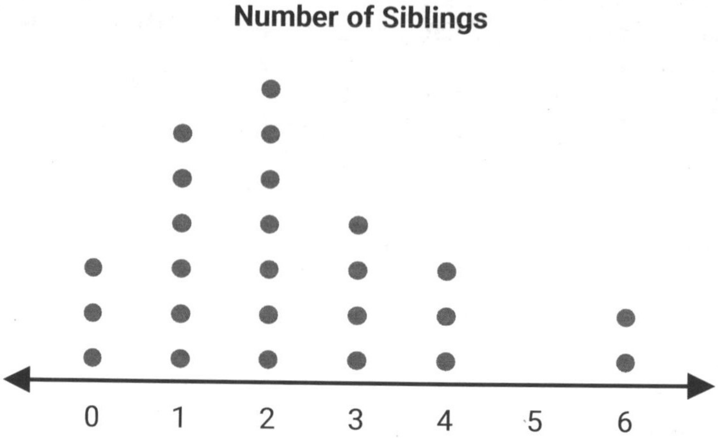

This dot plot shows the data from a survey of the 6th graders in a classroom. The survey gathered data about the number of siblings each 6th grader has in their family. The numbers along the bottom represent the number of siblings and the dots represent the number of students. Each dot is equal to one student. Based on this dot plot, you can tell that 7 people said that they have 2 siblings because there are 7 dots above 2.

The data from this dot plot can also be written in list form.

6, 6, 4, 4, 4, 3, 3, 3, 3, 2, 2, 2, 2, 2, 2, 2, 1, 1, 1, 1, 1, 1, 0, 0, 0

0, 0, 0, 1, 1, 1, 1, 1, 1, 2, 2, 2, 2, 2, 2, 2, 3, 3, 3, 3, 4, 4, 4, 6, 6

3, 2, 2, 3, 0, 1, 2, 1, 1, 6, 2, 4, 2, 3, 6, 0, 0, 1, 1, 2, 4, 2, 4, 3, 1

As you can see, each value is represented on the dot plot. Regardless, there are 2 people who have 6 siblings, 0 people with 5 siblings, 3 people with 4 siblings, 4 people with 3 siblings, 7 people with 2 siblings, 6 people with 1 sibling, and 3 people with 0 siblings.

Review Video: Line Plot Visit mometrix.com/academy and enter code: 754610

EXAMPLE

The dot plots show the number of miles two runners ran each week.

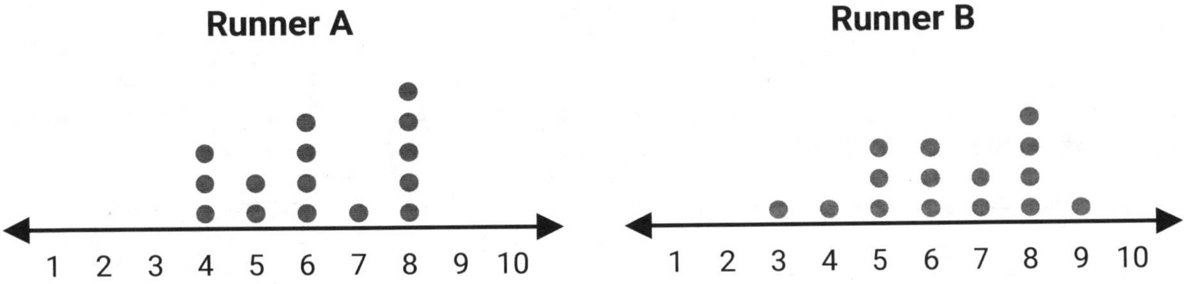

Which statement correctly compares these two data sets?

a. The range of the data for Runner A is greater than the range of the data for Runner B.
b. The mode of the data for Runner A is less than the range of the data for Runner B.
c. The mean of the data for Runner A is less than the mean of the data for Runner B.
d. The peak of the data for Runner A is greater than the peak of the data for Runner B.

To solve this problem, we will analyze the data from each dot plot and identify if each statement is true.

Choice A states that the range of the data for runner A is greater than the range of the data for Runner B. The range of the data is the difference, or distance, between the highest and lowest data point. For Runner A, the greatest data point is 8 and the lowest data point is 4, so the range of the data is $8 - 4 = 4$. For Runner B, the greatest data point is 9 and the lowest data point is 3, so the range of the data is $9 - 3 = 6$. The range of the data for Runner A is less than the range of the data for Runner B. Choice A is incorrect.

Choice B states that the mode of the data for Runner A is less than the range of the data for Runner B. The mode of the data is the data value that appears the most often. Runner 1 ran 8 miles more often than he or she ran the other distances. The range of the data for Runner B is 6. The mode of the data for Runner A is greater than the range of the data for Runner B. Option B is incorrect.

Choice C states that the mean of the data for Runner A is less than the mean of the data for Runner B. The mean of a data set is the sum of the data divided by the number of data points.

$$4 + 4 + 4 + 5 + 5 + 6 + 6 + 6 + 6 + 7 + 8 + 8 + 8 + 8 + 8 = 93$$

$$93 \div 15 = 6.2$$

The mean of the data for Runner B is also the sum of all miles run divided by the number of weeks recorded.

$$3 + 4 + 5 + 5 + 5 + 6 + 6 + 6 + 7 + 7 + 8 + 8 + 8 + 8 + 9 = 95$$

$$95 \div 15 = 6.\overline{3}$$

The mean of the data for Runner A is less than the mean of the data for Runner B. Choice C is supported by the data.

Choice D states that the peak of the data for Runner A is greater than the peak of the data for Runner B. On a dot plot, the peak is the data value with the highest column. The peak of the data for Runner A is 8. The peak of the data for Runner B is also 8. The peak of the data for Runner A is the same as the peak of the data for Runner B. Option D is incorrect.

The correct answer is C.

STEM-AND-LEAF PLOTS

A **stem-and-leaf plot** is a way to illustrate data with multi-digit values. This type of data representation is best used with a large number of data points that vary in value, say values from 0 to 100. Two common cases where stem-and-leaf plots are used are plotting the ages of a population and plotting temperature values.

In a stem-and-left plot, values are separated by place value. There is a list of numbers listed vertically along the left side; these are the stems. There is a list of numbers to the right of each stem; these are the leaves. There is a line dividing the stems from the leaves.

The stem-and-leaf plot below describes the ages of people at a family reunion.

Stem	Leaf
0	2, 2, 4, 5, 8, 8, 9
1	1, 2, 3, 3, 3, 4, 4, 5, 7, 9
2	0, 2, 8
3	2, 4, 6, 6, 7
4	3, 4, 9
5	0, 4, 5, 5, 6
6	4, 5, 5
7	0, 1
8	2
9	0, 4
10	2

Key:

9|4 = 94

10|2 = 102

You can see that there are values 0 to 9 on the left, a dividing line, and numbers to the right. The numbers on the left describe the tens place. The numbers to the right describe the ones place.

So, let's look at the second to last row, the 9's row. All these values have 9 in the tens place, and the listed value in the ones place. So, the values represented by this row are 90 and 94. This means that there are two people at the reunion in their 90s and their ages are 90 and 94.

Now let's look at the first row, the zero row. All these values have a zero in the ten's place. This means these are one-digit numbers. So, the ages represented in this row are 2, 2, 4, 5, 8, 8, 9. That means there are 7 people at the reunion under 10 years old. There are two 2-year-olds, a 4-year-old, a 5-year-old, two 8-year-olds, and a 9-year-old.

Now, sometimes your values will increase, like with our last row. We can see that 10 cannot technically be in the tens place, but this row gives the value 102. It is possible to see two digits in the stem part of the list.

Review Video: Stem-and-Leaf Plots
Visit mometrix.com/academy and enter code: 302339

EXAMPLE

The stem-and-leaf plot shows temperature readings in degrees Celsius.

Temperature Readings

Stem	Leaf
1	8, 9, 9, 9
2	2, 2, 3, 5, 6, 6, 6, 6, 7, 9
3	0, 1, 1, 1, 2, 3

Which statement best describes the data represented by the stem-and-leaf plot?

a. The number of readings between 10 and 20 degrees is greater than the number of readings 30 or above.
b. More than half of the readings were over 26 degrees Celsius.
c. The most common temperature reading was 9 degrees Celsius.
d. 50% of the temperature readings were in the 20s.

In this problem we are given a stem-and-leaf plot that has a series of temperatures. We need to select the statement that is true about the data represented by the plot.

To approach this type of problem, we should examine the statements and determine if they are true or not based on the data on the plot.

Choice A states that the number of readings between 10 and 20 degrees is greater than the number of readings over 30. To decide if this statement is true or not, we need to identify the number of readings that are between 10 and 20 and compare this to the number of readings over 30.

By reviewing the stem-and-leaf plot, we can see that there are 4 readings between 10 and 20: 18, 19, 19, and 19. We can also identify that there are 5 readings that are over 30: 31, 31, 31, 32, and 33. Because there are 5 readings above 30 degrees and 4 readings between 10 and 20, the number of readings between 10 and 20 is not greater than the number of readings 30 or above. This statement is not true, so A is not our answer.

Choice B states that more than half of the readings were over 26 degrees Celsius. To decide if this statement is true, we need to identify the number of readings over 26 degrees and compare this to the total number of readings.

By reviewing the stem-and-leaf plot, we can see that there are 8 readings that were over 26: 27, 29, 30, 31, 31, 31, 32, and 33. The total number of readings is 20. 8 is not more than half of 20 because half of 20 is 10, and 8 is less than 10. This statement is not true, so B is not our answer.

Choice C states that the most common temperature reading was 9 degrees Celsius. To decide if this statement is true, we need to review the data on the table. We can see that there are four 9s on the stem-and-leaf plot, but this does not mean the readings are 9 degrees. Instead, the readings with 9's are 19, 19, 19, and 29. Because there are no readings that read 9 degrees, this statement is not true, so C is not our answer.

While we have eliminated the untrue statements, we need to review the last choice to be sure.

Choice D states that 50% of the temperature readings were in the 20s. To decide if this statement is true, we need to identify the number of readings in the 20s and compare that to the total number of readings.

By reviewing the stem-and-leaf plot, we can see that there are 10 readings in the 20s: 22, 22, 23, 25, 26, 26, 26, 26, 27, and 29. We also know that the total number of readings is 20. 10 is half, or 50%, of 20, so this is a true statement.

The correct answer is D.

Circle Graphs

A **circle graph**, also known as a pie graph, is a type of graph used to represent the distribution of data. A circle graph uses a circle to represent the total data and each portion of the circle is divided based on the way the data is distributed. Circle graphs are commonly used with percentages and to illustrate how something is distributed across groups.

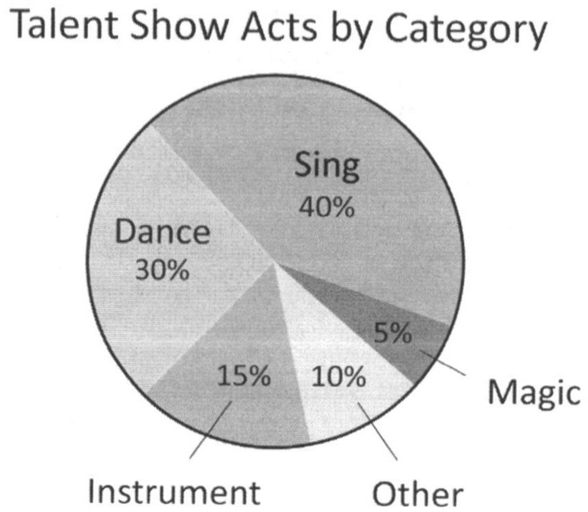

This circle graph shows the data collected from a middle school talent show. At the talent show, there were 80 students participating. 40% of the students performed a singing act, 30% of the students performed a dancing act, 15% of students played a musical instrument, 5% of students performed a magic act, and the remainder of the students, 10%, performed some other type of act.

A complete circle of the circle graph represents all students who participated in the talent show, or 100%. The size of each "slice" of the circle is proportional to the number of students who participated in a specific type of act.

EXAMPLE

A 7th grader spent 60 hours on their phone last week. The circle graph shows their phone's screen time report from last week.

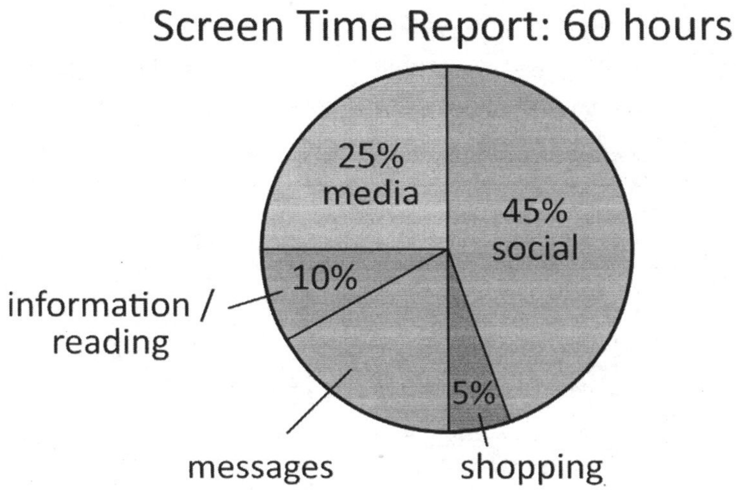

Based on the circle graph, how many hours were spent in messages?

A circle graph shows the percentage distribution of data from a data set. To solve this problem, we will need to identify the percentage of the hours spent in messages and identify the number of hours this percentage represents.

Based on the circle graph, we can see that this person spent 45% of the time on social, 25% on media, 10% on information/reading, 5% on shopping, and the rest in messages. We can use subtraction to find the percentage of hours spent in messages.

$$45\% + 25\% + 10\% + 5\% = 85\%$$
$$100\% - 85\% = 15\%$$

This person spent 15% of 60 hours in messages.

Now that we know the percentage of time spent in messages, we can set up a proportion and use cross multiplication to solve for the number of hours 15% represents.

$$\frac{15}{100} = \frac{x}{60}$$
$$15 \cdot 60 = 100x$$
$$\frac{900}{100} = \frac{100x}{100}$$
$$9 = x$$

This person spent 9 hours in messages last week.

ANALYZING DATA

QUALITATIVE PREDICTIONS AND COMPARISONS

Qualitative predictions are predictions based on observation and words rather than using numbers. Typical qualitative predictions include likelihood comparisons and uses words to describe the probability of an outcome. Qualitative predictions use the words more likely, less likely, very likely, or not likely to describe the probability of an outcome.

A group of 7th graders were asked, "If you could have any superpower, what would it be?" The results are shown in the table.

Superpower	Number of People
Super strength	5
Time travel	15
Fly	20

Based on the results of the survey, there are some predictions we can make about future surveys, and we can use qualitative statements to express these observations.

We can see that there were 40 students surveyed, $5 + 15 + 20 = 40$.

We can see that the superpower with the most votes was flight. Strength was chosen the least. Time travel was chosen three times as often as strength, and flight was chosen four times as often as strength.

We can make predictions about future surveys with this information.

It is more likely that time travel will be voted for than strength.

It is much more likely that flight will be voted for than strength.

It is less likely strength will be voted for than flight or time travel.

SHAPE OF A DATA DISTRIBUTION

The **shape** of data distribution describes the way that a set of data looks when it is represented visually. Graphs are visual illustrations of data, and we can observe the way data is displayed to make judgements. We can describe the shape of data based on symmetry, uniformity, peaks, gaps, clusters, and if it is skewed to one side or another.

SYMMETRY

A graph with **symmetry** is a graph that has a symmetrical shape, or it is the same shape on both sides. A symmetrical graph can be folded in half and look the same on both sides. Each side is a mirror image. The bar graph, dot plot, and box plot below show symmetrical sets of data.

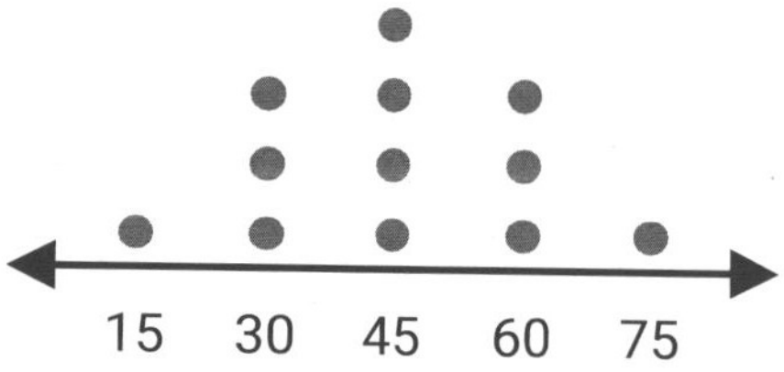

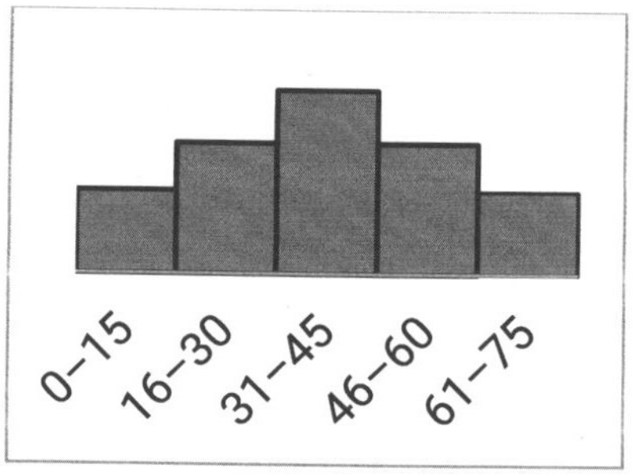

PEAKS

A **peak** on a graph is an area where there are more data points. A peak will be a tall part of a graph, where there is one area with the most data. The bar graph below shows a graph with two peaks. There is a peak at 16–30 and another peak at 46–60.

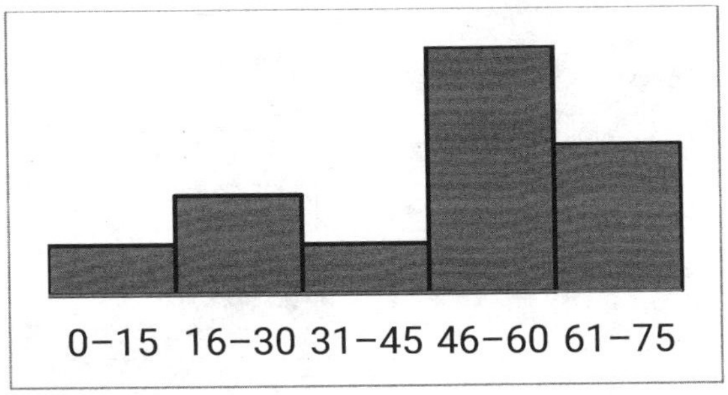

A **uniform** graph does not have any peaks.

GAPS

A **gap** on a graph is an area on the graph where there is no data and there is a blank area, or gap, in the graph. The dot plot below shows a graph with a gap at 60 because there is no data at 60, but there is data surrounding 60.

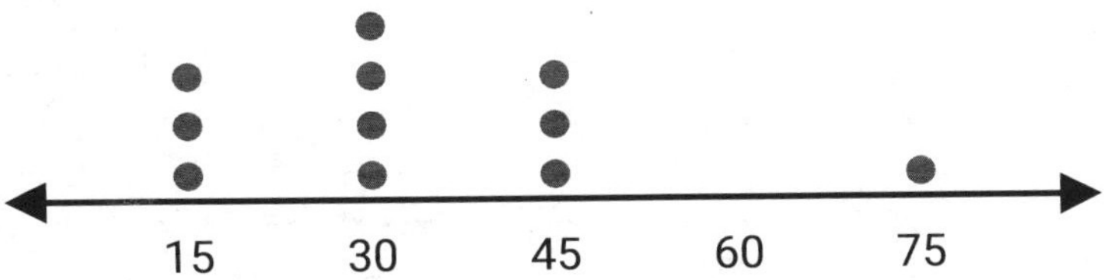

CLUSTERS

A **cluster** on a graph is an area where the majority of the data lies. The bar graph below shows a graph with a cluster from 0 to 45 because the majority of the data is at 0–15, 15–30, and 30–45.

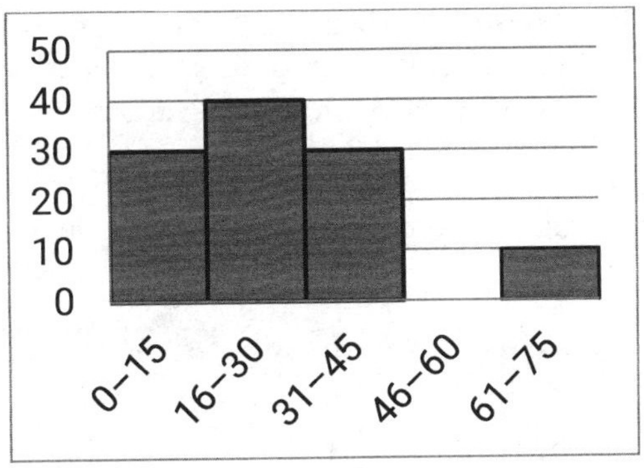

SKEWS

A **skewed** graph shows more data on one side of a graph than another. In a skewed graph, there is a peak and a tail. The peak in a graph is an area with the most data. The **tail** in a graph is an area with the least data. A graph with the tail to the right is described as "skewed to the right". A graph with the tail to the left is described as "skewed to the left".

Skewed to the right:

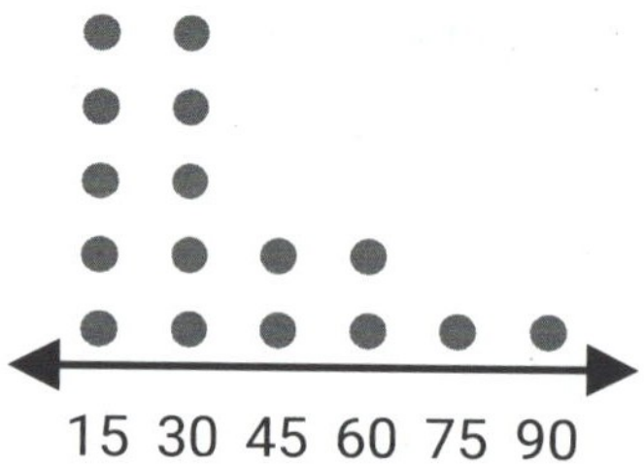

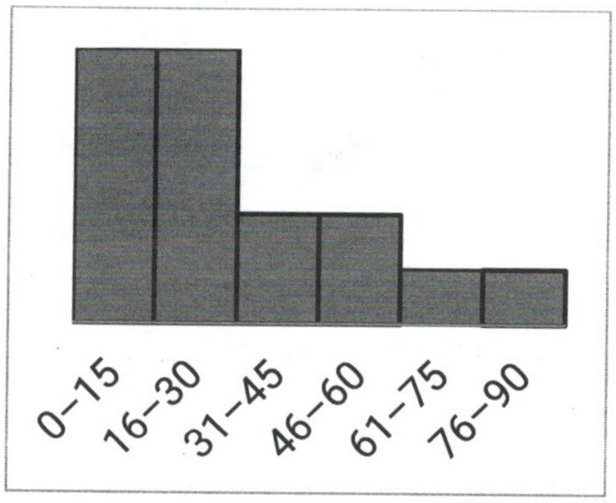

Skewed to the left:

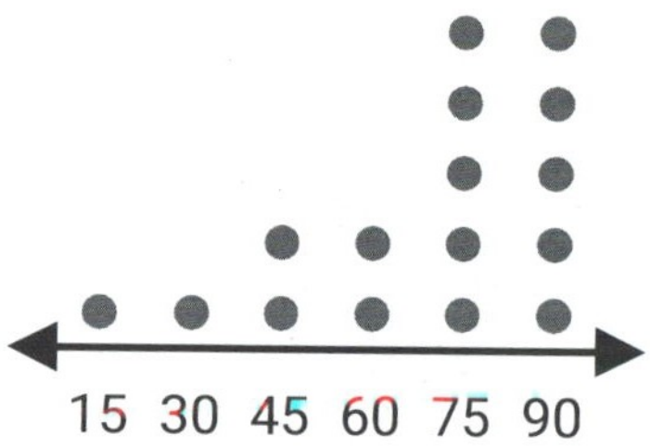

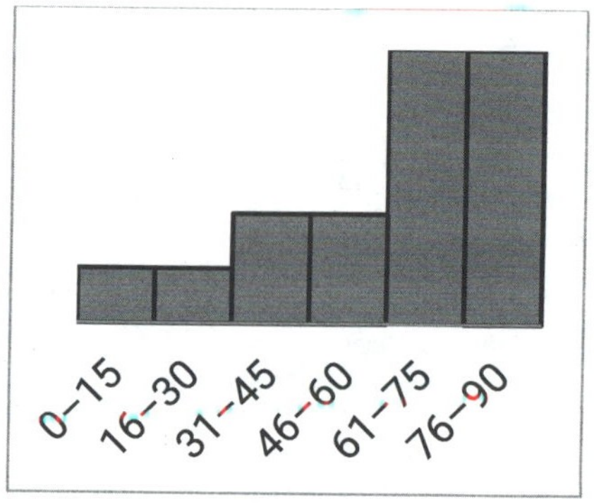

QUALITATIVE PREDICTIONS AND COMPARISONS

Qualitative predictions are predictions based on observation and words rather than using numbers. Typical qualitative predictions include likelihood comparisons and uses words to describe the probability of an outcome. Qualitative predictions use the words more likely, less likely, very likely, or not likely to describe the probability of an outcome.

A group of 7th graders were asked, "If you could have any superpower, what would it be?" The results are shown in the table.

Superpower	Number of People
Super strength	5
Time travel	15
Fly	20

Based on the results of the survey, there are some predictions we can make about future surveys, and we can use qualitative statements to express these observations.

We can see that there were 40 students surveyed, $5 + 15 + 20 = 40$.

We can see that the superpower with the most votes was flight. Strength was chosen the least. Time travel was chosen three times as often as strength, and flight was chosen four times as often as strength.

We can make predictions about future surveys with this information.

It is more likely that time travel will be voted for than strength.

It is much more likely that flight will be voted for than strength.

It is less likely strength will be voted for than flight or time travel.

QUANTITATIVE PREDICTIONS AND COMPARISONS

Quantitative predictions are predictions based on calculations. Experimental probability and theoretical probability are examples of quantitative predictions. These predictions are described using numbers whether it be a fraction or a percentage.

We can use quantitative predictions to express the probability of the outcome of future surveys.

We can see that there are 5 votes for strength, 15 votes for time travel, 20 votes for flight, and 40 total students surveyed. Based on this information, and what we know about probability, we can make predictions about future surveys.

> It is three times more likely for a student to vote for time travel than super strength.
>
> It is four times more likely for a student to vote for flight than super strength.

We can also make predictions about future surveys with numerical data.

> The probability of a student voting for strength is $\frac{1}{8}$.
>
> The probability of a student voting for flight or time travel is $\frac{7}{8}$.
>
> There is a 50% chance a student will vote for flight.

We cannot confirm what will happen in the future, but we can make educated predictions based on data from past events.

If there are 496 7th graders, what can be said about the outcomes of a survey of the whole 7th grade?

> There will be about $\frac{1}{8} \times 496 = 62$ votes for strength.
>
> There will be about $\frac{1}{2} \times 492 = 246$ votes for flight.
>
> There will be about $246 - 62 = 184$ more votes for flight than strength.

We make predictions about future outcomes using quantitative and qualitative predictions. Both of these predictions can be made by analyzing the data and comparing the probability of each outcome.

DATA AND EXPERIMENTAL PROBABILITY

Experimental probability is the probability of an outcome based on the results of an experiment. Experimental probability is described using fractions, decimals, or percentages. The experimental probability is the comparison of the frequency of an outcome, or how many times an outcome occurred during an experiment, and the total number of outcomes, or the total number of trials in an experiment.

$$\frac{\text{frequency of an outcome}}{\text{total \# of outcomes}}$$

Let's say there is bag of 50 buttons in different sizes. You pulled a button out of the bag at random and put the button bag in the bag before pulling a new button. The results of 10 pulls are recorded.

Size	Frequency
Large	1
Medium	6
Small	3

This is experimental data, so we can determine the experimental probability from the data. The frequency that a small button was pulled is 3 and the total number of pulls is 10. The experimental probability that a button pulled at random will be a small button is $\frac{3}{10}$, 0.3, or 30%.

$$\frac{\text{frequency of an outcome}}{\text{total \# of outcomes}} = \frac{3}{10} = 0.3 = 30\%$$

EXAMPLE

You flip two coins at the same time. The results of the experiment are represented in the table where H represents heads and T represents tails.

H, T	T, T	T, T	T, H	H, H
H, H	T, H	T, H	H, H	H, T
T, T	T, T	H, H	H, T	H, H

Based on the results, what is the experimental probability that the next time the coins are flipped, they will land with one coin on heads and one coin on tails?

To solve this problem, we will need to identify the frequency of the outcome and compare this to the total number of outcomes.

The trial shows 15 outcomes because there are 15 boxes with outcomes to the coin tosses. There are 6 outcomes where one coin landed on heads and one coin landed on tails. This means that based on the experimental data, the experimental probability that the coins will land with one coin on heads and one coin on tails the next time they are flipped is $\frac{6}{15}$. This can be written as a fraction, decimal, or percentage.

$$\frac{6}{15} = 0.4 = 40\%$$

DATA AND THEORETICAL PROBABILITY

Theoretical probability is the probability of an outcome based on calculations. The theoretical probability is the comparison of the possible frequency, the number of possible times a selected outcome could occur in the future, to the total number of outcomes.

$$\frac{\text{possible frequency of an outcome}}{\text{total \# of outcomes}}$$

Let's say there is a bag of 50 buttons in different colors. The contents of the bag are as follows:

- 5 green buttons
- 35 orange buttons
- 10 purple buttons

This data explains the frequency of button colors that appear in the bag. We can determine theoretical probability based on this information. There is no experiment performed, but we know the contents of the bag, which is enough information to allow us to calculate the probability of selecting a purple button.

The frequency that a purple button appears in the bag is 10 and there are a total of 50 buttons in the bag. The theoretical probability that a purple button will be selected at random is $\frac{1}{5}$, 0.2, or 20%.

$$\frac{\text{possible frequency of an outcome}}{\text{total \# of outcomes}} = \frac{10}{50} = \frac{1}{5} = 0.2 = 20\%$$

EXAMPLE

A variety snack pack contains 6 bags of potato chips, 4 bags of popcorn, 8 bags of fruit snacks, and 7 bags of trail mix, all of equal size. Your teacher selects a stack at random. What is the theoretical probability that your teacher will select a bag of popcorn from the snack pack?

To solve this problem we will identify the possible frequency of an outcome and compare this to the total outcomes.

In this story, there are 4 bags of popcorn in the snack pack. There are a total of 25 snack items in the snack pack. This means that the theoretical probability that your teacher will select a bag of popcorn is $\frac{4}{25}$. This can be written as a fraction, decimal, or percentage.

$$\frac{4}{25} = 0.16 = 16\%$$

Identifying Equivalent Expressions

Expressions Versus Equations

An **expression** includes numbers, variables, or numbers and variables separated with operation signs. Anything that stands alone or could belong on one side of an equal sign, is an expression. $3x + 4$ is an example of an expression. It contains numbers, a variable, and an operation. A single number is also considered an expression. Often, expressions are simplified. $2x + 4x - 1x$ is an example of an expression because there is no equal sign. It cannot be solved; you cannot solve for x in an expression, but it can be simplified. The expression below is simplified.

$$2x + 4x - 1x$$

$$6x - 1x$$

$$5x$$

Each step gives a more simplified version of the same expression. Each step in the simplification gives an equivalent expression.

Identify Equivalent Expressions with Variables

A **variable** is any unknown value represented by a letter or symbol, most commonly x. A **term** is a number or a number multiplied by a variable, like 3, or $3x$. Numerical expressions will include variable terms, and you may be required to identify or generate equivalent expressions that include these variable terms. When you encounter variables, it is important to remember that with each variable, any repetition of that variable is a **like term**. For example, x and y are not like terms because they are different unknown values. Also, x and 4 are not like terms because 4 is a whole number and x is an unknown term. However, x and $3x$ are like terms because they share the same variable. When encountering an expression with like terms, you may be required to simplify or expand the expression to find equivalent expressions.

Simplify the expression $4x + 2x + 7$.

Given the expression $4x + 2x + 7$, you have two like terms. We simplify these terms to find an equivalent expression. We can combine $4x + 2x$ to $6x$ because they are like terms.

So, $4x + 2x + 7$ is equivalent to $6x + 7$.

Expand the expression $4x + 2x + 7$.

Given the same expression $4x + 2x + 7$, we can expand the variable terms to find an equivalent expression. For example, $4x$ can be expanded to $(x + x + x + x)$, and $2x$ can be expanded to $(x + x)$.

So, $4x + 2x + 7$ is equivalent to $(x + x + x + x) + (x + x) + 7$.

When identifying equivalent expressions with variables, like terms can be combined, simplified, or expanded to generate an equivalent expression.

Using the Order of Operations

An **equivalent expression** is part of a set of expressions that have an equivalent value. The order of operations is essential to finding and identifying equivalent expressions. Finding equivalent expressions may require you to simplify or expand an expression. You may simplify the whole expression, or just part of the expression. For example, you may be required to simplify or identify an equivalent expression like $3(2 + 4) - 5$. There are many equivalent expressions that can be generated by this example. These are just a few possibilities.

Simplification

$3(6) - 5$ is an equivalent expression. The part of the expression in parentheses was simplified.

$18 - 5$ is an equivalent expression. The parentheses and multiplication parts of the expression were simplified.

13 is an equivalent expression. All components of the expression have been simplified.

Expansion

$3(2 + 2^2) - 5$ is an equivalent expression. The term 4 has been expanded to include an exponent.

$3(2 + 4) - (5 \times 1)$ is an equivalent expression. The term 5 has been expanded as 5×1.

There are many variations of the same expression. You may be required to simplify or expand an expression to identify equivalence.

Generating Equivalent Expressions

Using the Inverse Property

The **inverse property of addition** states that the sum of a number and its opposite is always equal to 0. Remember, the opposite of a number is a number that is opposite on the number line from zero, or the same number with the opposite sign. For example, −4 is opposite to 4, and 1,726.9 is opposite to −1,726.9. So, the inverse property of addition states that if you add opposite numbers, their sum is zero. For example, $5 + (-5) = 0$ and $-5 + 5 = 0$.

The **inverse property of multiplication** states that a number multiplied by its reciprocal is always equal to 1. The **reciprocal** of a number is its "flipped" fraction. For example, the reciprocal of 5 is $\frac{1}{5}$, or the reciprocal of $\frac{2}{3}$ is $\frac{3}{2}$. The inverse property of multiplication can be applied for these values, $5 \times \frac{1}{5} = 1$ and $\frac{2}{3} \times \frac{3}{2} = 1$. This is because when you multiply across, you get a fraction that is equal to 1.

$$\frac{2}{3} \times \frac{3}{2} = \frac{6}{6} = 1$$

EXAMPLES

Equivalent expressions can be generated using these inverse properties. There is an endless number of possibilities. Let's look at a few examples.

Given the expression $12 \times 0 + (4 - 6)$, we can use the inverse property of addition to generate equivalent expressions.

Using the inverse property of addition, we can say that $12 \times 0 + (4 - 6)$ is equivalent to $12(3 + -3) + (4 - 6)$. Alternatively, the expression $12 \times 0 + (4 - 6)$ is also equivalent to $12(-36 + 36) + (4 - 6)$.

We can do this because the sum of opposite numbers is equal to 0. In this example, we used $(3 + -3)$ and $(36 + -36)$ as equivalent expressions to 0. We could replace the 0 in the original expression with any expression that is equivalent to 0.

Given the expression $1 + (4 - 6)$, we can use the inverse property of multiplication to generate equivalent expressions. Using the inverse property of multiplication, we can say that $1 + (4 - 6)$ is equivalent to $\left(2 \times \frac{1}{2}\right) + (4 - 6)$, or $\left(\frac{5}{4} \times \frac{4}{5}\right) + (4 - 6)$. We can do this because when we multiply a number and its reciprocal, we get 1.

USING THE IDENTITY PROPERTY

The **identity property of multiplication** states that when a number is multiplied by 1, you get the same number. That is, anything multiplied by 1 is itself. For example, $2 \times 1 = 2$, or $1 \times -36 = -36$. Using the identity property of multiplication, we can identify and generate equivalent expressions. Let's say that we are given the expression $15 - (3 \times 4)$. We can generate equivalent expressions using the identity property. One equivalent expression example would be $(15 \times 1) - (3 \times 4)$. Another example would be $15 - (1 \times 3 \times 4)$. We can say these expressions are equivalent because the identity property of multiplication states that we can multiply any portion of an expression by 1 to get the same value.

The **identity property of addition** states that when 0 is added to a number, you get the same number. For example, $2 + 0 = 2$, or $0 + -3 = -3$. We can also use this property to identify and generate equivalent expressions. For example, if we are given the expression $2 \times (1 + 2)$, we could write the equivalent expressions $2 \times (0 + 1 + 2)$ or $(2 + 0) \times (1 + 2)$.

USING THE COMMUTATIVE PROPERTY

The commutative property applies to addition and multiplication and states that these operations can be completed in any order. The **commutative property of addition** states that numbers and terms can be added together in any order to still get the same value. For example, $3 + 4 = 7$ and $4 + 3 = 7$. Also, we can use the commutative property of addition to show that $3x + 4 + 2^2$ is equivalent to $4 + 3x + 2^2$ and $2^2 + 4 + 3x$. When adding terms, you can add in any order and get the same value.

The **commutative property of multiplication** states that numbers and terms can be multiplied in any order to get the same value. For example, 12×3 is equivalent to 3×12. Additionally, we can use the commutative property of multiplication to assume that $(5 + 3) \times (36 - 6)$ is equivalent to $(36 - 6) \times (5 + 3)$. You can multiply terms in any order and still get the same value.

USING THE ASSOCIATIVE PROPERTY

The **associative property of addition** states that if three or more terms are being added together, the value is the same regardless of the groupings.

For example, given the expression $3 + 4 + 6$, these terms can be grouped and added in any form. $3 + 4 + 6$ is equivalent to $(3 + 4) + 6$ and is also equivalent to $3 + (4 + 6)$. This can be applied to write equivalent expressions in a variety of ways.

For example, suppose we are given the expression $5 + (y + 2) + 4$. We can generate equivalent expressions knowing the associative property. Knowing that when three or more terms are added, the grouping is irrelevant, we can say that this expression is equivalent to $5 + y + (2 + 4)$, and it is equivalent to $(5 + y) + (2 + 4)$. It is even equivalent to $5 + y + 2 + 4$.

The **associative property of multiplication** states that if three or more terms are being multiplied together, the value is the same regardless of the grouping. We can use this property to identify and generate equivalent expressions.

For example, given the expression $2 \times 7 \times 3$, these terms can be grouped in any way and still get the same value. $2 \times 7 \times 3$ is equivalent to $(2 \times 7) \times 3$ or $2 \times (7 \times 3)$.

We can use this information to generate and identify equivalent expressions. Knowing that terms can be grouped in any way when dealing with multiplication, we can find equivalent expressions by regrouping terms.

An example would be given the expression $5 \times (2 \times y) \times 4$. Using the associative property of multiplication, we know that when three or more terms are multiplied, we can group them in any way, so $5 \times (2 \times y) \times 4$ is equivalent to $(5 \times 2) \times (y \times 4)$. It is also equivalent to $(5 \times 2) \times y \times 4$ and $5 \times 2 \times (y \times 4)$. It is even equivalent to $(5 \times 2 \times y) \times 4$ and $5 \times (2 \times y \times 4)$.

USING THE DISTRIBUTIVE PROPERTY

The distributive property is one of the most used properties when generating equivalent expressions. This concept is tested very often, so it is important to be able to use this property effectively. The **distributive property** states that when the sum of two or more terms is multiplied by a number, it is the same as adding the product of each term multiplied by that number. Let's look at the expression $4(3 + 2)$. With the distributive property, we can say that this expression is equivalent to $(4 \times 3) + (4 \times 2)$. This also applies to more simplified multiplication problems. For example, 6×87 can be expressed as $6(80 + 7)$ which is equivalent to $(6 \times 80) + (6 \times 7)$. This is very useful when simplifying expressions, especially when generating or identifying equivalent expressions.

Review Video: Commutative, Associative, and Distributive Properties
Visit mometrix.com/academy and enter code: 483176

EXAMPLE

Use the **distributive property** to identify an equivalent expression.

Which of the following is equivalent to the expression $2(y + 5) - 3$?

a. $2 + y + 2 + 5 - 3$
b. $2 \times y \times 2 \times 5 - 3$
c. $2 \times y + 2 \times 5 - 3$
d. $2 \times y \times 2 + 5 - 3$

We can approach this problem in a few ways. For this example, let's expand the given expression using the distributive property to identify an equivalent expression from the choices.

In the expression $2(y+5)-3$, we have the term $y+5$ being multiplied by 2. This means that each term can be multiplied by 2 to give the same value.

So, $2(y+5)$ is equivalent to $(2\times y)+(2\times 5)$.

Now, we have one operation left in our expression, –3. In this expression, $2(y+5)-3$, the entire expression $2(y+5)$ has 3 subtracted by it. This comes at the end of the simplification, so we can place this at the end of our expression.

So, we can say that $2(y+5)-3$ is equivalent to $(2\times y)+(2\times 5)-3$.

Review the answer choices. It looks like our options do not have parenthesis. Let's look at what we have so far: $(2\times y)+(2\times 5)-3$.

Knowing order of operations and the fact that the multiplication operation is done before the addition and subtraction operation, we can rewrite this expression without parentheses.

This means $(2\times y)+(2\times 5)-3$ is equivalent to $2\times y+2\times 5-3$.

Review our choices. Choice C is the expression that is equivalent to the given expression.

Additive Relationships

An **additive relationship** is a pattern where a value is added to x. For example, the two points (4,6) and (6,8) can be used to represent an additive relationship, since both points have a y-value that comes from 2 being added to the x-value. This pattern can also be described as $x+2$, where x is the previous number and 2 is added to it. Patterns may be expressed with a series of numbers separated by commas, or in a data table or graph.

x	y
2	4
4	6
6	8
8	10

This data table shows an additive relationship, $x+2$. When describing an additive relationship, we commonly use the equation $y=x+b$. This additive relationship can be written using the formula $y=x+b$ or $x+b=y$. In this example, x is the starting value, adding 2 is what happens to x, and y is the ending value. When we use values from the table to replace x and y in our equation, the sentence is true.

Multiplicative Relationships

A **multiplicative relationship** describes a pattern between x and y where x is multiplied by a number to get to y. Looking at the points (3,9) and (9,27), we can see that each x-value is multiplied by 3 to get the y-value. This is also called the **scale factor**.

x	y
3	9
9	27
27	81
81	243

This data table shows the same relationship in table form. This is a multiplicative relationship because the x-value is being multiplied by a number to get a y-value. We describe this multiplicative relationship using the formula $y=mx$, or $mx=y$, where x is the starting value, a is the scale factor, and y is the ending value. In this example, 3 is being multiplied by x to get to y, or y is 3 times as much as x, or x increases by a factor of 3. The equation to describe this relationship is $y = 3x$ or $3x = y$.

REPRESENTING ADDITIVE AND MULTIPLICATIVE RELATIONSHIPS

Patterns and relationships can be expressed using tables, equations, and graphs. These representations can be used interchangeably. They are different ways to illustrate the same information. In an additive relationship, a number is being added to x to get y. This is expressed using the equation $y = x + b$. This relationship can also be expressed using a table and a graph. Let's look at the equation $y = x + 3$. In this relationship, 3 is added to all x-values, or all y-values are 3 more than x. We can express this using a table.

x	y
1	4
2	5
3	6
4	7

This information can also be described using a graph by using the x- and y-values as coordinate pairs. We can plot each point on a graph to see the pattern graphically.

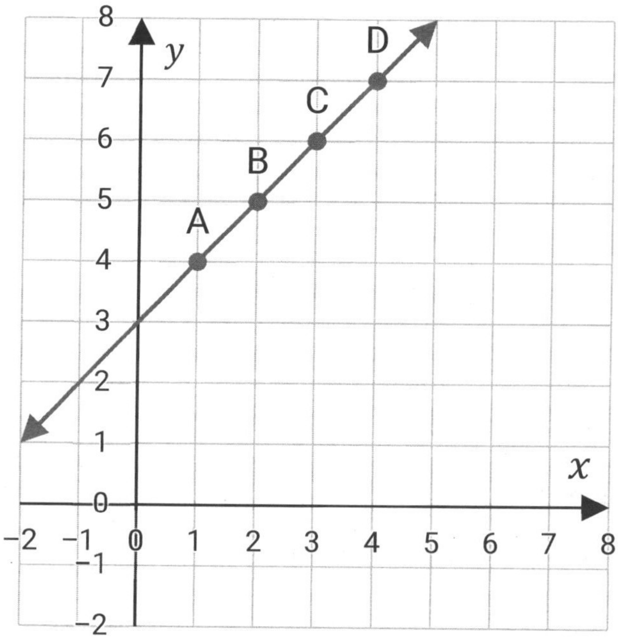

This graph uses the x and y-values from the table to create points. This line illustrates the information in the data table and describes the equation $y = x + 3$.

The equation, table, and graph all describe the same relationship, that y is 3 more than x.

Comparing Relationships and Patterns

We can use tables, graphs, and equations to compare relationships between x and y in additive and multiplicative relationships. To do this, we need to identify a pattern and use that information to compare. You may be given two sets of equations in the form $y = mx$ or $y = x + b$, two data sets, or two graphs, and asked to compare the relationships of x and y. Let's look at two equations and compare.

Equation #1	Equation #2
$y = 5x$	$y = x + 5$

Here we have two equations. You should ask yourself a few questions:

- What is the same in these relationships and how are they different?
- What is happening to x to get y?
- Are these additive or multiplicative relationships?

In this example, both equations have 5 as the m- and b-values. Equation 1 shows a multiplicative relationship where y is 5 times as great as x and equation 2 shows an additive relationship where y is 5 more than x.

Linear Relationships

A **linear relationship** is a relationship between x and y values where the relationship is constant. Linear relationships are expressed using the equation $y = mx + b$, where m represents the **slope** of the line or the rate of change between the independent and dependent quantities, and b represents the **y-intercept** or the point where the line passes the y-axis.

Linear relationships can be described verbally or using tables, graphs, and equations.

Let's look at the equation $y = 2x + 5$.

This is a linear relationship between x and y values. In the equation $y = 2x + 5$, we can see that the slope of the line this equation describes is 2, and the y-intercept to this line is 5.

This equation can be described using a table or a graph.

Representing Linear Equations in Tables

To describe this relationship using a table, we can use the equation and input various x-values to identify the corresponding y-values.

x	y
-5	
5	
10	

This table gives the x-values -5, 5 and 10. We can substitute these values into the equation to find the matching y values in this linear relationship.

Let's start with $x = -5$.

$$y = 2x + 5$$
$$y = 2(-5) + 5$$
$$y = -10 + 5$$
$$y = -5$$

Now, find y when $x = 5$.

$$y = 2x + 5$$
$$y = 2(5) + 5$$
$$y = 10 + 5$$
$$y = 15$$

And finally, $x = 10$.

$$y = 2x + 5$$
$$y = 2(10) + 5$$
$$y = 20 + 5$$
$$y = 25$$

Now the table can be completed.

x	y
-5	-5
5	15
10	25

This table can be used to describe the linear relationship between x and y values represented in the equation $y = 2x + 5$. It can also be used to graph the line that is represented by the equation.

Representing Linear Equations on Graphs

Linear relationships form straight lines on a graph. We can graph the linear equation in the form $y = mx + b$ in two ways.

Let's look at the equation $y = 2x + 5$. This is a linear equation in the form $y = mx + b$ where m, the slope, is 2 and b, the y-intercept, is 5.

We can use a table to identify 2 or more points along the line and connect the points, or we can use the y-intercept and the slope to graph the line.

The table represents three x and y value sets.

x	y
-5	-5
5	15
10	25

This table gives three coordinate pairs: $(-5,-5)$, $(5,15)$, and $(10,25)$.

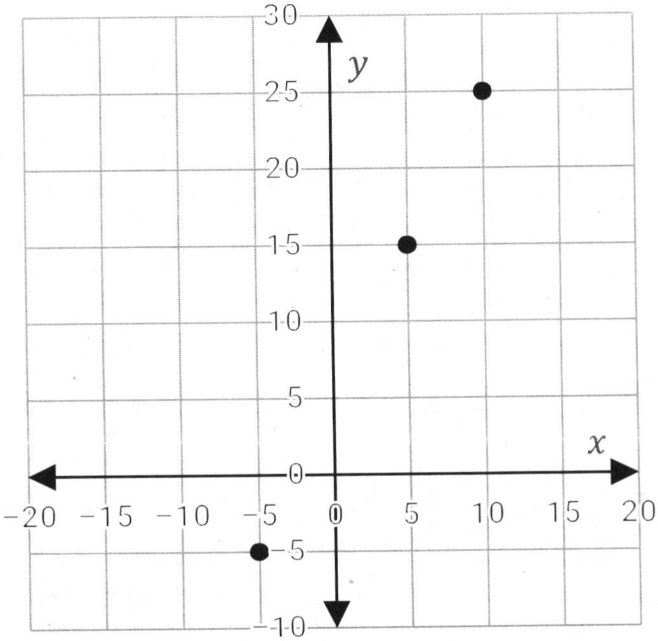

When these points are connected, they form the line $y = 2x + 5$.

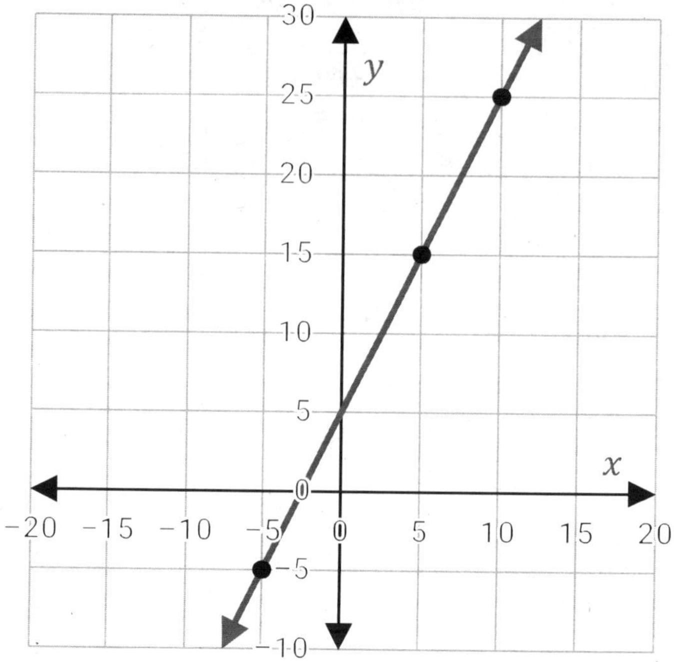

The other way we can graph a line in the form $y = mx + b$ is by identifying the slope and the y-intercept and graphing these attributes.

In the equation $y = 2x + 5$, the y-intercept is 5. This means that the point where the line crosses the y-axis has a y value of 5.

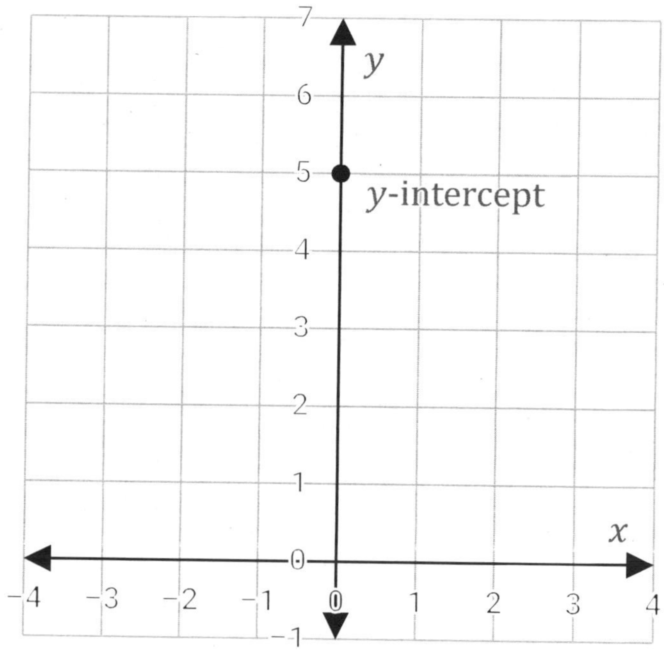

We also know that the slope of the line is 2. The slope of the line running between two points can be found by using the formula $m = \frac{y_2 - y_1}{x_2 - x_1}$. The slope is usually expressed as a fraction. The numerator is the change in y-values, also called the **rise**, and the denominator is the change in x-values, also called the **run**. The slope will be simplified to a whole number if the change in x-values is 1.

We can use the two points, $(5,15)$ and $(-5,-5)$, to find the slope. Let's say that $(5,15)$ will give us x_1 and y_1 and $(-5,-5)$ will give us x_2 and y_2.

$$m = \frac{y_2 - y_1}{x_2 - x_1}$$

$$m = \frac{-5 - 15}{-5 - 5}$$

$$m = \frac{-20}{-10}$$

$$m = 2$$

The slope of this line is 2, which means that the coordinate points on this line can be found by starting at a known point, moving up 2 y-values, then moving 1 x-value to the right.

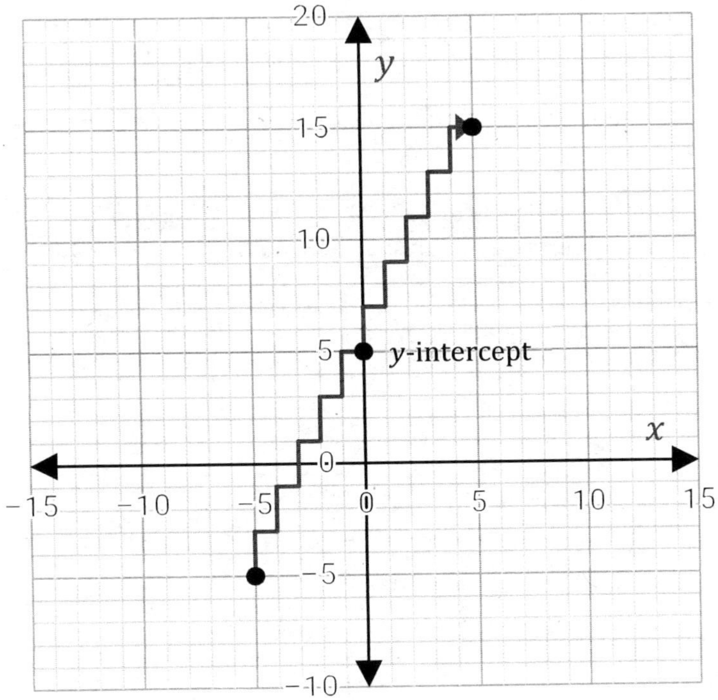

Now we can form a line.

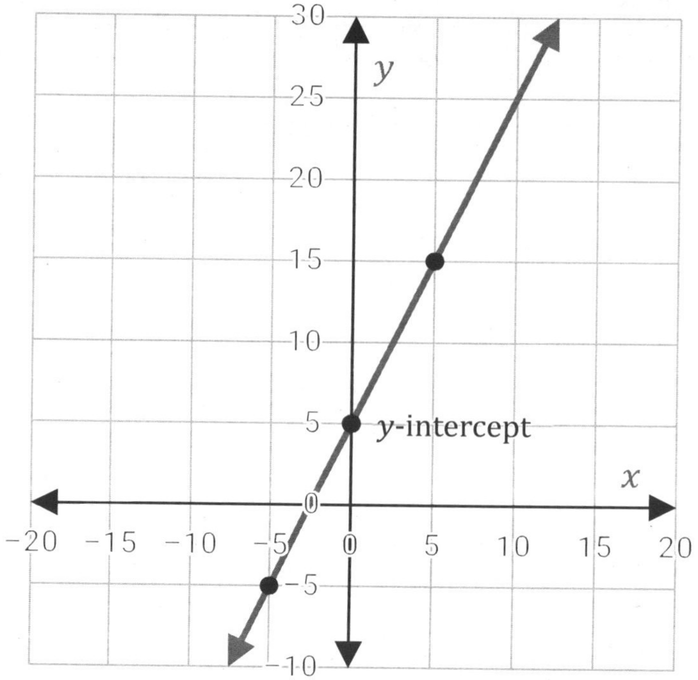

Both graphs created represent the same equation, $y = 2x + 5$. Both graphs include a line that intersects the y-axis at (0,5) and have a slope of 2.

Review Video: Graphing Linear Equations
Visit mometrix.com/academy and enter code: 479576

EXAMPLE

What equation best represents the relationship between x and y in the graph?

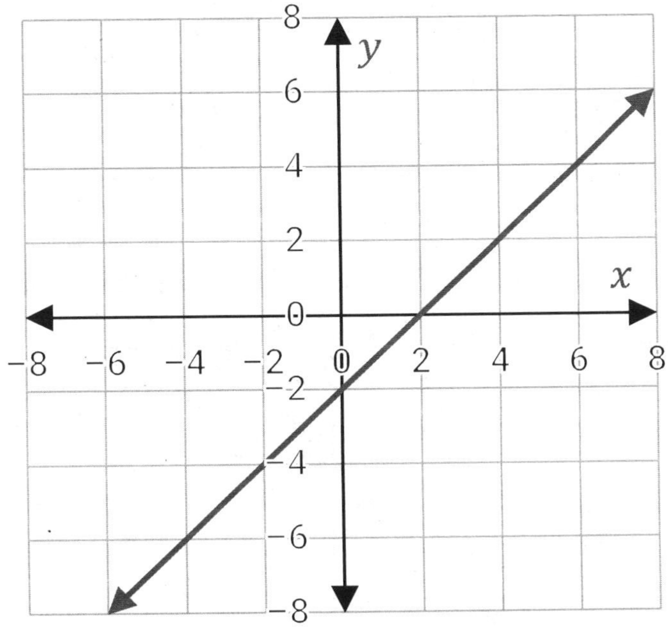

This is a line, so the equation will be in the form $y = mx + b$.

Based on the graph, we can see that the y-intercept is –2 because the point where the line crosses the y-axis is at $(0, -2)$. This means that $b = -2$ in our equation.

Next, we can identify the slope of the line. The slope of the line can be found by using the formula $m = \frac{y_2 - y_1}{x_2 - x_1}$. To find the slope, identify two points and plug their x and y-values into the formula.

Let's use the x-intercept, $(0,2)$, and the y-intercept, $(-2,0)$. The x-intercept gives us x_1 and y_1 and the y-intercept gives us x_2 and y_2.

$$m = \frac{y_2 - y_1}{x_2 - x_1}$$

$$m = \frac{0 - 2}{-2 - 0}$$

$$m = \frac{-2}{-2}$$

$$m = 1$$

Or we can use a graph.

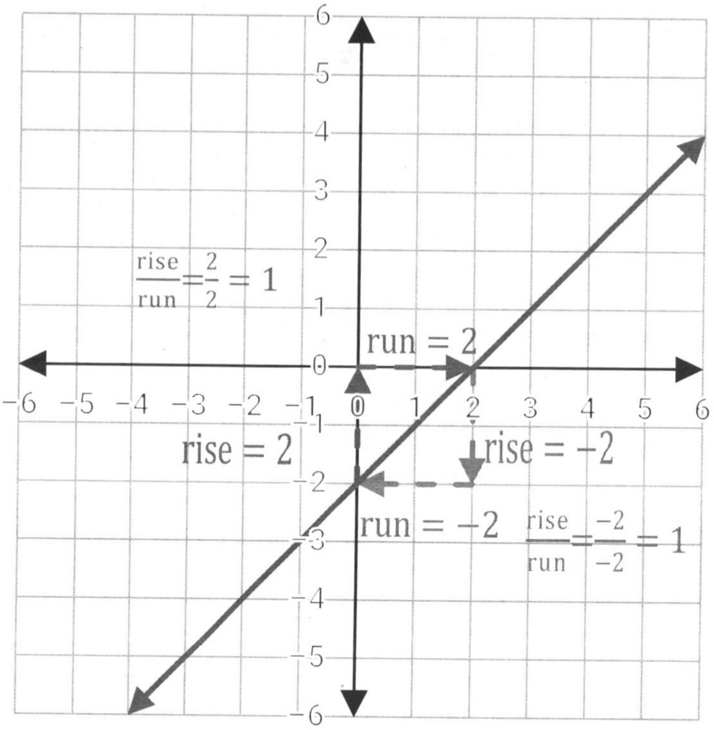

So, now we know that the y-intercept is –2 and the slope is 1. We can use these values to write the equation of the line.

$$y = mx + b$$
$$y = 1x + -2$$
$$y = x - 2$$

The equation that best represents the relationship between x and y is $y = x - 2$.

DETERMINING IF A PROPORTIONAL RELATIONSHIP EXISTS

Linear relationships can be proportional relationships if the y-intercept is equal to zero. This means that when the two quantities are graphed on the coordinate plane, the result is a straight line through the origin. If given a table, the ratio of y to x must be constant for all values of x and y besides zero for a proportional relationship to exist between the two variables. The value $\frac{y}{x}$ is the constant of proportionality.

EXAMPLE

For the graphs below, determine whether there exists a proportional relationship between x and y. If a proportional relationship exists, find the constant of proportionality and write an equation for the line.

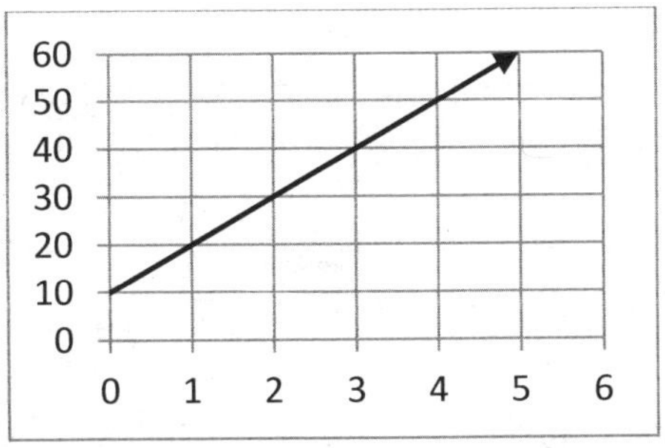

Though the graph of the relationship between x and y is a straight line, it does not pass through the origin. So, though y varies directly as x, the ratio $\frac{y}{x}$ is not constant: for instance, $\frac{20}{1} \neq \frac{30}{2} \neq \frac{40}{3}$..

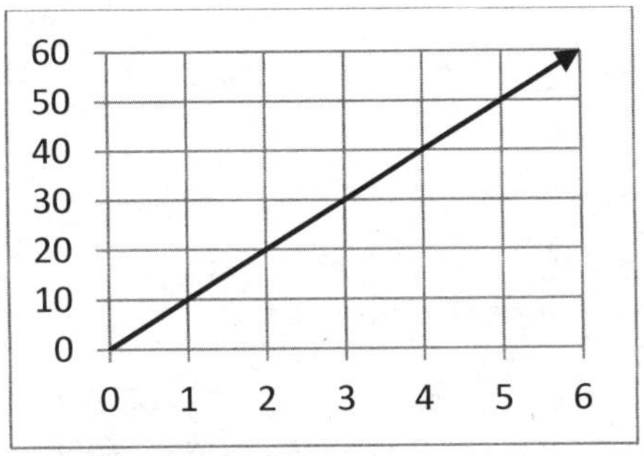

The graph of a proportional relationship is a straight line through the origin.

This graph is a straight line through the origin, so the relationship between x and y is proportional. The constant of proportionality is represented by the ratio $\frac{y}{x}$. This constant is the same as the unit rate. The constant of proportionality is equal to the y-value when $x = 1$. Since the ratio $\frac{y}{x}$ is 10 (see that $\frac{y}{x} = \frac{10}{1} = \frac{20}{2} = \frac{30}{3}$ and so on), or since $y = 10$ when $x = 1$, the constant of proportionality is 10. The relationship between x and y is represented by the equation $y = 10x$.

EXAMPLE

Determine whether there exists a proportional relationship between x and y. If a proportional relationship exists, find the constant of proportionality and write an equation to represent the relationship.

x	1	2	3	4
y	1	4	9	16

If the ratio of y to x is constant for all values of x and y besides zero, then there is a proportional relationship between the two variables. The value $\frac{y}{x}$ is the constant of proportionality.

The ratio of y to x is not constant; therefore, the values in the table do not represent a proportional relationship:

x	1	2	3	4
y	1	4	9	16
$\frac{y}{x}$	$\frac{1}{1} = 1$	$\frac{4}{2} = 2$	$\frac{9}{3} = 3$	$\frac{16}{4} = 4$

EXAMPLE

Determine whether there exists a proportional relationship between x and y. If a proportional relationship exists, find the constant of proportionality and write an equation to represent the relationship.

x	1	2	3	4
y	2.5	5	7.5	10

If the ratio of y to x is constant for all values of x and y besides zero, then there is a proportional relationship between the two variables. The value $\frac{y}{x}$ is the constant of proportionality.

The ratio of y to x is 2.5; therefore, the values in the table represent the proportional relationship modeled by the equation $y = 2.5x$:

x	1	2	3	4
y	2.5	5	7.5	10
$\frac{y}{x}$	$\frac{2.5}{1} = 2.5$	$\frac{5}{2} = 2.5$	$\frac{7.5}{3} = 2.5$	$\frac{10}{4} = 2.5$

LINEAR RELATIONSHIPS IN REAL-WORLD SCENARIOS

Linear relationships often appear in real world situations.

Let's say you are saving up to buy your first car. You work every Saturday to make \$50 each week, and all this money goes into savings. This is a linear relationship because you are making money at a constant rate of \$50 per week. We can describe the rate that you make money using the equation $y = 50x$, where y represents the number of dollars you have saved and x represents the number of weeks you have worked. But what if you already have money in savings when you start?

Let's say you started with \$250 in your savings account and *then* you start saving \$50 each week. This is still a linear relationship because you are saving money at a constant rate, but you already had some money to start with, so if we use the equation $y = 50x$, y would not give an accurate number of dollars in savings. Instead, we would use the equation $y = 50x + 250$ because you are making \$50 each week and you started with \$250.

This equation could then be used to find out how much money you would have after 25 weeks by plugging in 25 for x and solving for y.

$$
\begin{aligned}
y &= 50x + 250 \\
y &= 50(25) + 250 \\
y &= 1{,}250 + 250 \\
y &= 1{,}500
\end{aligned}
$$

This means that you would have \$1,500 in your savings account after 25 weeks.

EXAMPLE

This scenario can also be described using a table. If you have \$250 in savings and save \$50 each week, after zero weeks, you would have \$250. After 1 week, you would have $\$250 + 50 = \$300$.

A table describing how much money you would have saved after a given number of weeks can be created by inputting the appropriate x-value, number of weeks, into the equation $y = 50x + 250$.

Weeks (x)	0	1	2	5	10	15	30
Total \$ (y)	250	300	350	500	750	1,000	1,750

The relationship between x and y values is $y = 50x + 250$.

When $x = 0$, $y = 50(0) + 250 = 250$

When $x = 1$, $y = 50(1) + 250 = 50 + 250 = 300$

When $x = 2$, $y = 50(2) + 250 = 100 + 250 = 350$

When $x = 5$, $y = 50(5) + 250 = 250 + 250 = 500$

When $x = 10$, $y = 50(10) + 250 = 500 + 250 = 750$

When $x = 15$, $y = 50(15) + 250 = 750 + 250 + 1{,}000$

When $x = 30$, $y = 50(30) + 250 = 1{,}500 + 250 = 1{,}750$

This table, as well as the equation $y = 50x + 250$, can be used to express this linear relationship graphically. To represent this relationship graphically, we need to use the point on the graphic plane when $x = 0$ and at least one other point. Based on the table, we can see that when $x = 0$, $y = 250$, so the starting point is (0,250). We can choose any x-value to find another point that lies on the line. We can use $x = 2$, and when $x = 2$, $y = 350$, so we can use (2,350) as the other point.

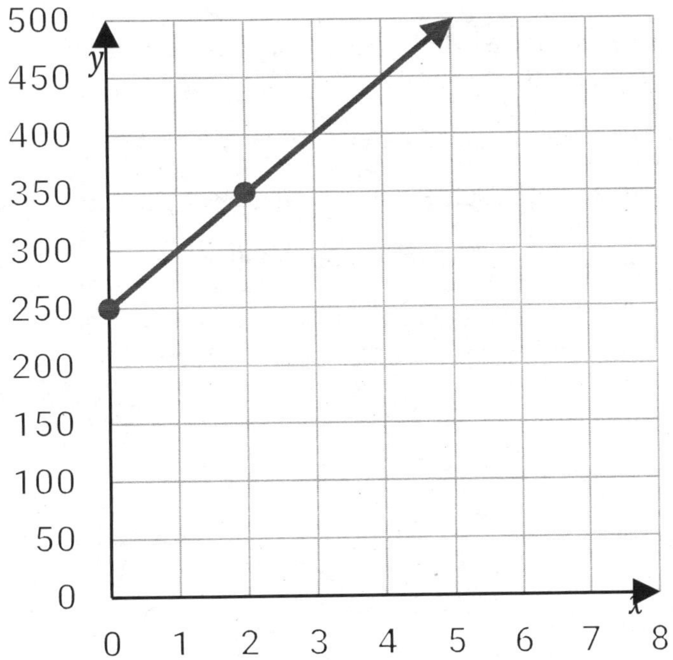

Now we have two points that lie on the line that represents the linear relationship. We can plot the points (0,250) and (2,350) on a coordinate plane and connect them with a line.

You started with \$250, which is evident by the fact that the y-intercept, the point that lies along the y-axis, is 250. Then, you saved \$50 each week, which is evident by the slope of the line, or relationship between x and y-values, where each week, the total cost along the line increases by 50.

EQUATIONS

WRITING EQUATIONS TO REPRESENT SCENARIOS

An **equation** is a set of expressions separated by an equal sign. In an equation, each **expression** is **equal** to the other. We can use equations to represent real-world scenarios. When we write equations from problems, we need to understand the given values and the unknown values. If we can see what we know, and identify what we need to find, we can use numbers and symbols to illustrate the problem. When we write equations, we use variables to stand for the unknown values. You will have to write an appropriate equation for a given situation using different math operations.

Let's say you are given this situation: You get paid \$250 every week from your new job and received a one-time \$500 bonus once you finished your first week of work. You have made a total of \$6,500 at your job so far. How many weeks have you been working?

In this problem, we know how much money you get per week, we know that you were given a bonus, and we know how much money you have now.

What do we not know? We do not know how many weeks you have been working. The unknown in a problem is usually going to be part of the question and what you want to find. We are trying to find out how many weeks you had to have worked at your job to make \$6,500.

If we know an end total, this can usually go on one side of our equal sign.

$$\$6{,}500 =$$

Now we have 1 side of our equation. How will we get to \$6,500? You make \$250 for a number of weeks. We do not know how many weeks you work, so we can use x to represent the number of weeks. Any letter can be used as a variable to represent an unknown value, but x is commonly used. If you make \$250 per week, then we can say you make \$250 times the number of weeks, or $250x$.

$$\$6{,}500 = 250x +$$

Now, you worked x number of weeks and made \$250 each week, and you got a one-time \$500 bonus.

$$\$6{,}500 = 250x + 500$$

When writing an equation, it is important to identify what you know and what you don't know. Then you can start understanding what the problem is saying. Every problem has a starting point, something that happens, and an ending point. When you can identify these things, you can build an equation.

EXAMPLE

You are dividing 245 inches of ribbon into sections. Each section is 5 inches long. You have cut 23 sections so far. Which of the following equations can be used to find *s*, the number of sections you have left to cut?

a. $\frac{245}{s} - 23 = 5$
b. $\frac{245}{5} - 23 = s$
c. $5s + 23 = 245$
d. $23 \cdot 5 \cdot s = 245$

We know that the ribbon is 245 inches long, we know that each section is 5 inches, and we know that you have cut 23 sections so far.

We do not know how many sections you have left to cut.

This story can be read as a division and subtraction problem. We have 245 inches divided into 5-inch sections with 23 sections cut so far where s represents the number of sections left to cut.

245 inches divided into 5-inch sections can be written as:

$$\frac{245}{5}$$

245 inches divided into 5-inch sections with 23 sections already cut could be written as:

$$\frac{245}{5} - 23 = s$$

The answer is B.

WRITING SCENARIOS FOR EQUATIONS

Situations can be expressed through equations. You can write an equation to match a situation or write a situation to match an equation. It is important to understand what is going on in an equation so that you can choose a situation that makes sense. An addition equation will include adding a value to an existing value and ending with a total. A subtraction equation will include a starting value, ending value, and a value being taken away. A multiplication equation will usually have a certain number of groups of a value, or a value being replicated a certain number of times, with an ending value. And a division equation will usually have a starting value that is broken into segments or groups a certain number of times.

A variable is an important part of an equation and represents an unknown value. A situation may include an unknown number that is added, subtracted, multiplied, or divided by a value. A situation may include two of these actions, which would be expressed by a two-step equation.

Once you identify what is happening in an equation, you can match a situation to the problem and vice versa.

EXAMPLE

Let's say we are given the equation $3x + 12 = 45$. We can write a situation to match the equation after understanding what is happening in the equation.

The expression $3x$ represents an unknown value multiplied by 3. We can describe this using words and real-world examples: 3 apples per tree, 3 words per second, 3 houses per block.

The expression $3x + 12$ describes an unknown value multiplied by 3 and added to 12. The other side of the equation is 45. This represents the total. The total could be anything: total number of apples picked, total number of words read, or total number of houses passed.

Now, we can put this all together to form some situations that represent the equation.

1. You go to an orchard to pick apples. You collected 12 apples off of the ground and then picked 3 apples per tree. At the end of the trip, you have 45 apples. How many trees did you pick apples from?
2. You read at a rate of 3 words per second. You have already read 12 words. At the end of a number of seconds, you have read 45 words. For how many seconds did you read?
3. You are riding your bike and notice that there are 3 houses on each block. You have already passed 12 houses. At the end of your ride, you have passed 45 houses. How many additional blocks did you travel?

Each situation can be expressed by the same equation. You have 12 of something. There is a rate of 3 per unit. At the end, you have a total of 45. $3x + 12 = 45$.

Then, you could use the equation to solve for the missing value, whether it is the number of trees you picked from, the number of seconds you spent reading, or the number of blocks you rode.

Solve Equations

The solution to an equation is the value of the variable. We can solve equations by performing inverse operations to isolate the variable. Isolating the variable means to get the variable by itself on one side of the equal sign.

Let's say we are given the equation $2x + 4 = 12$. This equation can be solved by performing operations to isolate x.

$$\begin{aligned} 2x + 4 &= 12 \\ 2x + 4 - 4 &= 12 - 4 \\ 2x &= 8 \\ \frac{2x}{2} &= \frac{8}{2} \\ x &= 4 \end{aligned}$$

The solution to the equation is $x = 4$.

Example

What is the solution to the following equation?

$9 = 7 + 8x$

The solution to this equation will be the value of x that makes this sentence true. Perform inverse operations to isolate x.

The first step to solve the equation is to subtract 7 from each side.

$$\begin{aligned} 9 - 7 &= 7 + 8x - 7 \\ 2 &= 8x \end{aligned}$$

The next step is to divide each side by 8.

$$\frac{2}{8} = \frac{8x}{8}$$

$$\frac{2}{8} = x$$

Simplify the fraction.

$$\frac{1}{4} = x$$

The solution to this equation is $x = \frac{1}{4}$ or 0.25.

Determining if a Value Makes an Equation True

The solution to an equation is the value of a variable that makes the sentence true. To identify if a given value makes an equation true, replace the variable with the given value and simplify. If both expressions, or both sides of the equal sign, are equal, then the equation is true. If the expressions are not equal, the given value is not a solution.

Let's say we are given an equation and two solution possibilities.

$$3x - 12 = -21$$

The two possible solutions are $x = 11$ and $x = -3$.

To identify which value is the solution, we can replace x with each of the given values and simplify the expression. If the simplified expression is a true statement, the given value is a solution.

We can start with 11.

$$\begin{aligned} 3x - 12 &= -21 \\ 3(11) - 12 &= -21 \\ 33 - 12 &= -21 \\ 21 &\neq -21 \end{aligned}$$

Since 21 does NOT equal -21, so $x = 11$ is NOT a solution.

Now we can try $x = -3$.

$$\begin{aligned} 3x - 12 &= -21 \\ 3(-3) - 12 &= -21 \\ -9 - 12 &= -21 \\ -21 &= -21 \end{aligned}$$

This number sentence is true, so $x = -3$ is a solution to the equation.

Inequalities

Writing Inequalities to Represent Scenarios

An **inequality** is a math sentence that connects two expressions with a comparison. These expressions are compared using a **greater than**, $>$, **less than**, $<$, **greater than or equal to**, $\geq$, or **less than or equal to**, $\leq$, sign.

There are some situations that can be illustrated by inequalities. In these scenarios, we need to identify what we know, what we don't know, and what the comparison is.

For example, imagine you go to the grocery store to buy avocados and one bag of tortillas. Avocados are $0.70 each, and a bag of tortillas costs $1.50. You only brought 5 dollars. An inequality can be used to illustrate how many avocados you can buy.

We know that avocados are \$0.70 each and a bag of tortillas is \$1.50. We know that you can't spend more than \$5. We know that you want to buy a number of avocados and a bag of tortillas, but we don't know how many avocados we can get. That must be the unknown.

We can write an inequality using a for avocados.

We can't go over \$5, but the total cost can be equal to \$5. The cost of the avocados and the bag of tortillas has to be less than or exactly \$5.

$$\text{total cost} \leq 5$$

Now, we want avocados, and each one is \$0.70, so the other side of our inequality will have to include \$0.70 times the number of avocados.

$$0.70a \leq 5$$

We also want to get a bag of tortillas which cost \$1.50. This must be added to the avocado side of the inequality.

$$0.70a + 1.5 \leq 5$$

Inequalities can be solved in a way similar to solving equations, using inverse operations. Solving this inequality would reveal number of avocados you could buy without spending more than \$5.

EXAMPLE

A bathtub holds 42 gallons of water. A faucet fills the bathtub at a rate of 3.5 gallons per minute. There are 5 gallons of water in the bathtub so far. Which inequality can be used to represent all possible number of m, minutes, the faucet can run before the bathtub overflows?

a. $42 \leq 3.5m + 5$
b. $42 \leq 5m + 3.5$
c. $42 \geq 3.5m + 5$
d. $42 \geq 5m + 3.5$

In this story, a bathtub holds 42 gallons of water. Water fills the bathtub at a rate of 3.5 gallons per minute and there are 5 gallons in the bathtub so far. We want to identify the inequality that represents all possible number of minutes the faucet can run before the bathtub overflows.

The bathtub fills at a rate of 3.5 gallons per minute, which can be represented by the expression $3.5m$, where m represents the number of minutes.

$$3.5m$$

There are 5 gallons in the bathtub already, which means we have started with 5 gallons. This can be represented by the expression $3.5m + 5$ because there are 5 gallons in the bathtub already and the water increases at a rate of 3.5 gallons per minute. This is one side of the inequality.

$$3.5m + 5$$

This expression represents the number of gallons in the bathtub after the faucet runs m number of minutes.

The bathtub holds 42 gallons of water. We need to know all number of minutes the faucet can run without the bathtub overflowing. This means that the expression $3.5m + 5$ must be less than or equal to 42 for the bathtub to not overflow.

$$3.5m + 5 \leq 42$$

This inequality can also be written as

$$42 \geq 3.5m + 5$$

The correct answer is C.

Writing Scenarios for Inequalities

Real-world scenarios can be expressed through inequalities, and we can also write situations based on an inequality. Inequalities usually use the language, "fewer than," "more than," "no more than," "no less than," "a maximum of," "a minimum of," etc. This language gives us clues that we are dealing with values that are greater than, less than, greater than or equal to, or less than or equal to a quantity.

If there is a number divided into some pieces, and there is no more than 5, that means the value is less than or equal to 5. If there is a value and some number is added and the total is more than 10, that means the value is greater than 10. If there is a value multiplied by a number and the total is at least 25, that means the value is greater than or equal to 25. If the value is less or more, you will use greater than or less than. If the value is less or more, but can also be that number, you will use less than or equal to, or greater than or equal to. It takes a little practice and logic to really think about what is happening in the situation.

Example

Which situation can be represented by this inequality?

$15y + 67 \geq 250$

a. You have 15 coins in your coin collection. You add 67 coins each year. How many years of collecting will result in a collection of at least 250 coins?
b. You have 15 coins in your coin collection. You add 67 coins each year. How many years of collecting will result in a collection of 250 coins, at most?
c. You have 67 coins in your coin collection. You add 15 coins each year. How many years of collecting will result in a collection of at least 250 coins?
d. You have 67 coins in your coin collection. You add 15 coins each year. How many years of collecting will result in a collection of 250 coins, at most?

To solve this problem, we can identify the inequality that describes each situation and match this to the given inequality.

Choice A describes having 15 coins and adding 67 coins each year. This means that you begin with 15 coins and add 67 each year for y years. So, after y years you will have $15 + 67y$ coins. The answer choice asks for the number of years it takes to collect *at least* 250 coins. If you want at least 250 coins, that means $15 + 67$ must be greater than or equal to 250. This situation can be represented by the inequality $15 + 67y \geq 250$.

Choice B describes having 15 coins and adding 67 coins each year. This means that you begin with 15 coins and add 67 each year for y years. The solution is every possible number of years that will result in at most 250 coins. If you want at most 250 coins, that means that the solution will give a total that is either 250 or less than 250. This story can be represented by the inequality $15 + 67y \leq 250$.

Choice C describes having 67 coins and adding 15 coins each year. This means that you begin with 67 coins and add 15 each year for y years. The solution is every possible number of years that will result in at least 250 coins. If you want at least 250 coins, that means that the solution will give a total that is either 250 or more than 250. This story can be represented by the inequality $67 + 15y \geq 250$.

Choice D describes having 67 coins and adding 15 coins each year. This means that you begin with 67 coins and add 15 each year for y years. The solution is every possible number of years that will result in at most 250 coins. If you want at least 250 coins, that means that the solution will give a total that is either 250 or less than 250. This story can be represented by the inequality $67 + 15y \leq 250$.

The only situation that gives an inequality that is equivalent to the given inequality is choice C. The correct answer is C.

Representing Inequalities on a Number Line

Inequalities can be represented on a number line. Inequalities are two expressions connected by a greater than, less than, greater than or equal to, or less than or equal to sign. We express solutions to these sentences using number lines and a series of arrows, open circles, and closed circles. You may be asked to draw or identify the number line that represents an inequality, including inequalities with variables.

When representing solutions to an inequality on a number line, we are identifying the number or group of numbers that makes the statement true.

We can represent the inequality $2x + 5 > 21$.

What are the possible values of x?

The first step to solving this inequality is to solve as you would solve an equation. Perform inverse operations to each side of the inequality to isolate x.

$$\begin{gathered} 2x + 5 > 21 \\ 2x + 5 - 5 > 21 - 5 \\ 2x > 16 \\ \frac{2x}{2} > \frac{16}{2} \\ x > 8 \end{gathered}$$

This tells us that the value of x must be any value that is greater than 8.

The value must be greater than 8, but not exactly 8 because the symbol used is "greater than," not "greater than or equal to," so we will identify 8 on our number line with an **open circle** because the value cannot be 8. Open circles are used when the comparison is "greater than" or "less than" to show that the number that the circle identifies is not included in the possible values of x.

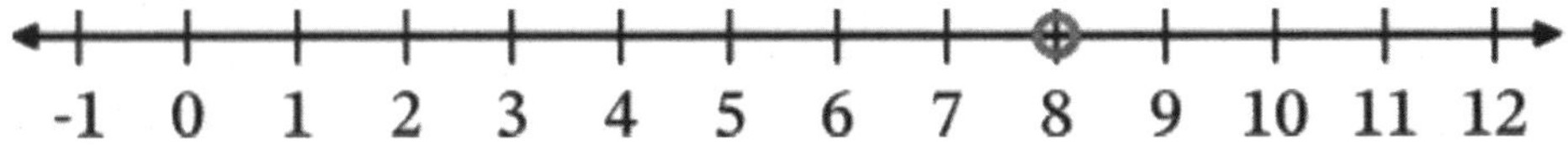

All numbers greater than 8 can be a solution, so we will place an arrow to the right to identify all numbers greater than 8.

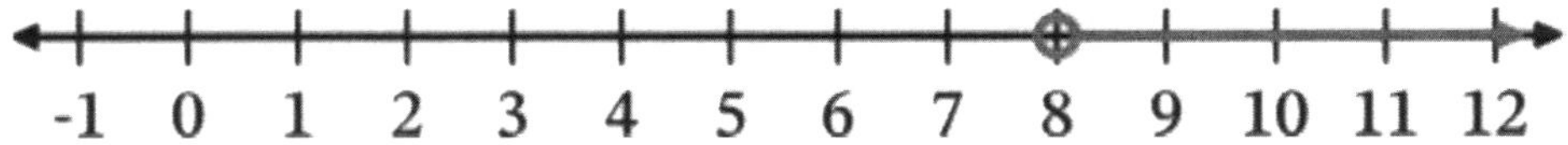

Let's look at another example. Consider the inequality $2x + 5 \leq 21$.

To solve this inequality, use inverse operations to isolate x.

$$\begin{gathered} 2x + 5 \leq 21 \\ 2x + 5 - 5 \leq 21 - 5 \\ 2x \leq 16 \\ \frac{2x}{2} \leq \frac{16}{2} \\ x \leq 8 \end{gathered}$$

This tells us that the value of x must be any value that is less than or equal to 8.

The value must be less than or equal to 8, so the value could be exactly 8. We will identify 8 on our number line with a **closed circle** because 8 is included as a solution to the inequality. Closed circles are used when the comparison is "greater than or equal to" or "less than or equal to" to show that the number that the circle identifies is included as a possible value of x.

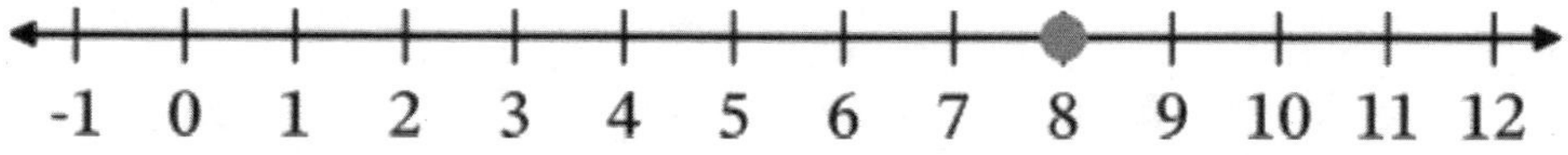

We know that the value of x is all values less than or equal to 8, so we can identify these values by placing an arrow to the left of 8 to identify all values less than 8, and the closed circle identifies 8 as one of the possible values.

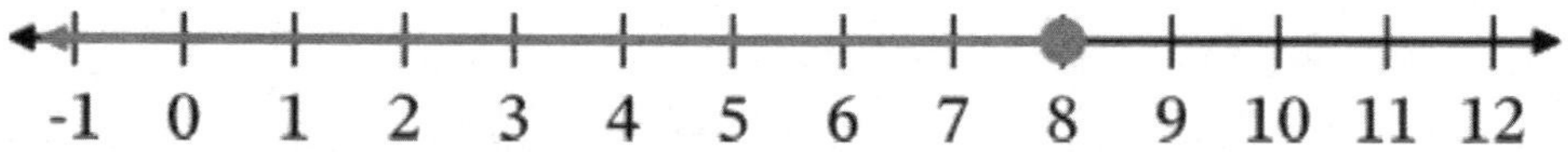

This number line appropriately represents all possible solutions to the inequality $2x + 5 \leq 21$.

> **Review Video: Solving Inequalities Using All 4 Basic Operations**
> Visit mometrix.com/academy and enter code: 401111
>
> **Review Video: Graphing Solutions to Inequalities**
> Visit mometrix.com/academy and enter code: 391281

EXAMPLE

Draw a number line that represents the solution to $42.5 \geq 9x - 2.5$.

To find all possible solutions to this inequality, we will solve the inequality by performing inverse operations to isolate x.

$$42.5 \geq 9x - 2.5$$
$$42.5 + 2.5 \geq 9x - 2.5 + 2.5$$
$$45 \geq 9x$$
$$\frac{45}{9} \geq \frac{9x}{9}$$
$$5 \geq x$$

This states that 5 is greater than or equal to x. This can also be read as $x \leq 5$, or the value of x is less than or equal to 5.

If the value of x is less than or equal to 5, then the solution to the inequality is all values less than 5 or exactly 5. If a possible solution is exactly 5, then we can notate 5 on the number line with a closed circle.

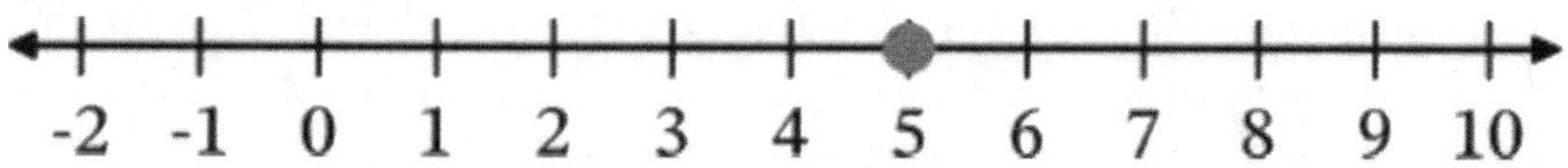

Now, the possible values of x are 5 and all values less 5. This means we can notate all possible solutions by drawing an arrow to the left of 5 to highlight all values less than 5.

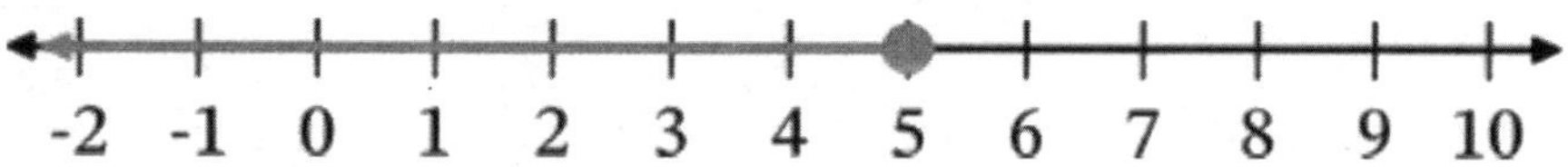

This number line appropriately represents all possible solutions to the inequality $42.5 \geq 9x - 2.5$.

EXAMPLE

Which number line represents the solution to the inequality $3.5x + 11.5 > 18.5$?

a. 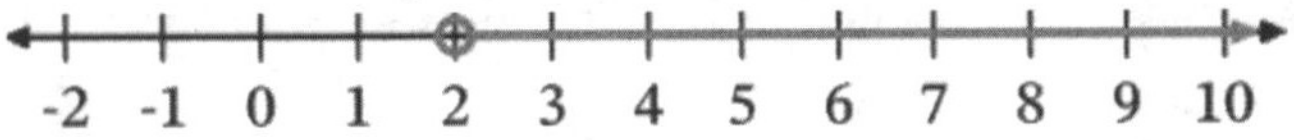

b. 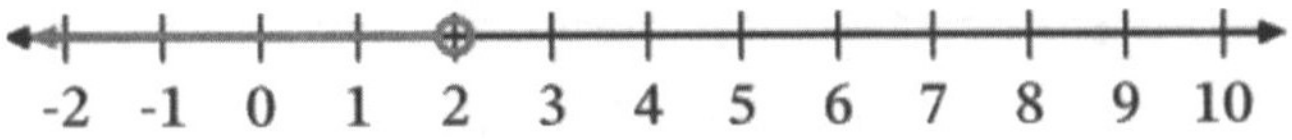

c. 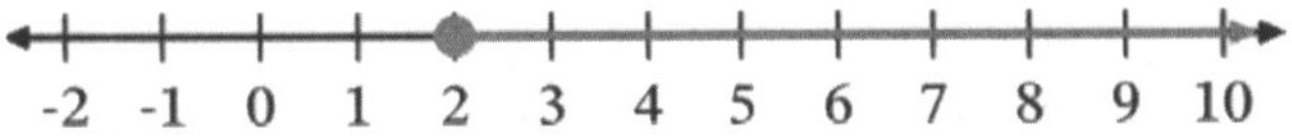

d. 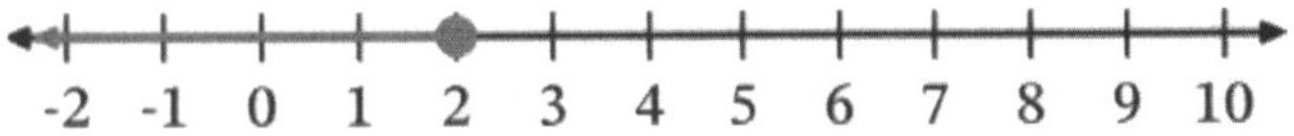

To identify the number line that represents all possible solutions to the inequality, we will perform inverse operations to isolate x.

$$3.5x + 11.5 > 18.5$$
$$3.5x + 11.5 - 11.5 > 18.5 - 11.5$$
$$3.5x > 7$$
$$\frac{3.5x}{3.5} > \frac{7}{3.5}$$
$$x > 2$$

This shows that the solution to the inequality is all values greater than 2.

This can be shown on a number line by notating 2 with an open circle and an arrow to the right of 2 because the solution is all values greater than 2, but not exactly 2.

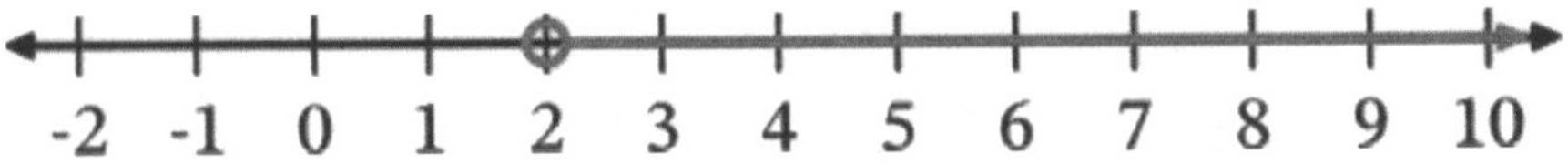

The correct answer is A.

SOLVING INEQUALITIES

The solution to an inequality describes all possible values of a variable and is called a solution set. The solution is a set, or group, of solutions because there is more than one possible value that makes the inequality true. To find all possible solutions to an inequality, isolate the variable in an inequality. This can be done the same way as solving an equation: by performing inverse operations to get the variable alone on one side of the comparison.

Let's say we are given the inequality $15 > 2x + 4$. The solution set to this inequality can be found by performing inverse operations to isolate x.

$$15 > 2x + 4$$

The first step to solving the inequality is to subtract 4 from each side.

$$15 - 4 > 2x + 4 - 4$$
$$11 > 2x$$

The next step is to divide each side by 2.

$$\frac{11}{2} > \frac{2x}{2}$$

$$5.5 > x$$

The solution set to the inequality is $5.5 > x$, or $x < 5.5$, or the value of x is all values less than 5.5. The solution set is $x < 5.5$.

EXAMPLE

What is the solution set for the inequality below?

$$\mathbf{6 + 2x < 4}$$

a. $x < 6$
b. $x < -6$
c. $x < 1$
d. $x < -1$

To find the solution set for the inequality, we can perform inverse operations to isolate the variable.

$$6 + 2x > 4$$
$$6 - 6 + 2x > 4 - 6$$
$$\frac{2x}{2} > \frac{-2}{2}$$
$$x > -1$$

The solution set is all values greater than –1, or $x > -1$.

The correct answer is D.

SOLVING INEQUALITIES THAT INCLUDE NEGATIVE NUMBERS

The solution to an inequality can be found using a process similar to solving for an equation. However, there is an exception when you encounter negative numbers. When solving an inequality, and you must multiply or divide each side by a negative number, you must also flip, or reverse, the inequality symbol. This means that if you had a less than symbol and have to multiply or divide by a negative number, you will perform the operation AND change to a greater than symbol. Same if you had a greater than or equal symbol and must multiply or divide by a negative number, you will perform the operation and then change to a less than or equal to symbol.

Let's say you are given the inequality $-x + 8 \geq 15$ and you need to find the solution set.

First, solve the inequality like you would any other inequality or equation, by performing inverse operations to each side.

$$-x + 8 \geq 15$$
$$-x + 8 - 8 \geq 15 - 8$$
$$-x \geq 7$$

Now, the next step is to divide each side by –1 to remove the negative sign from the variable. Because we are dividing by a negative, we will also flip the inequality symbol.

$$\frac{-x}{-1} \geq \frac{7}{-1}$$
$$x \leq 7$$

We divided by –1 and flipped the symbol, so the solution set to the inequality is all values less than or equal to 7, or $x \leq 7$.

EXAMPLE

What is the solution set for $-6x - 10 \leq 38$?

a. $x \leq 8$
b. $x \geq 8$
c. $x \leq -8$
d. $x \geq -8$

To find the solution set, we will perform inverse operations to isolate the variable. When dividing by a negative value, change the direction of the inequality symbol.

$$-6x - 10 \leq 38$$
$$-6x - 10 + 10 \leq 38 + 10$$
$$-6x \leq 48$$
$$\frac{-6x}{-6} \leq \frac{48}{-6}$$
$$x \geq -8$$

The solution set for the inequality is all values greater than or equal to –8.

The correct answer is D.

DETERMINING IF A SET OF VALUES MAKES AN INEQUALITY TRUE

The solution set to an inequality is the set of values of a variable that make the simplified sentence true. To identify if a given set of values makes an inequality true, there are two main strategies. One strategy is like finding if a solution is true for an equation; replace each value with the variable and simplify to see if the simplified sentence is true. If the sentence is true, then the given value is a solution. If the sentence is not true, then the given value is NOT a solution.

Let's say we are given an inequality and a set of possible values.

$$3x - 12 \leq -21$$

The value set is $\{-10, -5, 0, 5, 10\}$.

One way to solve this problem is to replace x with each given value to see if they make the sentence true. Consider $x = -10$.

$$3x - 12 \leq -21$$
$$3(-10) - 12 \leq -21$$
$$-30 - 12 \leq -21$$
$$-42 \leq -21$$

This sentence is true, so $x = -10$ is one of the possible solutions.

Consider $x = -5$.

$$3x - 12 \leq -21$$
$$3(-5) - 12 \leq -21$$
$$-15 - 12 \leq -21$$
$$-27 \leq -21$$

This sentence is true, so $x = -5$ is another possible solution.

Consider $x = 0$.

$$\begin{aligned} 3x - 12 &\le -21 \\ 3(0) - 12 &\le -21 \\ 0 - 12 &\le -21 \\ -12 &\le -21 \end{aligned}$$

This sentence is not true, so $x = 0$ is not a possible solution.

Consider $x = 5$.

$$\begin{aligned} 3x - 12 &\le -21 \\ 3(5) - 12 &\le -21 \\ 15 - 12 &\le -21 \\ 3 &\le -21 \end{aligned}$$

This sentence is not true, so $x = 5$ is not a possible solution.

Consider $x = 10$.

$$\begin{aligned} 3x - 12 &\le -21 \\ 3(10) - 12 &\le -21 \\ 30 - 12 &\le -21 \\ 18 &\le -21 \end{aligned}$$

This sentence is not true, so $x = 10$ is not a possible solution.

This means that -10 and -5 are the only possible solutions from the given set of values.

EXAMPLE

Which values from the set $\{-12, -8, -4, 0, 4, 8, 12\}$ are valid solutions to the following inequality?

$$\frac{x}{2} + 3 > -1$$

To solve this problem, there are two useful strategies. One is to substitute each value from the value set for x in the inequality and simplify to see if the sentence is true, and the other is to solve the inequality and compare the solution set to the value set. Solving the inequality and comparing is the quickest strategy, so this is the strategy we will practice.

To solve the inequality, we will perform inverse operations to isolate the variable.

$$\frac{x}{2} + 3 > -1$$
$$\frac{x}{2} + 3 - 3 > -1 - 3$$
$$\frac{x}{2} > -4$$
$$2 \cdot \frac{x}{2} > -4 \cdot 2$$
$$x > -8$$

The solution set to the inequality is $x > -8$, or all values greater than -8.

The given value set is $\{-12, -8, -4, 0, 4, 8, 12\}$, and the values in the set that are greater than -8 are -4, 0, 4, 8, and 12. These are valid solutions to the inequality.

MODELING EQUATIONS AND INEQUALITIES

Equations and inequalities can be modeled using pictures and symbols. A model may have a key of labeled pictures or symbols and will express that each expression is either equal to, less than, greater than, less than or equal to, or greater than or equal to the other expression.

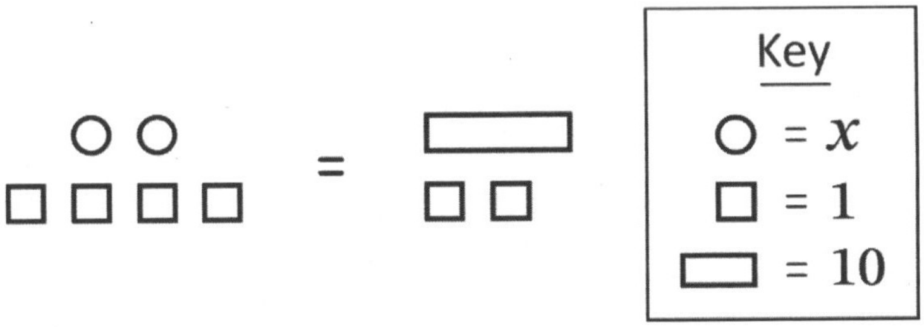

This model represents an equation. Both sides are equal because the equal sign separates each expression. The expression on the left side of the equal sign represents $2x + 4$ because there are two circles that represent x and four boxes that represent 1. The expression on the right side of the equal sign represents 12 because there is one rectangle that represents 10 and two boxes that represent 1. This model represents the equation $2x + 4 = 12$.

Reading

Word Analysis and Vocabulary

ROOT WORDS AND AFFIXES

A **root word** is a word that can be added onto. An **affix** is a prefix or suffix that is added onto a root word. Often, the affixes in the English language come from Latin or Greek origins. A **prefix** is added to the beginning of a root word and a **suffix** is added to the end of a root word.

For example, the word "inscription" is made up of three sections. The root *script* means "write" or "writing." There are two affixes in the word. The prefix *in-* can mean various things such as "not," but also "on." In this case it means "on." The suffix *-tion* means "action" or "process." So, put together, the word "inscription" means "the act of writing on." Studying roots and affixes is important because it allows you to decode words you might not otherwise understand with relative ease.

COMMON GREEK AND LATIN ROOT WORDS

Root	Meaning	Example
gen	born	genealogy (the study of ancestry)
luc	light	translucent (something light can be seen through)
log/logue	spoken	monologue (a speech performed by one person)
mis/mit	to send	transmit (to send something to another place)
omni	all	omniscient (all knowing)
phil	loving	philanthropist (someone that acts for the good of others)
photo	light	photon (a small particle of light)
scrib/script	to write	transcript (a written copy of spoken words)
sens/sent	to feel	sensory (an experience related to one of the five senses)
vac	empty, void	vacant (the state of being empty)
vid/vis	related to sight	video (a recording that is viewed, or watched)

Common Prefixes

Prefix	Meaning	Example
dis-	not	disagree (not agree)
im-	not	impossible (not possible)
in-	in, into, not	injustice (an action that is not just)
mis-	wrongly	misspell (to spell wrongly)
non-	not	nonpaid (not paid)
pre-	before	preview (to view before)
sub-	under	submerge (to sink below the surface)
super-	over or greater than	superhuman (greater than a regular human)
trans-	across, through, or change	translate (to write or say in a different language)

Common Suffixes

Suffix	Meaning	Example
-able	can be done	likeable (can be liked)
-er	a person connected with	teacher (a person connected with teaching)
-ful	full of	wonderful (full of wonder)
-it/ity	state of	activity (state of being active)
-ive	cause to, tend to, or doing	creative (a person who tends to make new things or think of new ideas)
-logy	study of	biology (study of life)
-ment	the result	payment (the result of being paid)
-ness	state of being	darkness (being dark)
-y	characterized by	cloudy (characterized by clouds)

Example

Use knowledge of affixes to figure out the meaning of the word *mournful* in the following sentence:

> "Well, it being away in the night and stormy, and all so mysterious-like, I felt just the way any other boy would a felt when I see that wreck laying there so *mournful* and lonesome in the middle of the river." (From *The Adventures of Huckleberry Finn* by Mark Twain).

Mourn means to grieve for something, while *-ful* refers to being "full of". Putting the two components together, *mournful* means "full of grief or sadness". This definition makes sense in the context of the sentence. The "wreck" in the sentence is sad looking because it is in the river by itself.

When trying to determine the meaning of a word, always look for a root word and any prefixes or suffixes that have been added on to the root word. If a component of a word is not familiar, decipher what is clear about the word, then look at the word as used in context.

Denotative and Connotative Meanings

The **denotative meaning** of a word is the exact dictionary definition of the word. The **connotative meaning** of a word is the emotion conveyed by the use of the word in context. The word may have associated meaning in addition to its dictionary definition. A good way to remember the difference between denotative and connotative is to think "direct" or "dictionary" in relation to denotative.

An example of a denotative meaning for the adjective *ablaze* would be "burning", as in the logs burning in a fireplace. A connotative meaning for the adjective *ablaze*, based on the context of the word, may indicate a level of comfort while sitting in front of a fireplace. For instance, in the context: "A logs were *ablaze* in the fireplace, radiating heat out into the corners of the snow-enclosed room", the word *ablaze* implies comfort and coziness within the space described. The connotative meaning of a word can often have an emotional association for the reader.

Example

Define the denotative and connotative meaning of the word *palace* in the following sentence:

> The golden *palace* gates opened slowly to reveal an expansive garden that was well-tended by precise gardeners all wearing the king's insignia.

In the example, the denotative meaning of the word is that a *palace* is literally a place where royalty lives. A *palace* implies, or connotes, a place of riches and is usually associated with wealth. The words "golden", "expansive garden", and "king's insignia" all give clues that the *palace* can be viewed as a place of importance, one that is well taken care of.

When looking for the denotative meaning of a word, remember to think "direct", or the literal meaning of the word. The connotative meaning of the word is implied and not directly stated; the connotative meaning is often associated with emotion and feeling about the typical context of the word.

Using Context to Determine the Meanings of Words

Readers of all levels will encounter words that they have either never seen or that they have seen before but still don't know what it means. The best way to define a word in **context** is to look for nearby words that can assist in learning the meaning of the word.

Context Clues

Context clues are hints about the meaning of a word. They are the words or phrases in the sentence or sentences before and after a new or unfamiliar word. Context clues give the reader an idea about what a word means. A context clue may also contain words that help define the new word or an example of what the new word means. A context clue in the form of an example may contain the words including 'such as', a dash, or a colon before stated information.

Using context clues to figure out meaning can be helpful when learning a new set of vocabulary words or reading a difficult text. The dictionary definition of a word can always be looked up to double-check intended meaning.

Review Video: Reading Comprehension: Using Context Clues
Visit mometrix.com/academy and enter code: 613660

EXAMPLE

Using context clues, determine the meaning of *gregarious* in the following excerpt.

> Beverly is the most *gregarious* person I have ever known. She loves people and spends a lot of her time talking to her friends and arranging get-togethers. She doesn't mind spending hours cooking as long as she knows that her house will be filled with people.

This excerpt says Beverly loves people and spends a lot of her time talking with friends and arranging get-togethers. It also says that she likes her house filled with people. These clues in the sentence help the reader determine that *gregarious* means Beverly is someone who likes to talk with other people, so she is "sociable."

EXAMPLE

Read the sentence and explain the meaning of *sense of foreboding:*

> All day long Ron kept thinking about Sue. For some unknown reason he was worried about her. He had a strong *sense of foreboding* that something was about to go wrong in Sue's city. Then he heard about the earthquake there. Luckily Sue was not injured.

To figure out the meaning of the phrase *sense of foreboding*, the reader needs to look for context clues in just the same way the reader would do to figure out the meaning of a single word. The excerpt says that Ron was "worried" about Sue for "some unknown reason." It also says that he felt that "something was going to go wrong in Sue's city." Ron also heard about an earthquake taking place in Sue's city. A "sense of foreboding" must mean that Ron had an idea that something bad was going to happen. The context clues help the reader figure out the meaning of the phrase.

SUBSTITUTION TO FIND MEANING

One way to find out if you have figured out the correct meaning of a new word is to **substitute** the meaning for the word. Using the example for *basin*, if the reader substituted in "depression in the earth," the sentence would read:

> The "depression in the earth" had filled with water over the summer months, so that the rocky bottom was no longer visible to the casual hiker.

This is a way for the reader to confirm that they have used the context clues in the sentence correctly.

MULTIPLE-MEANING WORDS

A multiple-meaning word has different definitions, depending on the contextual use of the word. A multiple-meaning word is also called a **homonym**. A homonym is defined as a word that has more than one meaning, but is spelled and pronounced the same for all of them. For example, look at the word *leaves* in the following two sentences:

1. Michelle *leaves* the building at 5 o'clock every day.
2. The *leaves* fell off the oak tree in September.

In the first sentence, *leaves* means exits. In the second sentence, *leaves* refers to parts of a tree. By looking at the rest of each sentence, the reader can understand which definition of the multiple-meaning word the author is referring to.

Synonyms and Antonyms

When you understand how words relate to each other, you will discover more in a passage. This is explained by understanding **synonyms**, which are words that mean the same thing, and **antonyms**, which are words that mean the opposite of one another. As an example, *dry* and *arid* are synonyms, and *dry* and *wet* are antonyms.

Review Video: Synonyms and Antonyms
Visit mometrix.com/academy and enter code: 105612

Definition Within a Text

An author may **define** a word in the text. For example, an author may write, "The company did not have sufficient capital, that is, available money, to continue operating." The author defined "capital" as "available money." Authors will use words and phrases, such as "that is," "or," "meaning," and "which is," to let the reader know that they are defining the word.

Analogy

Analogies are used to **compare relationships**. For example, the analogy "restaurant is to eating as store is to shopping." A restaurant is a place where you eat, and a store is a place where you shop. The analogy compares locations and the things people do at those locations. **Analogies** can also be used to show the meaning of unfamiliar words. For example, consider the analogy "author is to writing as artisan is to crafting." *Artisan* may be an unfamiliar word to some. However, this analogy begins with "author is to writing." An author writes to create books, articles, and poems. The first part of the analogy pairs a person's job title with the action that their job requires. Based on this, a reader can conclude that an artisan is someone who crafts things.

Examples That Clarify Meaning

An author may use a word and then give examples that reveal its meaning. Consider this text: "Those who do not know sign language can communicate with people who are deaf or hard of hearing by using gestures. These may include pointing their fingers to indicate which direction to look or go or holding up a hand to indicate stopping." The author of this text has used the word *gestures* and then followed it with examples. This shows a reader who is unfamiliar with the word that gestures are hand motions. Readers can find examples by looking for signal words like "for example," "for instance," "like," and "such as."

Contrast

Readers can use these **contrasting** words and **opposites** as context clues to help them understand unfamiliar words. For example, an author may write, "Our conversation was not cheery. We sat and talked very solemnly about the events." Because the author says the conversation was "not cheery," a reader who is not familiar with the word "solemnly" can see that "solemn" means the opposite of cheery. This shows that *solemn* must mean serious or sad.

Cause and Effect

A text that discusses a **cause and effect** can also show the meaning of an unfamiliar word. Consider the following sentence: "The student was mortified after she learned that she accidentally sang the wrong song at the talent show." *Mortified* may be an unfamiliar word. However, this sentence shows that the student became mortified as a result of her mistake. The reader can understand that making a mistake in front of many people is the cause. Usually, this would have the effect of making someone very embarrassed. *Mortified* means "extremely embarrassed," which is supported by the event in the sentence.

Dictionary

A print or digital dictionary can be used to find out many things about a word. A dictionary will show the correct pronunciation of a word, provide its meaning, and identify what part of speech the word is. It will also tell how the word was derived—that is, what words it came from originally. A dictionary will have a **pronunciation guide** for each word that shows how to sound it out and where its syllables start and end. It will use symbols to indicate sounds, and will also use sample sounds (the "a" in "bad," for instance). A dictionary lists all of the meanings of a word and the parts of speech the word can be used as.

EXAMPLE

Philippe used his dictionary to check the various meanings of the word *eliminate*. He found this entry:

eliminate \ i-'li-mə-ˌnāt \ verb

1. to put an end to or get rid of
2. to expel from the living body
3. to cause to disappear by combining two or more equations

Identify which definition of *eliminate* is used in the following sentence:

> Harold couldn't wait to *eliminate* the other team from the playoffs by winning the first two games.

The correct answer is meaning 1: "to put an end to or get rid of." If you substitute that definition for the word, the sentence makes sense. Meanings 2 and 3 do not fit with the context of the sentence. When considering which meaning is being used, always check for context clues in the sentence or in the sentences before or after the sentence in which the word is used. Dictionaries also tell you how to pronounce words and often the derivation of the word, although that is not given here.

THESAURUS

A thesaurus is a reference book that gives **synonyms** of words. It is different from a dictionary because a thesaurus does not give definitions. A thesaurus can be helpful in finding the meaning of an unfamiliar word when reading. If the meaning of a synonym is known, then the meaning of the unfamiliar word will be known. Another time in which a thesaurus can be helpful is when writing. Using a thesaurus helps authors to vary their word choice.

GLOSSARY

A glossary is a **list of terms and their definitions** that can be found **at the back** of certain types of books, such as textbooks or reference books. A glossary does not have the definitions of all words, like a dictionary, but instead gives the definitions of the important terms within that particular book which are either uncommon or newly introduced. One may use a glossary when reading a book about economics or a chapter in a science textbook, for example, to define some of the technical terms within the text.

Literal and Figurative Language

Imagery

Imagery is the use of **descriptive language** to add life or feeling to a work of literature. Many authors add literary and sound devices to create vivid pictures in the minds of their readers. Most of the time, imagery is thought to be one of the best ways to help readers fully understand and remember a work.

The most common forms of imagery are those that appeal to the sense of sight and sound. Imagery that appeals to the sense of sight, or **visual imagery**, helps the reader picture an event in their mind, usually by including specific details in the text that are not strictly necessary for the purpose of the story, but allow the reader to more easily "see" the scene. Some common forms of figurative language can help create visual imagery.

Literal and Figurative Language

Many types of text use both **literal language**, which means just what it says, and **figurative language**, which allows the writer to expand the way in which he or she uses language. When an author uses figurative language, she connects things in an exaggerated and non-literal way in order to create a memorable image, which helps to describe a situation in a new way for the reader.

Review Video: Figurative Language
Visit mometrix.com/academy and enter code: 584902

Simile

- Shows similarity between two ideas or objects, using the words "**like**" or "**as**"
- For example, an author might write "The princess is as beautiful as a rose" to compare the appearance of a woman to a beautiful flower.

Metaphor

- Puts one idea in place of another to draw a parallel between the two ideas.
- For example, an author might write "Her room was a pigsty," to compare a person's bedroom to a dirty spot where pigs sleep.

Symbolism

- Using one object to stand for something else.
- For example, an author may include a flag flying high throughout a story to show pride in the characters' country and to represent the idea of patriotism.

Hyperbole

- An extreme exaggeration of an idea.
- For example, a character might say "I'm starving to death!" to show that they are really hungry. Most of the time a character who says this is not literally going to die from hunger, they are just ready for a snack.

Irony

- Uses sarcasm or humor (usually with an emphasis on the opposite) to show difference from literal meaning.
- For example, if a character says "Well today must be my lucky day!" after they left their homework on the kitchen table, they are being ironic. The irony used here helps show that it is definitely *not* the character's lucky day.

Personification

- Gives life or human characteristics to an inanimate object
- For example, if an author writes "The trees whispered to each other across the wide blue sky," they are using personification to help the reader imagine the scene. Trees are not human beings, so they do not whisper, but the image created in the reader stands out more than a literal description would.

Example

Based on current knowledge, identify whether metaphor, simile, or hyperbole is used in this sentence:

> The chiming bell was a beacon of hope for the downtrodden villagers.

A **metaphor** is used in this sentence to draw a parallel between "the chiming bell" and "a beacon of hope." The bell is being compared to something else in the sentence, which indicates the use of metaphor or simile, but the reader knows that the sentence does not contain a simile, because the words **like** and **as** are not used to show the comparison. The sentence also does not contain an exaggeration of facts, so the reader can see that hyperbole is not used.

Example

Discuss the kind of figurative language used in the following poem by the Scottish poet Robert Burns.

> O my luve's like a red, red rose
> That's newly sprung in June;
> O my luve's like the melodie
> That's sweetly played in tune.

The poet uses **similes** to create an image in this poem. The two similes here occur when the speaker says that his love is "**like** a red, red rose" and that she is also "**like** the melodie." These are examples of similes because they use the comparing word 'like' to compare two things. They are not metaphors because metaphors do not use the comparing words 'like' or 'as.' The poem paints an image of the speaker's love by comparing her to a red rose that has newly sprung and a melody that is sweetly played.

Example

Read the following excerpt from "The Raven" by Edgar Allan Poe, identify the metaphor, and discuss how it impacts the text:

> And the raven, never flitting, still is sitting, still is sitting
> On the pallid bust of Pallas just above my chamber door;
> And his eyes have all the seeming of a demon's that is dreaming

One **metaphor** in the excerpt from "The Raven" by Edgar Allan Poe is: 'And his eyes have all the seeming of a demon's that is dreaming' The metaphor compares the raven's eyes with a demon, which shows that the speaker thinks there is evil in the bird. This helps contribute to the overall tone of the poem and the reader's understanding of how the speaker views the bird.

Example

Read the excerpt from a poem by William Blake and describe what form of figurative language it uses.

> The wild winds weep,
> And the night is a-cold;
> Come hither, sleep,
> And my griefs unfold.

This poem contains several examples of **personification**. In the poem, the speaker says "The wild winds weep," thereby giving the winds the human characteristic of weeping. Later it says "Come hither, sleep," which is another use of personification asking that sleep to go somewhere as though it were a person. The poem gives the winds and sleep human characteristics. This is the definition of personification. It is not an example of simile because there is no comparison using the words "as" or "like." It is not a metaphor because there is no comparison between two things sharing a similar quality. And it is not an example of hyperbole because there is no exaggeration. The poem does contain some alliteration, however; the repetition of the letter "w" in "wild winds weep" qualifies as alliteration, which is another literary technique.

Author's Purpose and Craft

Author's Purpose

The purpose of a text is the author's main reason for writing the text. As the reader reads a text, they should always try to figure out the author's purpose for writing as this will help them to better understand the message that the author is trying to convey.

Informational Texts

- Inform the reader on a topic that they previously knew nothing about, such as many non-fiction texts.
- The author will usually include sources of information for an informative piece.
- For example, an informative paper on early Native American Indian tribes would detail where Native American Indians lived, what types of foods they ate, how they bartered for goods, and other aspects of their culture.

Persuasive Texts

- Influence the reader to think a certain way about a topic, calling them to action or pointing them toward resources that would help them to learn more about the topic.
- A **proposition and support** paper would be an example of this, where an author gives their opinion and then tries to convince the reader to see something from their point of view.
- An author will often use positive expert testimonials when trying to persuade the reader to accept a given point-of-view.
- For example, an author may try to persuade the reader that technology is negatively affecting social interaction, and that limits should be set on how much people can use their technological devices.

Expressive Texts

- Express the author or speaker's opinion or emotions about a topic. Generally, expressive texts include descriptive words to clearly show the reader how the author or speaker feels.
- For example, the author may think that history is important for all people to study, and express the opinion that education without history class would be incomplete.

Entertaining Texts

- Entertain the reader, such as in most fictional texts.
- For example, Lois Lowry, the author of *The Giver,* entertains his readers with the story of a young boy named Jonas who is learning how to navigate his unexpected life assignment.
- Entertaining texts can be either fiction or non-fiction, but are usually stories such as a fairy tale or fictional piece of writing. Entertaining texts usually follow a chronological order.

Authors usually write to entertain, to inform, or to persuade their readers. The organization structure or pattern they use is related to what the author's purpose is. It is important to choose the pattern that best presents the information, as not all patterns will work for every piece of writing.

Determining the Purpose of a Text

When reading, the reader should always determine the purpose of a text. to do so, ask yourself what effect the writing has on you. Does the text try to explain or persuade you of something? Perhaps the text is making an appeal to your emotions. The signs that a text is attempting to persuade you include an author offering an opinion and explaining why she thinks this way. On the other hand, if a text is simply informative, it will have many facts that will give details about an event, person, or idea without trying to persuade you of anything. Manuals that come with equipment are clearly not persuasive, simply instructive.

Review Video: Understanding the Author's Intent
Visit mometrix.com/academy and enter code: 511819

Review Video: Sensory Language
Visit mometrix.com/academy and enter code: 177314

LANGUAGE AND THE AUTHOR'S VIEWPOINT

The way that a writer uses language to decribe an idea or an event tells the reader a lot about how the author feels about the subject. In most works, the tone, voice, and mood are consistent with one another to provide a unified feel throughout a text, but these aspects of how the author writes can be manipulated to cause the reader to feel a specific way. For instance, the subject matter can be something that is generally considered good, like a sunny day at the park, but can be cast with tones that make the subject feel scary.

EXAMPLE

> The sun peered out of the blue expanse, leaving nowhere to hide from its heat. Jenny's ice cream was quickly melting, along with the hope that she could delay any longer. Her dad brought her a brand-new bike and, with it, an expectation that she would be riding on her own within the hour.

Sometimes authors use subtle hints by manipulating the tone and mood in ways that contradict what they are literally saying. Readers need to be aware that the author may be saying one thing, but can be implying something different by shading the language.

Types of Texts

Literary Genres

Literature contains many different **genres**, which are categories that texts can be divided into. Genres are used to group types of writing together for purposes of study, reading, or simple organization. Some common literary genres are

- **Realistic fiction** -A story that could actually happen and reflects life in a realistic way.
- **Adventure stories** -Short, mostly fictional stories that follow characters as they go on an adventure or quest.
- **Historical fiction** -Often strays from historical reality in order to tell a story and make a true historical event more interesting to the reader.
- **Mysteries** -Fiction stories about solving crimes or revealing secrets.
- **Humor** –Stories, mostly fictional, full of fun and excitement meant to entertain readers. Can be seen in stories from all genres.
- **Myth** -A legend or traditional narrative, often based on a historical event. The story reveals something about human behavior or the natural world, and often involves actions of gods.
- **Fantasy** -Fictional stories that contain unusual and other worldly settings and characters. The sense of "realness" in other stories is not present. The fantasy genre is known for including elements like magic and imaginary creatures like fairies, dragons, and elves.
- **Science fiction** -Fiction based on what could happen if actual, imagined, or possible scientific advances occurred. Usually set in the future, a modified past, or on other planets.

Poetry

Poet Versus Speaker

The author of a poem is called a **poet**. Many poems are written in first person, which means the **stanzas** (groups of lines) include words like "I" and "me." However, the poet is not always the **speaker** of the poem. In a novel, the author can create characters with different points of view. The characters can argue or have different roles to play in telling the story. Similarly, a poet may write a poem from a different point of view or even include more than one voice. The speaker is the voice of the poem, and is not always the same person as the poet him or herself. The reader or listener should know that the person telling the story is a character, and not always a real person.

For example, this excerpt from a poem by Dr. Seuss reads:

> When you think things are bad,
> when you feel sour and blue,
> when you start to get mad...
> you should do what I do!
> Just tell yourself, Duckie,
> you're really quite lucky!
> Some people are much more...
> oh, ever so much more...
> oh, muchly much-much more
> unlucky than you!

Even though one line has the word "I" in it, the poem is not from the perspective of Dr. Seuss. He is the author of the poem, but not the speaker. The person saying "I" is a character, just like in a story.

Meter, Rhyme, and Repetition in Poetry

The **meter** of a poem refers to the number of syllables per line as well as the pattern of emphasis on those syllables. The use of meter gives a poem a rhythmic context and contributes to the poem's flow. Certain types of meter can also make a poem more appealing to the reader or represent natural speech rhythms.

Rhymes repeat the ending sound of words: "So very soon/We will fly to the moon." Here the "oo" sound is repeated in the words *soon* and *moon*. Rhymes are frequently used in poetry, mostly older forms of poetry rather than modern poems.

Another type of repetition is **alliteration**. Alliteration repeats beginning sounds, usually consonants: "Rah, rah, rah," the crowd cried, "rah, rah, rah." It is often used in poetry as well as in spoken forms of writing.

Rhyme Scheme

When determining what a poem's rhyme scheme is, readers should look at the last word of each line to see which words rhyme with each other. Words that rhyme are assigned a letter of the alphabet, beginning with "a." The next time words rhyme, if the rhyme is different than the last one, they assigned a new letter, going forward in order of the alphabet until the poem is over or there are no more rhymes. This sounds complicated, but it's easy with practice.

Let's take a look at an excerpt from Dylan Thomas' poem "Do not go gentle into that good night":

Do not go gentle into that good night,
Old age should burn and rave at close of day;
Rage, rage against the dying of the light.

Though wise men at their end know dark is right,
Because their words had forked no lightning they
Do not go gentle into that good night.

The words at the end of the lines are *night, day, light, right, they,* and *night.*

We know that the first rhyme is assigned the letter "a," and can clearly see that *night, light,* and *right* all rhyme, so we can mark the poem like this

Do not go gentle into that good night, **a**
Old age should burn and rave at close of day;
Rage, rage against the dying of the light. **a**

Though wise men at their end know dark is right, **a**
Because their words had forked no lightning they
Do not go gentle into that good night. **a**

Now, we'll look at the only other rhyme in the poem, which is made up of the words *day* and *they.* This rhyme does not rhyme with the first set of words, so it gets a new letter, "b."

Do not go gentle into that good night, **a**
Old age should burn and rave at close of day; **b**
Rage, rage against the dying of the light. **a**

Though wise men at their end know dark is right, **a**
Because their words had forked no lightning they **b**
Do not go gentle into that good night. **a**

After looking at all six lines and determining how they rhyme, we can confidently say that the rhyme scheme for this excerpt is a, b, a, a, b, a.

Rhymes are used at the discretion of the poet and are not always mandatory. Many modern poems—actually, most of them—use a blank verse, where there are no rhyme schemes. However, there are many formal poetic types, such as the sonnet, that have a specific rhyme scheme that poets must follow to achieve that kind of poetic form.

EXAMPLE

Explain the rhyme scheme of the following excerpt from a poem entitled "Alone" by Edgar Allan Poe.

> From childhood's hour I have not been
> As others were; I have not seen
> As others saw; I could not bring
> My passions from a common spring.
> From the same source I have not taken
> My sorrow; I could not awaken
> My heart to joy at the same tone;
> And all I loved, I loved alone.

The rhyme scheme that Edgar Allan Poe uses in this excerpt from his poem "Alone" is: a, a, b, b, c, c, d, d, e, e. Every two lines rhyme, but the rhyme is not repeated in the other lines. This is a rather unusual rhyme scheme; many others have lines that repeat the rhyme scheme, but not in a consecutive order, such as a, b, a, b or a, b, c a, b, c.

GRAPHICAL ELEMENTS IN POETRY

Graphic elements in a poem such as capitalization, line length, and word position can call special attention to words or phrases. **Capitalization** can signal the beginning of a sentence, or all caps may be used to provide emphasis. **Line length** can be used to help create a shape, like in concrete poems, or to create a bold statement, like a one-word line. A poet can create tension by using line length and punctuation independently of one another. **Word position** can be used to contribute to a feeling, or it can also be used to help create a shape, so poets are often careful where they end lines.

LINE BREAKS

Line breaks are used to end a line of poetry. Poets use **line breaks** to control the **length** of **each line**. The length of lines in a poem can impact the poem's meaning and the **speed** at which the poem is read. **Long** lines are usually read more **quickly**, while **short** lines cause the reader to briefly pause and look to the next line, so their reading is **slowed**. These effects often contribute to the reader's experience when reading the poem, so poets aim to make the effects match the tone of their message in the poem.

PUNCTUATION

The punctuation in each line of a poem causes the reader to **pause** after certain words. This lets the poet **emphasize** specific **ideas** or **images**. Similar to the effects of line length, punctuation at the end of a line can guide the **speed** at which the reader reads each line. Lines with a punctuation mark at the end cause readers to pause, while lines that do not end with a punctuation mark carry a sentence to the next line. This creates an effect that is like the effect of long lines.

CAPITALIZATION

Poets also use capitalization to **highlight** certain words in their poetry. Authors will often capitalize words that are not proper nouns so that the reader pays more attention to them. While this is not grammatically correct, it is used in poetry to create a certain effect and guide the reader as they read and form their understanding of the poem.

Drama

Dramas are texts that are written to be performed by people reading the lines or acting the stories out. They can also be presented as monologues (one character speaks), dialogues (two character speak to each other), or pantomimes (body movements are used instead of spoken words). Dramatic texts are called plays or **scripts**, and they are written differently than other texts.

Text Structure in Drama

Plays are divided into **acts** (large units) and **scenes** (small sections inside acts) instead of chapters. There are also **stage directions**, which are instructions from the playwright about where items go, where actors should move, and what the characters should be doing during the scene. Stage directions are usually in italics to set them apart from other parts of the play. When it is time for a character in a play to speak, there will be **character tag** on the left side of the page which shows the name of the character (all letters of the name are capitalized) followed by a colon.

Here is an example of how a page from a play might look:

Title of Play

Act Number

Scene Number

The setting of the scene is being described here. The reader is being introduced to the characters and the things happening around them. Characters will enter speak to one another during the scene.

CHARACTER 1:
I am speaking. These are words I say. *(stage directions)* I am still speaking.

CHARACTER 2 *enters and does something.*

CHARACTER 2:
Now I am speaking. This is my dialogue.

Dialogue and Stage Directions

Dialogue refers to what the characters say in a play when they are talking to each other, talking to themselves, or even talking to the audience. The type of speech, word choice, and accent a character uses is specific to the role he is playing. For example, a person cast to play a cowboy would have certain words in his vocabulary that a character from a big city in the North would not have.

A playwright also uses stage directions to make the play flow smoothly. Character interaction helps the viewer to understand the mood of the scene. If two characters are confrontational, the viewer is aware that there is some type of conflict occurring. Stage directions create order when all the characters are on stage together.

Informational Text

Structural Features of Informational Text

Texts which intend to inform the reader about a topic are often accompanied by visual aids or graphics. Some common examples are listed below.

- **Forewords** appear before the actual text. Usually, forewords are not written by the author of the text. They are written by a different person who is well-respected in a related field of work or study. The author of the foreword usually provides some information about the texts and explains why they support the text.

- **Prefaces** are written to provide the reader with supporting information that was not included in the text. This information may help the reader better understand the text or may show the reader why the topic of the text is important or interesting to the author.
- **Introductions** usually appear as the first paragraph in a text. An introduction is used to catch the reader's attention and let the audience know what the text is about and how the topic will be covered by the text.
- **Insets and sidebars** show additional information related to the text in boxes or on the sides of the page. Insets can contain pictures or text, and sometimes have different colored backgrounds or font types to make them stand out from the text.
- **Visual aids** include features like diagrams, graphs, and charts. These can help the user think about information in a different way. They do this by visually presenting the relationship between the information in the text.
- **Bullet points** list items separately, making facts and ideas easier to see and understand.
- **Numbers** can also be used to list separate items. Usually, numbers are used to show that the items are part of a sequence. For example, in a list of instructions, each instruction may be numbered to show the reader the order in which each instruction should be completed.
- **References** are the sources of the information the author included in the text. In most works, the references will all be listed after the last page of the main text. These may be included on a page titled "Bibliography," "Works Cited," or, simply, "References." Reviewing the author's sources and reviewing their credibility can show the reader whether the work itself is credible, unbiased, and accurate.
- **Acknowledgements** appear near the end of books, after the main text and any resources that the author has included for the reader. The acknowledgements section is used by authors to thank the people that helped them create the work. People who encouraged the author, assisted the author with writing and editing, or made it possible for the work to be published are usually named in the acknowledgements section.

Argumentative Texts

Identifying the Claim

In a persuasive or argumentative text, the author is writing in order to make and support a claim. A claim is similar to the key idea of an informational text. However, a claim can be argued, which means that some readers may not agree with it. The author of the text will need to use the body of the text to support the claim and show readers why they should agree with it. To identify the claim of a text, first identify the topic. Then, read the introduction text to see what the author writes about the topic.

The claim should be clearly stated in the introduction. However, if the claim is still not clear, read the body to see what kind of evidence the author uses to support the claim. The way that the author gives and applies evidence may also show what the claim of the text is.

Call to Action

Another strategy is to look for a call to action in the text. A call to action is a statement that instructs the reader to do something after reading the text. Often, the call to action will tell the reader to do something that shows that he or she agrees with the author's claim. For example, if an author's claim is that reading is better than watching a movie, the author may include a call to action that says "Turn off the TV and dig in to a new book today!" By including this statement, the author is telling the readers to show their agreement by choosing to read rather than watch a movie.

Identifying How the Author Supports a Claim

In a persuasive or argumentative text, the author must use information to support his or her claim. This information is called evidence. Below are common types of evidence an author may use to support a claim:

- **Facts:** Authors may use facts that show that their claim is true. For example, a claim that fish are better pets than dogs can be supported by the fact that fish cannot make a mess inside a house.

- **Personal Anecdotes:** A personal anecdote is a story from a person's own experience. Authors can use personal anecdotes to tell stories that show why their claim is true. For example, an author can support the claim that people should wear elbow pads when riding a bike can be supported by sharing a story about their experience of scraping their elbow after falling off of a bicycle.
- **Statistics:** Statistics are observations that are based on a collection of data. Statistics can show trends or preferences among members of a group. An author can use statistics to support a claim by sharing the statistic says is likely to happen or be true for many people.
- **Examples:** Authors may give examples of events or experiences that suggest that their claim is true. For example, an author may claim that people should exercise because it will make them healthier. The author could give an example of how exercise can improve a person's health in order to support this claim.
- **Quotes:** An author can support a claim by using quotes from other people or texts. If the person or text makes a statement that shows that the author's claim is true, the author can include that quote in his or her text. When authors include quotes in their work, they must always tell the reader where the quote came from.

The author must use enough evidence to support the claim. If the evidence does not fully support the claim in the text, then the author must continue working to find evidence for the claim. The evidence used to support a claim must also be believable and come from a reliable source.

Counterarguments

A counterargument is a claim that seeks to disprove another claim. Sometimes, an author of a persuasive or argumentative text will include a **counterargument** to their own claim in a text. Doing this allows the author to show why someone may disagree with his or her claim and then show why the counterargument is wrong. Authors include counterarguments in order to strengthen their own argument and show the reader why claims that oppose their own are incorrect.

Identifying the Intended Audience

Authors of persuasive and argumentative texts want to convince others to agree with a claim or take a certain action. Because of this, they will often write to a specific audience. Often, the target audience will include people who disagree with the author's claim. The author's desire is to give these people information that will lead them to change their minds or actions.

Strategies for Identifying the Intended Audience

One way to identify the intended audience of a persuasive or argumentative text is to first identify the author's claim. Then, consider who would disagree with the author's claim. This group of people is likely the group that the author wants to persuade.

Another way to identify the audience is to look for clues in the text. Sometimes, authors will clearly state which people are included in the intended audience. For example, imagine that an author includes the statement, "Teachers should reward their students every time they make a good grade on a test." This shows that the text is written to persuade teachers who do not already reward their students for good test grades. Similarly, a call to action may show who the target audience is by instructing the members of the audience to take a certain action.

Main Idea and Supporting Details

Key Ideas and Supporting Details

Identifying **key ideas** helps the reader see what a text or story is mostly about. They are the **most important ideas** in a text, and everything else in the text builds around and supports them. Every piece of writing has key ideas. The **supporting details** in a story, such as the characters, events, and settings, will work together to reveal the key ideas. The details are not key ideas, themselves. They make the key ideas clear and show the reader the author's purpose for writing the text.

Controlling Idea

The controlling idea, also called the main idea or thesis, of a passage is usually located in the first paragraph or two of text. Having the controlling idea near the beginning of the passage allows the author to grab the reader's attention and let them know what the rest of the passage will discuss.

To find the controlling idea in a passage, there are questions the reader can ask while reading: What is this passage about? What does the author want the reader to know about the topic? The supporting details will provide evidence that the controlling idea is correct and are found in the body of a passage. The supporting details often provide examples of the controlling idea.

For example, a passage may contain the controlling idea: "Ellis Island was an entry-point to America for many immigrants during the Industrial Revolution." A supporting detail for the controlling idea may be "Immigrants were examined for contagious diseases at Ellis Island before being granted entry to America."

Review Video: Thesis Statements
Visit mometrix.com/academy and enter code: 691033

Example

Determine the controlling idea the following sentence tells the reader and indicate what details support the controlling idea:

> Her breath billowed out in clouds of white and disappeared into the quiet air.

The controlling idea is what the author wants the reader to understand about the text. Details help to explain or support that controlling idea. A controlling idea usually states the point of an entire essay, article, or book, but can be simply stated in one sentence. The controlling idea in the sentence above is that a girl is outside in the cold. Details to support this statement include the word 'her,' showing that the character is a girl, and 'clouds of white,' which indicate that the air is cold. in order to conclude that the girl is out in the cold, the reader needs to understand that breath can be seen when the air is cold.

Supporting Details

Authors use supporting details to provide evidence and backing for the main point. All texts contain details, but they are only classified as supporting details when they serve to reinforce some larger point. Supporting details are most commonly found in informative and persuasive texts. in some cases, they will be clearly indicated with words like **for example** or **for instance**, or they will begin with words like **first**, **second**, and **last**. However, these special words are not a requirement. As a reader, it is important to consider whether the author's supporting details really back up his or her main point. Supporting details can be factual and correct but still not relevant to the author's point. Sometimes, supporting details can seem important but they might not support the controlling idea in the story well because they are based on opinion that cannot be proven.

Example

Decide whether the following sentence is the main point or a supporting point of a text, and state where the information would be placed in an outline:

> One type of horseback riding, bareback horseback riding, involves sitting on a moving horse without a saddle and grasping the horse's mane.

This sentence is a supporting point, with the main point of the entire text likely about horseback riding in general. As a supporting point, this sentence would go further down in an outline, next to any numeral after numeral I. This sentence can be followed by additional sub-points that further explain the concept of bareback horseback riding. When a supporting point is used to clarify a main point or topic, the supporting point helps to break the topic down into smaller pieces.

Transitions

Transitions

Transitions between sentences and paragraphs guide readers from idea to idea and show relationships between sentences and paragraphs. Writers should use transitions carefully and only when they are truly helpful. They should also be selected to fit the author's purpose. Transitions can show relationships such as time, comparison, an order of events, and cause and effect. Transitions are often used at the beginning of a phrase, sentence, or paragraph, since this helps prepare the reader for the next piece of information.

Review Video: Transitions in Writing
Visit mometrix.com/academy and enter code: 233246

Types of Transitional Words

Time	Afterward, immediately, earlier, meanwhile, recently, lately, now, since, soon, when, then, until, before, etc.
Sequence	too, first, second, further, moreover, also, again, and, next, still, besides, finally
Comparison	similarly, in the same way, likewise, also, again, once more
Contrasting	but, although, despite, however, instead, nevertheless, on the one hand... on the other hand, regardless, yet, in contrast.
Cause and Effect	because, consequently, thus, therefore, then, to this end, since, so, as a result, if... then, accordingly
Examples	for example, for instance, such as, to illustrate, indeed, in fact, specifically
Place	near, far, here, there, to the left/right, next to, above, below, beyond, opposite, beside
Repetition, Summary, or Conclusion	as mentioned earlier, as noted, in other words, in short, on the whole, to summarize, therefore, as a result, to conclude, in conclusion
Addition	and, also, furthermore, moreover

Review Video: Transition Words
Visit mometrix.com/academy and enter code: 707563

Point of View

Point of View

Authors choose which character tells the story they are writing. This is called **point of view**. The point of view affects the story in many ways. There are three general types of point of view:

First Person

- Tells a story through the eyes of one character.
- Uses the pronouns 'I,' 'me,' 'we,' and 'my.'
- The reader gets only one side of the story, without any other angles on what may have happened in the text

Second Person

- Tells a story using the pronoun 'you.'
- The least common point of view.

Third Person

- Tells a story about a character or group of characters from an outside viewpoint.
- Uses the words 'her', 'his,' 'they,' or a name to talk about a character or characters.
- A common way to show action in a story which allows the author to easily and realistically tell a story from more than one person's viewpoint.
- Gives readers a more complete view of a story as it is told from many different perspectives.

Different Forms of Third Person

When an author writes in third-person point of view, there are a few options to choose from:

- **Third person omniscient** - There is an all-knowing narrator telling the story as well as interpreting events, and relating thoughts of the characters.
- **Third person limited (or closed)** - The author writes in the third person, but does so from only one character's point of view. There are two different variations of this type of narration: the narrator can either stay with the same character throughout or cycle through different characters over the course of the story.

Subjective and Objective Point of View

The point of view of a character or narrator can either be **subjective** or **objective**. When a character or narrator is describing a person, object, or idea using phrases that are based on opinions or motivated by feelings, their point of view is subjective. When they use phrases based on facts or something that can be proven, their point of view is objective. For example, if a character describes a person walking toward them and they say "Her shirt was a beautiful shade of yellow, which made her blonde hair shine even brighter" they are speaking in subjective point of view. The yellow color they think is beautiful could be someone else's least favorite color. If the same character described the situation objectively, they might say "As she walked by, I noticed her shirt was yellow and her hair was blonde." The narrator doesn't comment on his opinion of the color, just that it is factually yellow.

Elements of Story

Setting

The setting is where a story **takes place**. The setting of a story may stay the same for the entire story, or change as events in the story unfold. For example, an entire story may take place in one room or cross continents as the reader follows the characters along on a trail of events.

The setting of a story is described by the author in terms of what it looks like, how the character feels, and anything else that is happening at that location at the time. For example, a character may be caught on a doorstep on a cold, rainy day. The character may feel frustrated as they shiver in the doorway, waiting for the heavy rain to let up a bit.

Shaping a Character with Setting or Plot

The setting of a story shapes character because it helps to define the situation that a character finds herself in. A character is limited to the setting of a story. For example, if a story takes place in a cold environment filled with snow and ice, this is certain to impact what actions a character can and will take. Frequently, the setting changes the way characters behave based on time. For example, the character of a woman who is a single mother in 1920 would be seen and behave very differently than a single mother in 2020.

Example

Read the excerpt and determine how the setting influences the character in this excerpt.

> She had swum too far out. The waves were higher than she thought. She was struggling hard to get to shore. She wondered if she would make it. She thought of her childhood. Had she been right to run away from home, she wondered? Just then, a lifeguard grabbed her and helped her to shore.

The setting of the ocean and the high waves creates a conflict in the character. She is worried. She thinks about her childhood and her parents. She doesn't know if she will make it to shore. This is how the setting affects the character in this excerpt. Without the high waves and the struggle, she would not become so worried and start to think about her past. She probably would not have questioned herself. This is an example of how a setting influences a character. If the waves had not been high, there probably would not have been a struggle or any self-searching of the swimmer's past.

Historical and Cultural Setting

Historical context influences literature in a number of ways. The style of the author's writing can be impacted by the historical period during which it was written (e.g., Dickens wrote at a time when authors were paid by the word; this is why his novels are so long). Obviously, the setting of the book includes its historical context. In addition, dialect may be a function of the historical period of the book. When a reader understands the historical context of a particular book, he or she can have a deeper understanding of the novel. Knowing about the time period during which the author wrote, as well as the time period discussed in the novel, helps the reader understand some of the author's choices, including character motivations.

Example

Slavery used to be the norm in Southern states. One of the major ways in which the historical context of slavery impacted literature coming out of the South was the birth of the slave narrative. Slaves wanted to have their experiences documented. After the Civil War, former slaves wrote their stories. These slave narratives have given historians valuable firsthand accounts of life in the South. From a literary perspective, slave narratives are one of the most important genres of African-American writing. Slavery influenced literature by delving into themes of power, racial injustice, and equality. Literature from this time period can help the reader better understand the perspectives and experiences of the slaves themselves, as well as the slave holders.

Patterns Related to Settings

The setting of a story can allow the reader to draw on personal experience about where the story takes place. If a story takes place on a farm, the reader will likely picture a rural, peaceful setting, which may go along with (or be in contrast to) the actual plot of the story. For example, a reader would not expect a scary story to occur on a farm on a sunny day. Conversely, a reader may view a dark subway as a dangerous place, while the plot of a story set there may be based on a very calm series of events. When an author is crafting a story, they need to consider what the audience may already think about a particular setting in order to properly present the events of a story for greatest impact.

Style, Voice, Tone, and Mood

Style, tone, and mood all play an important role in the development of a story. The reader's impression of a story can vary based on the style, tone, and mood established by the author.

- **Style** refers to the way an author uses words, phrases, and sentence structure. The style of the text can change depending on whether the author uses short, choppy sentences, long, elaborate sentences, formal language, or informal language.
- **Voice** refers to the characteristics of a text that show the author's personality and distinguish the author from other writers. An author's voice may be recognized through the way they use words or the way they organize and present their thoughts. Voice is specific to each writer, and it can be as specific and unique as personality.
- **Tone** refers to the attitude of the writer toward the subject matter. The tone can change throughout the text or stay the same. There are many ways to describe the tone of the text, such as light, playful, questioning, humorous, serious, solemn, or tense. The reader can identify the tone by paying attention to the author's word choice.
- **Mood** refers to the overall feeling conveyed by a setting. For example, a story may be dark in terms of setting, characters, and events that occur. If a story is presented in a picturesque countryside location where the characters are content and the style of speaking is elaborate, the reader will have a different impression of the story than if the setting is in a rundown house with a pale, unhappy caretaker that rarely speaks.

Review Video: Style, Tone, and Mood
Visit mometrix.com/academy and enter code: 416961

Plot

The storyline of any text is also called a **plot**. The characters and events in the story determine what the plot will be. Readers may find a **plot line** useful as they try to put the events in the text in order and determine the relationships between events.

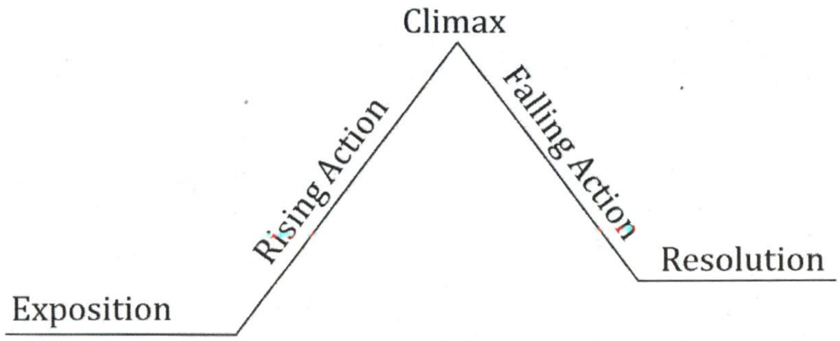

Review Video: Plot Line
Visit mometrix.com/academy and enter code: 944011

Every plot will begin with **exposition**, which introduces the characters and the setting of the story. The plot will continue to develop as new ideas and events centered on the main conflict in the story are revealed, which is called the **rising action**. The action in the story will rise until a **climax** is reached within the conflict. The climax can also be referred to as the turning point in the story, since the climax is where each character makes an important decision. After the climax, the action starts to wind down during the **falling action**. At this point, the characters begin to follow the paths they chose in during climax. The events of the story reach **resolution** in some way by the end of the story. Some conflicts are left open-ended, so that the reader is left to decide what really happened at the end of the story. Keep in mind that not all resolutions are happy or peaceful.

EXAMPLE

Read the following plot and analyze what event is missing from the plot sequence.

> Martin's family decided to go camping at the local park over the weekend. They packed all the camping necessities and drove to the park. Thick sheets of rain poured down all day, so they were stuck in their tent.

Martin and his family forgot to check the weather forecast before they left for their camping trip. to fill in the missing detail, the author may write: "Martin and his family checked the forecast and saw that it was going to rain, but decided to go camping anyway." the flow of the story is broken up by the sudden realization that it is raining, something that could be prevented by adding in the missing detail.

When details are missing from a plot sequence, the audience has trouble following the action in a story. By adding in additional details, the point of each step in a story can be made clearer to the audience.

CONFLICT

An important part of analyzing the plot of a passage is identifying the **main conflict**. There will likely be many smaller conflicts in the story, but there will be one main problem that influences the characters and events. to identify the main conflict, first look at who the main character is. Now ask yourself what they want. They may want to something to happen or not happen, another character to do or not do something, or to confront or avoid a problem, among other things. Once you know what they want, now ask yourself what is standing in the character's way. It may be a person, an event, or something less tangible like the passing of time. Combining what the main character wants and why they do not currently have leaves the reader with a summary of the main conflict.

EXAMPLE

Read the following sentence from the *Call of the Wild* by Jack London and describe the main conflict in the sentence. Explain how the conflict may be resolved.

> The breaking down of discipline likewise affected the dogs in their relations with one another.

Based on the information in the sentence, an event has caused the dogs, the characters in the story, to not follow their regular routine. The sentence indicates that there has been a breaking down of discipline which is affecting how the dogs relate to each other. in order to solve this conflict, discipline needs to be restored. However, in order to return to previous relations between the dogs, any problems that are in the way of conflict resolution need to be taken care of. The word *likewise* means *also*, which tells the reader that other parts of the story are being affected besides the relations between the dogs.

EXAMPLE

Read the following sentence and explain the main conflict between the two characters:

> Joe stared angrily at Jamie's retreating back as Jamie raced away down the field with Joe's soccer ball.

The main conflict in the sentence is that Jamie has Joe's soccer ball. There may be additional conflicts between the two characters, but none are evident from the evidence shown in the sentence. in any story, a conflict may be minor and only affect part of the story, or be the main focus, taking an entire story to solve a conflict between characters. in the context of the sentence, it is not clear whether or not the entire story will revolve around Jamie taking Joe's soccer ball.

RESOLUTION

The term **resolution** usually indicates the result of a conflict in a story. Conflict between characters, within a character, or against an external element is necessary in order to have a plot for a story. without conflict, no events would occur to form the story. A conflict will come to a climax, and then conclude in some way. The resolution of a problem may be open-ended, end tragically, or end in a way that is good for everyone involved. The problem resolution typically occurs near the end of a story, after the climax has happened. A problem may be resolved by the characters involved within the conflict or by an external event; an upcoming resolution may be foreshadowed in the text, or may be completely unexpected by the reader. If the resolution is completely unexpected, it is considered to be a **twist** in the story.

FORESHADOWING

Foreshadowing is a technique authors use to give readers **hints** about events that will take place later in a story. Sometimes, foreshadowing is also used to build **suspense**. Foreshadowing most often takes place through a character's dialogue or actions. Sometimes the character will know what is going to happen and will purposefully allude to future events. For example, consider a protagonist who is about to embark on a journey through the woods. Just before the protagonist begins the trip, another character says, "Be careful, you never know what could be out in those woods!" This alerts the reader that the woods may be dangerous and prompts the reader to expect something to attack the protagonist in the woods. This is an example of foreshadowing through warning.

Alternatively, a character may unknowingly foreshadow later events. For example, consider a story where a brother and sister run through their house and knock over a vase and break it. The brother says, "Don't worry, we'll clean it up! Mom will never know!" However, the reader knows that their mother will most likely find out what they have done, so the reader expects the siblings to later get in trouble for running, breaking the vase, and hiding it from their mother.

NON-LINEAR PLOT DEVELOPMENT

Some texts contain a **non-linear plot**, which means the plot is not told in chronological order, or is not told from "beginning to end" in one straight line. There are several devices that authors can use to make their plot non-linear, including:

- **Foreshadowing:** the author gives the reader hints early on in a work about something that will become clearer (or more important) later on.
- **Flashback:** the author shows the reader an event that happened in the past to explain something about the present.
- **Subplot:** a side story, usually about a supporting character, is told along with the main story. Sometimes subplots occur within flashbacks.
- **Parallel plot:** two stories are told alongside each other, often narrated by two different characters in alternating chapters. The events in the stories usually end up overlapping or coming together at some point, most often the climax of the text.

CHARACTERS

CHARACTER TRAIT

The traits of a character may include how they act and physical characteristics; a character trait is a behavior or physical characteristic that is unique to a specific character. For example, a character may be outgoing, which means he or she likes to talk a lot, or they may have bright red hair. These are both character traits.

An author uses character traits to describe a character in a story and help the reader to learn more about how the character acts and what they look like. By comparing the character traits in a story, the reader can see similarities and differences between characters. The author includes character traits to help the reader understand why a character may act a certain way in the story. For example, a character who is shy may not want to talk with a lot of people in a new classroom, but a character who is outgoing may want to talk with many people.

An author typically provides many details about a character so that the reader can learn more about the character's traits, motivations, relationships, and any conflicts they may have in the story. The traits of a character may include how they act and how they look. Characters are often motivated by things that have already happened in their life or how they feel about a topic. The author will often give the reader enough information about the character so that the reader can figure out why the character responds to a situation in a certain way. The author will also often give details about the relationships between characters and points they may conflict on. For example, a character may be good friends with another character; however, the two characters may disagree on where to play outside if one character likes being near the water and the other character does not.

EXAMPLE

Read the following description of a character and decide, logically, whether the character is likely to go hiking outdoors:

> Jeremy lived in a high-rise in Chicago. He was studious, and not very athletic. Jeremy preferred to stay indoors and read a book, rather than enjoy outdoor weather.

Based on the description of the character's traits, preferences, and personality, he is not likely to go hiking outdoors. The description indicates that the character prefers reading, rather than enjoying outdoor weather. In addition, the character lives in a tall building in the middle of a large city, in order for him to enjoy the outdoors, he would have to travel away from where he lives. The character is not likely to change his preferences. A situation may lead the character to go hiking, but he is not likely to initiate the action on his own. A description of a character that is likely to go hiking outdoors may include a preference for outdoor activity and living near trails.

CHARACTER CHANGES AND RESPONSES

Characters can change in a multitude of ways throughout a story; however, there are main aspects of a character that change. A character's identifying **characteristics**, such as personality or behavior traits, may change as the result of a prominent event in the story, current **motivations**, and conflicts. As **conflicts** change or are resolved, a character may no longer be motivated by striving toward a goal that was previously important to them. Furthermore, a character's development may also lead them to make **different choices**, which can **impact the plot**. As the plot of a story moves along, characters can constantly change in relation to events that occur. Relationships between characters and the points of view of characters may change throughout a story as well.

Each story will have many different types of characters and each of these characters will have a different relationship with other characters. Stories usually have a protagonist, antagonist, and a variety of other characters including round, flat, and stock characters.

PROTAGONIST

The main character in a drama, movie, novel, or other fictional text. The author portrays the protagonist in a way that the audience is most like to identify with themselves. The protagonist is generally undertaking some type of personal challenge throughout the story. The author writes the story so that the reader becomes aware of the protagonist's emotions and is generally able to empathize with the personal challenge.

ANTAGONIST

The character that actively opposes the protagonist by trying to prevent them from succeeding. The antagonist is usually presented in such a way as to make the audience dislike them, and want them to fail at stopping the protagonist. The protagonist and antagonist oppose each other, so their relationship is almost always one of dislike.

Flat Character

Does not have any substantial changes throughout the story. They stay the same despite the conflict, and do not learn any lessons. They are usually minor characters that might interact with the main character in some way.

Round Character

Major characters in the story that will be more fully developed than other minor characters. They will usually encounter some type of conflict that they must overcome, and usually learn a lesson about life or themselves along the way.

Stock Characters

Often get their characteristics and mannerisms from stereotypes of people that are widely recognized. These types of characters are often repeated and well-known. Readers should be aware that stereotypes are rarely accurate in reality, and are generally intended to be humorous or dramatic. Some examples are evil stepmothers, unintelligent blondes, rude athletes, and loyal servants.

Characters' Influence on the Plot

There are many ways in which the action of a story may be driven. Dialogue is one of them. What a character says either to another character or about a situation may propel the action by revealing what a character is thinking or what he may do. Similarly, what a character says will tell the audience what he is like. His manner of speaking, what he says, and how he says it are all clues to his personality. Dialogue can also provoke a decision by showing what the character intends to do in the future. Incidents in a story also propel the action because the plot is made up of events that build on events. Incidents such as a confrontation could reveal aspects of a character or provoke a decision.

Example

Read the excerpt and tell how this incident propels the action of the story and provokes a decision.

> It was a perfect day it seemed, until Sam saw the thunderheads roll in. He knew that it would be dangerous to be in a rowboat in the middle of the lake during a thunder and lightning storm. Suddenly the sky became darker and he heard a clap of thunder.

This incident certainly propels the action of the story. It would appear that Sam is in a rowboat in the middle of the lake having a lovely time when he hears a clap of thunder. He realizes that a lake is a dangerous place to be so this event means that Sam must take action. What that action is would be of interest to the reader because it will help form the plot of the story. The incident also forces Sam to make a decision about what he should do. This will help the reader better understand Sam as a character.

Themes

Theme

The **theme** of a story is a unifying idea that is used throughout the text; it can take the form of a common setting, idea, symbol, design, or recurring event. The theme of a story may vary according to place, time, and characters, but theme is often based on common human experience. A plot line is built around the theme of a story. Most themes are about life, society, or human nature. The theme is often why a passage is written. It helps give a passage unity. The theme is created through the development of the story. The events of a story help shape the kind of theme the passage. A theme is not usually stated explicitly. The reader **infers** the theme from the topic, information, or plot of a passage.

For example, a series of events in a story may be based upon people being willing to trust the actions of others. The story may be centered on why people need to trust others in order to carry out important actions. For example, a character may trust that a bus driver will stay on the road while the bus driver, in turn, trusts that the passengers stay in their seats so that they do not distract him.

The theme of a story is not the same as the topic of a story. The topic is what the story is about, but the theme is what a reader is meant to learn. When readers are discussing theme, they can determine both theme topics as well as theme statements.

Theme topics are broad ideas that apply to the text. Examples include:

- Love changes people
- Man versus man
- Man versus nature
- Man versus himself
- Fate versus free will
- Triumph over adversity
- Coming of age
- The importance of friendship
- Good vs. evil
- The circle of life

Themes may also be complete statements written in sentence form. Examples are:

- Acts of courage can bring positive changes to the world.
- True friendship can withstand the hardest challenges.

Review Video: Themes in Literature
Visit mometrix.com/academy and enter code: 732074

Example

Tell why the theme of the following excerpt should be "Overconfidence can lead to a fall."

> Bella was happy. She auditioned for the starring role in the school play and she felt sure she'd got the part. Afterwards, she told her friends she would be starring in the play. But on Tuesday when the director said they had offered the part to Sara Goodwin, she started crying.

The excerpt tells the story of a girl who has an audition and thinks she got the starring role. She is so confident that she even tells her friends that she has the part. But then she learns that the role was offered to someone else and she starts to cry. She was overly confident about her success and was subsequently devastated when she learned of her failure, and that is the lesson of the story. If you are overly confident you may have a fall. That is the theme of the story. A theme is the lesson that a story teaches. This particular theme is found often in literature. A theme is not stated in a passage: the reader must deduce it from the plot of the story.

Universal Themes

Some themes are fairly common. These themes are called **universal themes** and they suggest things about life, society, and human nature. If a reader is trying to decide whether a theme is universal or not, they must consider whether the theme they have identified can be applied to other works as well. Some examples of universal theme topics are:

Good Versus Evil

- The universal theme of a small number of people invested in doing good works becoming a powerful force against those doing evil works can be seen in multiple texts, including the *Harry Potter* series by J.K. Rowling, *The Hunger Games* by Suzanne Collins, and *Cinder* by Marissa Meyer.

CHANGE VERSUS TRADITION

- *The Giver* by Lois Lowry, the *Divergent* series by Veronica Roth, and *Children of Eden* by Joey Graceffa all reveal the universal theme of the ongoing struggle for societies to welcome change rather than being stuck in tradition.

MAN VERSUS MAN

- Learning that people are capable of committing horrifying acts against other people is a universal theme evident in *The Boy in the Striped Pajamas* by John Boyne, *A Long Walk to Water* by Linda Sue Park, and *All the Light We Cannot See* by Anthony Doerr.

Organizational Patterns of Texts

Organizational Patterns

When writing there are a variety of ways that an author can choose to organize their text. It is important for them to choose the pattern that best presents their information, as not all patterns will work for every piece of writing. Some examples are

Advantage/Disadvantage

The author chooses a topic or concept and addresses both the advantages and disadvantages (or pros and cons) of the subject. In this type of text the author is not trying to persuade their audience to choose a side, but rather, to inform the reader of all the possible positive and negative effects.

Cause and Effect

The author will write about relationship between two events that occur, where the second event occurs as a result of the first.

For example, a text may discuss a school policy stating that when a student is late to school too many times, they receive a detention. Later in the text, we might see a student repeatedly arriving late to school, after which he is given a detention. In this example, the **cause** is the student being late to school, and the **effect** is the student receiving a detention.

Classification

The author chooses a topic and divides it into smaller parts or groups in order to discuss them individually. These types of texts address how parts work within a whole, or what characteristics can be used to classify a given subject or concept.

Chronological Order

The author organizes the progression of events based upon when they occurred and what was included in each step of the story. By organizing the text in this way the author presents all necessary information about the six questions readers can ask to help themselves understand the text: who, what, when, where, why, and how.

Compare and Contrast

The author will show similarities and differences between items or events.

For example, the author may write about cats and dogs. They might start by giving a brief description of the two. Then they will want to point out all of the similarities, such as; they both have tails, and both are kept as pets. Next, they will explain the differences, such as; dogs are canines, while cats are felines. They will try to provide as much detail as possible about both the similarities and the differences.

Definition

Authors introduce a concept or word and then explain or describe it. This type of text often included examples that will help the reader gain understanding of what is presumably a new concept for them.

Inductive / Deductive

Authors organize ideas from general to specific or specific to general. If ideas are organized **inductively**, they are arranged from specific facts to general conclusions. If ideas are organized from general conclusions to specific facts, they are organized **deductively**. A reader can make a logical assumption about a topic based on the facts that are presented in the text.

For example, in these two sentences the ideas are organized deductively, from general to specific.

> Many canoers use the lake in the summer. Jeff learned how to canoe last summer, and is on his way to the lake now.

The idea that "Many canoers use the lake in the summer" is a general idea. The facts that Jeff already knows how to canoe and is headed to the lake are specific to him as a character.

Order of Importance

The author puts the information in the text in order of what is most important. **Order of importance** can be either increasing or decreasing, depending on how the writer wants to structure the work.

Proposition and Support

The author states a proposition that they believe to be true, and then provides support for that proposition in the paper. The topics that use this type of structure are generally things that reader might feel uncertain about or might not already have an opinion about. The support that the author gives for the proposition should include facts, statistics, logic, and reasoning. The more hard evidence an author can give the reader, the better it will help convince them to see things from the author's point of view.

Identifying Organizational Strategies

Example

Explain which organization pattern would be the best choice for this writer and why.

> Sara is writing a report on sea turtles. She has researched the various dangers that they face: their predators, the difficulties they encounter in their life cycle starting with their birth, their migration to the ocean, and the dangers that await them as they mature. She is unsure of how to organize her report.

A cause and effect order would seem to be the best idea for Sara because she would be able to identify the causes and effects of the dangers that sea turtles encounter. She could organize the report so that each paragraph deals with a different threat, using headings to identify what would be in each section. A chart would also be useful because it puts the same information in a clear format so that readers would be able to refer to it. She might also consider using a video showing baby turtles migrating towards the open sea, which would give her audience an even greater understanding of the turtles' plight.

Example

Identify the text structure that is used in the following sentences:

> Madison and her brother Jake used to live on a wind-torn island in the Chesapeake Bay. Last year they moved to Baltimore, a city in Maryland. Next summer they plan to visit the island where they grew up.

Chronological order is used as a text structure in the example sentences, as they are organized according to the passage of time. Note that each sentence refers to a point in time. The first sentence refers to where the siblings lived in the past. The second sentence refers to the siblings' move to Baltimore last year. The final sentence refers to what the siblings plan to do in the future. By referring to a specific place in time, the reader can see what occurred in the story during that time period. An author will often use flashback to indicate what happened in the past, and foreshadowing to give the reader a glimpse of what may occur in the future.

Example

Identify the text structure that is used in the following sentences:

> Three cousins lived in the same small town. One day the cousins decided to journey together to enter a singing contest across the country. The cousins won the contest and made their hometown fans proud.

The information in the story can be organized according to the passage of time, called chronological order. The story will start based in the cousins' hometown, to give some background on where the cousins come from. Subsequent events in the story will occur over time based on the cousins' motivations due to their background. The story will end by referring back to how far the cousins have come from their small-town roots.

Example

Read the following thesis statement and discuss the organizational pattern that the author will use:

> Throughout his life, Thomas Edison used his questioning and creative mind to become one of America's greatest inventors.

Based on the thesis statement, the reader can assume that the author is going to use chronological order to organize the information in the rest of the essay. The words "throughout his life" clue the reader in to the chronological organizational structure, which presents information in the order than it occurred. The author will probably discuss Edison's childhood and initial inventions first and then move on to his later queries and inventions. Chronological order is often used as the organizational structure in biographies as a way to logically present the important events in a person's life.

Graphic Features in Texts

Print and Graphic Features

An author may show information in a chart, a graph, in paragraph format, or as a list. Information may also be shown in a picture or a diagram. The way an author chooses to show information is often based on the purpose of the text and the audience that the text is meant to reach.

A reader may be asked to answer questions based on the graphic by itself, how the graphic relates to the text, or how the text would best be shown in a graphic form. Some common examples of graphics are cause and effect organizers, circle graphs, bar graphs, illustrations, and diagrams.

Cause and Effect Graphic Organizers

Cause-and-effect graphic organizers are often used to map the **elements of a story**. A reader might read a story about a string of events and then be asked to correctly fill in either the **cause** or **effect** of an event in the story.

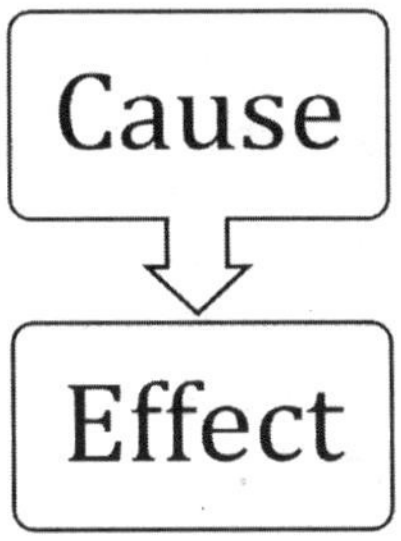

Example

Read the following excerpt from *Ramona Quimby, Age 8* by Beverly Cleary and decide what the cause of the hectic morning at the Quimby house is.

> With all four members of the family leaving at different times in different directions, mornings were flurried in the Quimby household.

A **cause and effect** graphic organizer for this excerpt might look something like this:

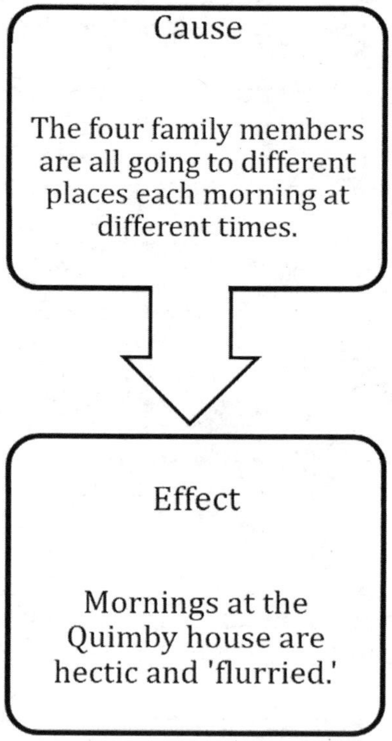

LINE GRAPHS

Line graphs are used for measuring general **trends over time**. For example, this line graph shows an overall upward trend in the amount of candy bars sold for four weeks.

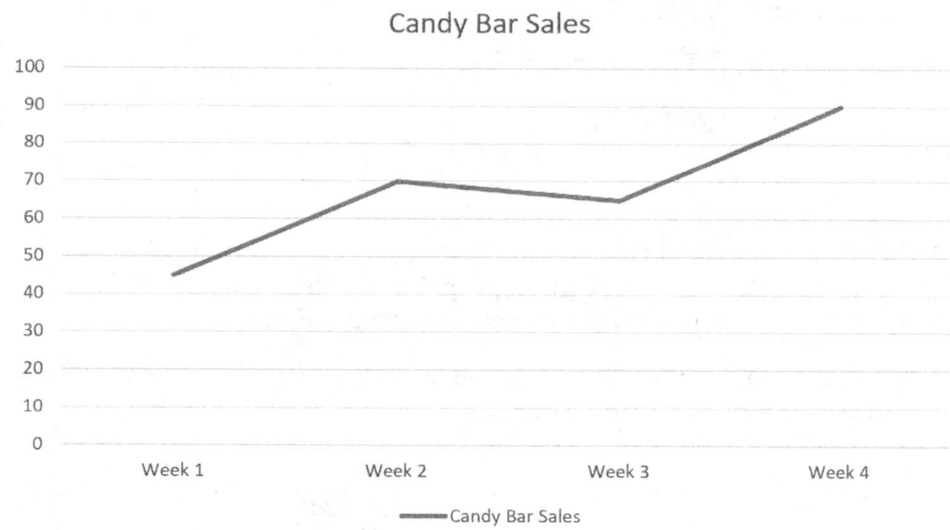

CIRCLE GRAPHS

Circle graphs, also called pie charts, are often used to represent information that can be shown as **parts of a whole**. For example, this graph shows the results of people being asked about their favorite color:

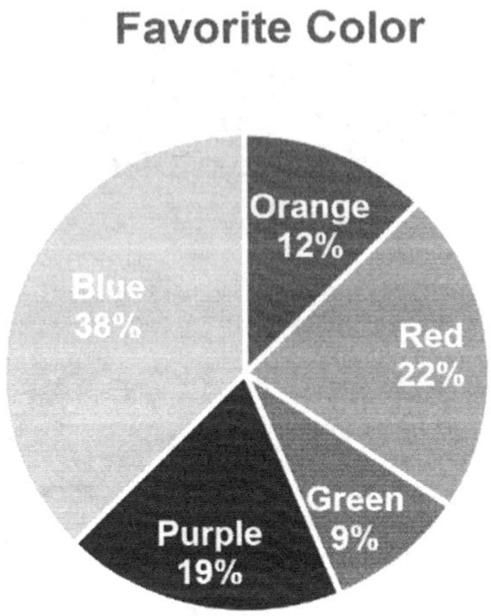

BAR GRAPHS

Bar graphs are used to show information about **numbers**. For example, this graph is a different way of representing the same results as those in the circle graph.

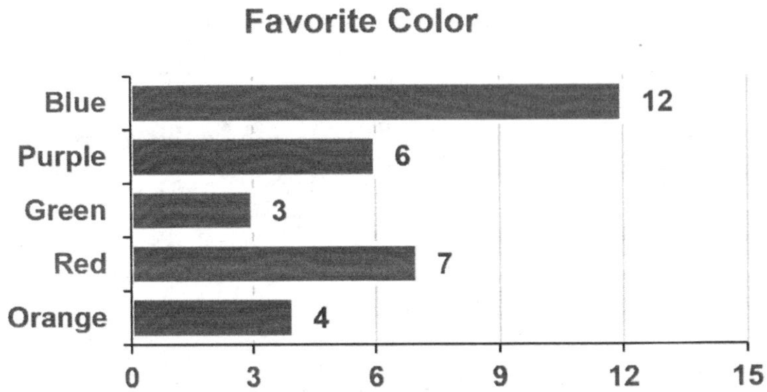

ILLUSTRATIONS AND PHOTOGRAPHS

Authors may choose to include **illustrations** or **photographs** (or both) with their texts. These two image types both show something from the text or give more information about the text.

Illustrations are drawings of an object. They may be based on reality, or they may represent an artist's abstract idea. For example, this is an illustration of a 1903 automobile:

Photographs are pictures of objects. They are generally extremely realistic, and most often show an object as it actually existed at that moment in time. For example, this is a photograph of a 1917 automobile:

Both illustrations and photographs give the reader another way to relate to and understand the text. The reader may be asked how the image relates to the text, what type of caption the image should be given, or why the author chose to include the image with the text.

DIAGRAMS

Diagrams are used to show information in a visual way. There are many different types of diagrams, including:

Diagrams that show the parts of an object, how they work together, or how they should be put together. This is an example of a diagram which shows how gears turn together

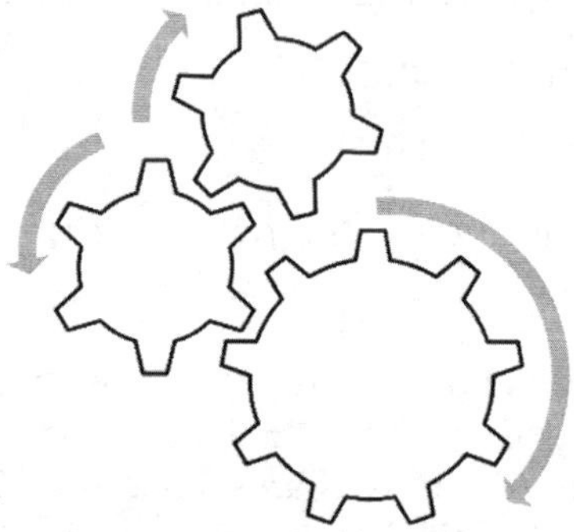

Diagrams that show how information is related are called **Venn Diagrams**. These are ways to visually see the way in which two different ideas overlap. This is an example of a Venn Diagram comparing cats and dogs:

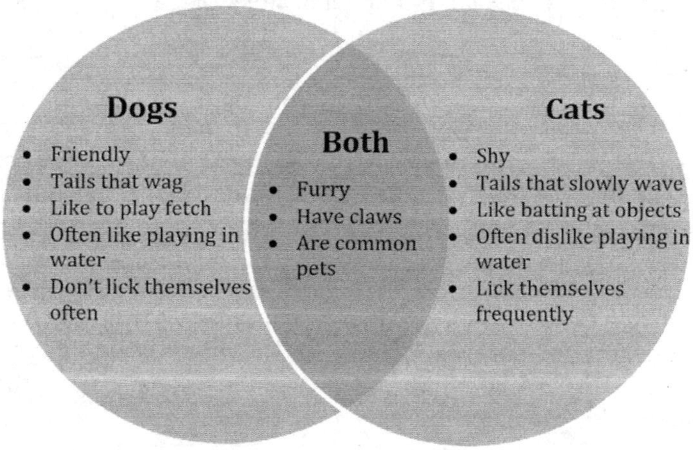

Paraphrasing and Summarizing

Paraphrasing and Summarizing

Paraphrasing and summarizing are two ways readers can work to understand what they read. Both involve reading a text and recalling the main points in an accurate way, but they differ in several ways.

How to Paraphrase	How to Summarize
State the message in the text in the reader's own words, while keeping the original meaning of the text Take all of the original ideas and word them in a way that the reader can better understand Put what the reader has read into their own words, rephrasing what the author has written	State main points of the text clearly and to-the-point. Take information and state it simply, in a much shorter form. Put information in a short form that keeps the main points of the whole text. Do not include many details, just the main idea of the text

Paraphrasing is often done for individual ideas, while summarizing is done for an entire block of text or ideas. Often times, a summary can be done in just one sentence, boiling down the author's words into just main idea.

Review Video: Summarizing Text
Visit mometrix.com/academy and enter code: 172903

Paraphrasing the Main Point of a Sentence

Paraphrase the main point of the following two sentences:

> Emmanuel went swimming in the lake by his house, where the water reached a depth of twenty feet in the middle. He did not venture out more than six feet into the water, however.

When paraphrasing a couple sentences or an entire paragraph, always include the main point of the text being reviewed, this is what the reader needs to know about the text. in the example, the reader needs to know that Emmanuel went swimming in the lake, but not more than six feet out. A paraphrase of the text may include: Emmanuel went swimming six feet out in the lake by his house. That is the main point that the audience needs to know.

Recall that a paraphrase is stating the author's ideas in the reader's own words. A summary typically involves including the main points of a longer text, such as a novel or full story.

Example

Read the following paragraph and then give a one sentence summary statement:

> When choosing a pet, people need to think about what type of home they can offer the animal. For example, a small apartment might not be a good fit for a large dog, but could be a comfortable home for a kitten. A house that has a big yard would be great for a puppy, but a rabbit does not need a large yard.

In order to summarize, one has to identify the main idea and any supporting ideas in the author's work. The summary is an overview of the author's paragraph and will tell what it is about without getting into any of the details. The summary needs to be broad enough to cover all of the information in the author's paragraph. Here is a possible summary statement for the above paragraph:

> People need to consider a number of factors, particularly the available space they have, when choosing a pet.

Example

Read the following sentences and then paraphrase the material:

> The government is debating a new health care system for our country. The Senate and the House of Representatives have both passed bills; now they need to resolve these two bills into one bill that a majority can agree on.

When paraphrasing information, one needs to read carefully and pay attention to details, then put the material away and write or tell it in their own words. One does not want to look at the material while paraphrasing to avoid plagiarizing by accident. Here is one example of a way to paraphrase the sentences:

> Our government is trying to adopt a new health care system. The Senate has passed a bill and so has the House of Representatives. Their bills are different so now they have to compromise on one bill that can be passed.

Summarizing Literature to Support Comprehension

When reading literature, especially demanding works, summarizing helps readers identify important information and organize it in their minds. They can also identify themes, problems, and solutions, and can sequence the story. Readers can summarize before, during, and after they read. They should use their own words, as they do when describing a personal event or giving directions. Previewing a text's organization before reading by examining the book cover, table of contents, and illustrations also aids summarizing. So does making notes of key words and ideas in a graphic organizer while reading. Graphic organizers are another useful method; readers skim the text to determine main ideas and then narrow the list with the aid of the organizer. Unimportant details should be omitted in summaries. Summaries can include description, problem-solution, comparison-contrast, sequence, main ideas, and cause-and-effect.

Drawing Conclusions and Making Inferences

Facts and Opinions

Writers and readers must always be aware of the difference between fact and opinion. A **fact** can be tested and proven to be true. An **opinion**, on the other hand, is someone's personal thoughts or feelings. Opinions are often not changed by information. If an author writes that a newborn elephant is about five times taller than a newborn giraffe, then he or she is stating a fact. If the author writes that giraffes are more interesting than elephants, then he or she is giving an opinion because this cannot be proven to be true or false. Opinions are often supported by facts. For instance, the author might use a comparison between the way that giraffes eat and the way elephants eat as evidence of how giraffes are more interesting. An opinion supported by facts tends to be more convincing. On the other hand, when authors support their opinions with other opinions, readers should seriously think about and read the argument carefully to see whether it is logical and trustworthy.

> **Review Video: Distinguishing Fact and Opinion**
> Visit mometrix.com/academy and enter code: 870899

Text Evidence

The term **text evidence** refers to information found in a text that supports a reader's claim about the text. A reader can draw conclusions or inferences based upon information found in a text. Often, the author will deliberately include information that supports the main point of the text to help the reader make conclusions and inferences that align with the author's purpose for writing the text.

Drawing Conclusions Based on Text Evidence

Readers often need to use prior experience and background information to draw an accurate conclusion about the passage they are reading. Sometimes interpreting the information in a sentence can be difficult, especially if the reader is unfamiliar with some of the words used in a sentence. Looking at the words that the reader does understand in the sentence can help. By taking a pen or pencil and underlining important information in a sentence, the reader can better understand what the author is trying to say and draw a clearer conclusion from that.

Example

Draw a conclusion based on the following sentence:

> New Orleans then was a mere huddle of buildings around Jackson Square; but with the purchase of the Louisiana territory from France, and the great influx of American enterprise that characterized the first quarter of the last century, development was working like yeast...

The sentence describes how New Orleans grew after the "purchase of the Louisiana territory" and how "development was working like yeast". Yeast multiplies rapidly, so the reader can conclude that New Orleans was growing rapidly.

Example

Read the following sentence. Draw a conclusion based upon the information presented.

> "A rosy-faced servant-maid opened the door, and smiled as she took the letter which he silently offered."

The reader can conclude, based on the sentence, that the servant-maid is friendly. The words "rosy-faced" and "smiled" lead the reader to this conclusion. People who are friendly are often described as having rosy complexions and smiling as a common sign of pleasantness. The reader can also assume, from the sentence, that the letter does not present any threat or unpleasantness to the servant-maid. The person presenting the letter does not have anything to say upon offering it, so perhaps he is waiting to see how the servant-maid will react.

When interpreting a sentence, always look for key words that describe a character. The author carefully crafts a description of each character, to form a picture in the reader's mind about what the character is like.

Making Inferences and Drawing Conclusions

An **inference** is a **conclusion** or generalization that the reader makes based on the information provided within a text. Certain facts are included to help a reader come to a specific conclusion. It is what the story may hint about, and what a reader can conclude as a result of what the author says in the passage. It is also the best guess that a reader can make based on what happened or was said or in a story. A good inference is based on or supported by details in the passage.

Readers may come to their own conclusion about a topic, or the author may state a conclusion at the end of a story. When readers are in the middle of a story, they can predict what will happen at the end of it based on the events that have occurred so far and the typical characteristics that have been presented by the author up to that point. A reader needs to consider all of the information that an author has presented, including the main point and supporting points, to make logical conclusions and inferences about the story.

For instance, if a passage says that Joan is holding her mouth and moaning, you might conclude, or **infer,** that she has a sore mouth or a toothache. You cannot be sure of this, but it is the best conclusion that you can reach using the information at hand. Inferences are considered **implicit information**. They are not found directly in a passage, but they can be supported by explicit information from the passage.

Review Video: Inference
Visit mometrix.com/academy and enter code: 379203

Finding Explicit Information

Explicit information is the term for information that is **directly stated** in a story or passage. It is what **the author tells you**. It is not information that is hinted at or that you have to make a conclusion about. Explicit information can be facts or details about an event, something or someone. There is usually a lot of explicit information in a story and this information is often used to make an inference or draw a conclusion. to answer questions that ask about explicit information, simply reread the story until you find the answer. in fiction, details about characters, events, and setting are often explicit.

Example

Read the following excerpt. Tell whether it contains explicit information or not.

> I think the most famous person in the Old West is Annie Oakley. Annie is the best rifle shot who ever lived. She almost never missed. Many men challenged her to contests of speed and accuracy. She won them all.

Most of the information in the excerpt is explicit information. The information tells the reader about Annie Oakley: that she was the best rifle shot who ever lived and that she almost never missed. It also says that many men challenged her to contests and she won them all. This information is found right in the excerpt. It is not suggested or hinted at. Everything that is said is clearly what it means. The first sentence is a personal opinion; it is also explicit because the reader does not have to guess what the author thinks of Annie Oakley.

Implicit Information

Implicit information is information that is **not directly stated** in a text, but can be inferred from something that the author explicitly states. For instance, the author may say "Seth buys a new TV, laptop, and home theater system every year." from this the reader could infer several things. For instance, Seth probably likes electronics and has a lot of spending money.

EXAMPLE

Draw a conclusion based on the implicit information in the following sentence from the *Adventures of Tom Sawyer* by Mark Twain:

> He had discovered a great law of human action, without knowing it—namely, that in order to make a man or a boy covet a thing, it is only necessary to make the thing difficult to attain.

The reader can clearly see from the sentence that the character did not set out to learn something, but through an action, the character learned that people will want what is hard to attain. Although it's not explicitly stated, the reader can draw the conclusion that the character gained the experience of coveting (or desiring) something that was hard to get.

EXAMPLE

Read the passage and discuss why the conclusion that the Vikings were searching for new farmland is valid.

> The Vikings set out in their boats in summer. The number of people in Scandinavia was growing fast. They needed to grow more food. In the late 900s, Eric the Red sailed across the Atlantic to Greenland. In 985, Viking farmers settled in Greenland.

The passage says that the Viking population was growing and that they needed to be able to grow more food. It is logical to guess that they sailed in search of new farmland. There is really not another possibility. Remember, inferences are assumptions that are hinted at or suggested by the text. They are not like explicit information; they are implicit in the text based on the explicit information that is found there. They are the best guess a reader can make.

EXAMPLE

Read the following sentence and draw a conclusion based upon the information presented:

> "You know the reason Mother proposed not having any presents this Christmas was because it is going to be a hard winter for everyone; and she thinks we ought not to spend money for pleasure, when our men are suffering so in the army." (from *Little Women* by Louisa May Alcott, p. 3)

Based on the information in the sentence, the reader can conclude, or infer, that the men are away at war while the women are still at home. The pronoun 'our' gives a clue to the reader that the character is speaking about men she knows. In addition, the reader can assume that the character is speaking to a brother or sister, since the term Mother is used by the character while speaking to another person. The reader can also come to the conclusion that the characters celebrate Christmas, since it is mentioned in the context of the sentence. In the sentence, the Mother is presented as an unselfish character who is opinionated and thinks about the well-being of other people.

EXAMPLE

Draw a conclusion based on the following sentence from *The Adventures of Tom Sawyer* by Mark Twain:

> He had discovered a great law of human action, without knowing it—namely, that in order to make a man or a boy covet a thing, it is only necessary to make the thing difficult to attain.

The reader can conclude from the sentence that the character did not set out to learn something, but through an action, the character learned that people will want what is hard to attain. The character learned a fact about human nature: that a person will value something more if they have to work hard for it, than if it is simply given to them. The word *covet* means to desire, which the character learns can be manipulated by making an item or an outcome more difficult to grasp. In everyday life, this could apply toward taking a hard test and doing well. If someone studies for a hard test and does well, the person will value their score more than if the test was very easy and he or she did not study for the test.

Analyzing Ideas Within and Between Selections

Making Connections to Enhance Comprehension

Reading involves thinking. For good comprehension, readers make text-to-self, text-to-text, and text-to-world connections. Making connections helps readers understand text better and predict what might occur next based on what they already know, such as how characters in the story feel or what happened in another text. Readers can make connections before, during, and after reading. Venn diagrams and other graphic organizers can help readers visualize connections.

Text-to-Self

Reading while looking for connections with the reader's life and experiences makes literature more personally relevant and meaningful to readers. Sentences showing text-to-self connections may begin with these examples

- This is similar to a time when...
- I understand how the character feels because...
- The setting makes me think of...
- I experienced this same thing when...

Text-to-Text

Reading while looking for connections to other texts helps the reader learn to identify the way authors use genre, setting, characters, plot elements, literary structure and devices, and themes to create meaning. Sentences showing text-to-text connections may begin with these examples

- The character in this story reminds me of the character in...
- These two stories are alike because...
- The conflict in this story is similar to the conflict in...
- The relationship between the friends in this story is different than the relationship in...

Text-to-World

Reading while looking for connections to the world helps the reader begin to see literature as a reflection of real life and notice patterns in history and current events. Sentences showing text-to-world connections may begin with these examples

- The event in this story sounds like the event in history when...
- The actions of this character sound like...
- This is like what happened in real life when...
- I heard about this on the news when...

Synthesizing a Text With Existing Knowledge

Synthesizing is similar to summarizing but it takes it one step further. Synthesizing involves taking the main points of a text and comparing it with existing knowledge to create a new idea, perspective, or way of thinking.

Another term for knowledge that you already have is **schema**. The plural form of this word is **schemata**. Schemata contain all the ideas you have about something. Synthesizing is all about how schemata change over time with the introduction of new information.

EXAMPLE

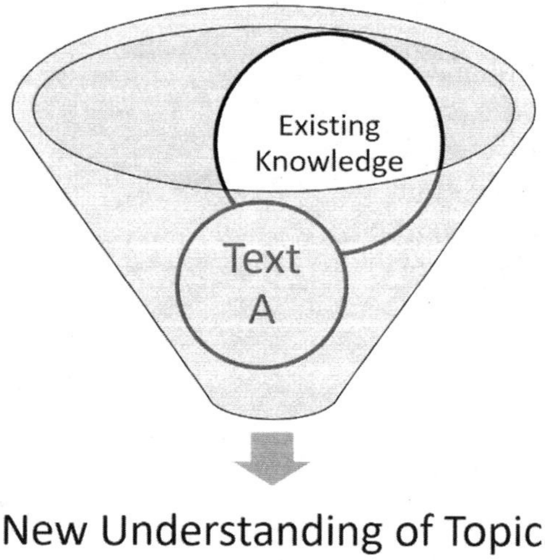

Using self-questioning strategies can help readers synthesize texts with their schemata to increase or change their understanding of topics. These questions include

- What do I already know about this topic?
- Is any of this new information?
- Has my perspective changed now that I've read this?
- What do I understand now that I didn't before?
- What are the main ideas of this text?
- How do the parts of the text fit together to create meaning?
- Are there any text-to-text, text-to-self, or text-to-world connections here?

SYNTHESIZING TEXTS WITHOUT EXISTING KNOWLEDGE

If the reader is completely unfamiliar with the topic, they will have no background knowledge. In this case, instead of using existing knowledge, synthesizing may instead be done by combining the ideas provided in two or three different texts. The reader must make connections between the texts, determine how the ideas fit together, and gather evidence to support the new perspective.

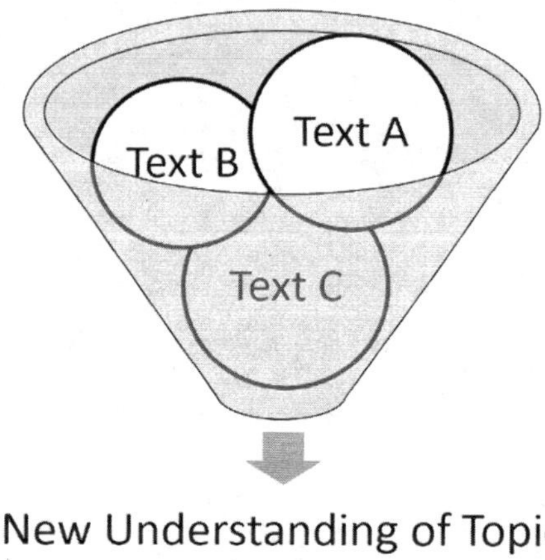

Using self-questioning strategies can help readers synthesize texts to increase their understanding of topics. In this case, readers are creating new schemata as they read. These questions include

- What do these texts have in common?
- What is different between these texts?
- What new information have I learned?
- What do I understand now that I didn't before?
- How do these texts relate to one another?
- If I think of these texts as parts of one whole, what meaning do they create together?
- What predictions can I make about this topic?

Mathematics Practice Test

1. Ana has completed approximately $\frac{2}{7}$ of her research paper. Which of the following best represents the percentage of the paper she has completed?

a. 24%
b. 26%
c. 27%
d. 29%

2. Simplify the expression: $2n + (3n - 2)^2$

____

3. Elijah has prepared $2\frac{1}{2}$ gallons of lemonade to distribute to guests at a party. If there are 25 guests, how much lemonade is available to each guest, given that each guest receives an equal amount?

a. $\frac{1}{8}$ of a gallon
b. $\frac{1}{6}$ of a gallon
c. $\frac{1}{12}$ of a gallon
d. $\frac{1}{10}$ of a gallon

4. The points M, N, and O are plotted on the number line below. Plot point P based on the equation: $N - M + O = P$

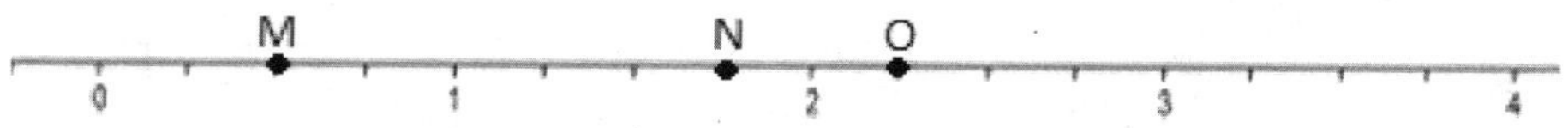

5. Which of the following figures show parallelogram *WXYZ* being carried onto its image *W'X'Y'Z'* by a reflection across the *x*-axis?

a.

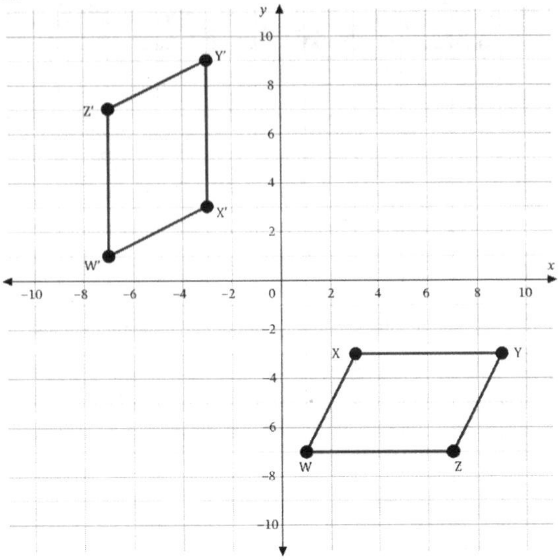

b.

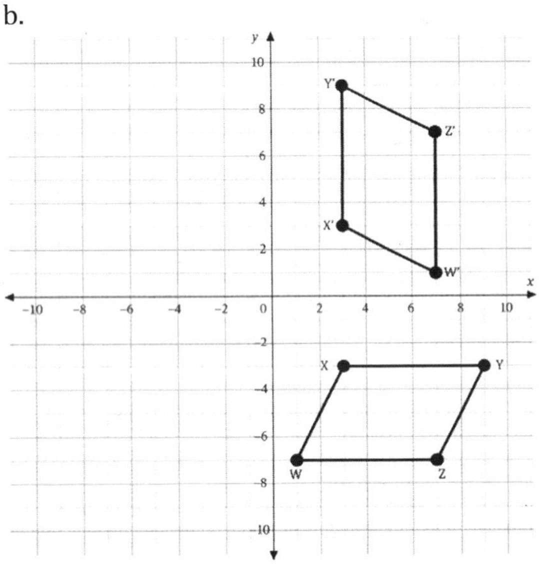

c.

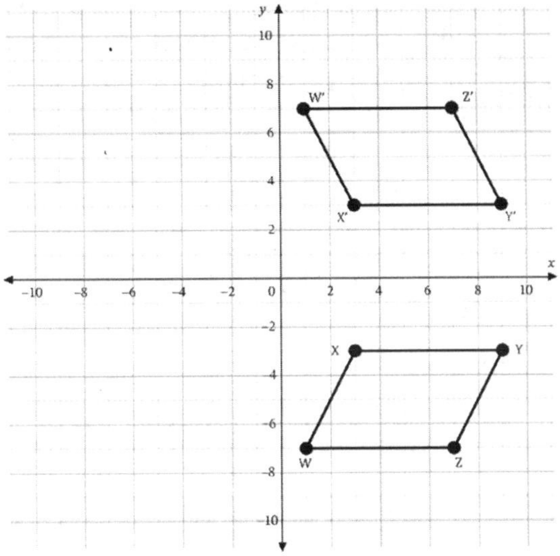

d.

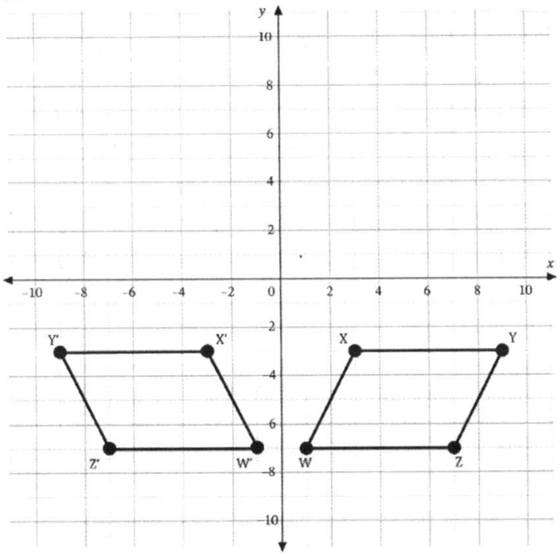

6. A bag of coffee costs \$9.85 and contains 16 ounces of coffee. Which of the following best represents the cost per ounce?

a. \$0.67
b. \$0.64
c. \$0.65
d. \$0.62

7. Which of the following is equivalent to $4^3 + 12 \div 4 + 8^2 \times 3$?

a. 249
b. 393
c. 211
d. 259

8. The ingredients needed for a cake are given below:

- 2 eggs
- $1\frac{3}{4}$ cups of flour
- 2 teaspoons baking soda
- ½ cup butter
- $1\frac{1}{4}$ teaspoons vanilla extract
- $\frac{3}{4}$ cup of milk

What is the ratio of butter to flour?

a. 1:3
b. 2:5
c. 2:7
d. 3:2

9. Two similar triangles A and B are defined by the coordinates:

$$\boldsymbol{A} = \{(\mathbf{1},\mathbf{1}),(\mathbf{-3},\mathbf{4}),(\mathbf{-4},\mathbf{-6})\}$$
$$\boldsymbol{B} = \{(\mathbf{1},\mathbf{6}),(\mathbf{-3},\mathbf{9}),(\mathbf{-4},\mathbf{-1})\}$$

Triangle B can be generated from triangle A by:

a. Reflection
b. Adding 5 to the coordinates
c. Translation
d. Rotation

10. Martin and his friends are taking a road trip from Houston, TX to Las Vegas, NV. The trip will take two days and they will spend the night in El Paso, TX. The first day they drove for 11 hours at a rate of 69 miles per hour. The next day they drove for 10 hours at a rate of 72 miles per hour. How far is it from Houston to Las Vegas?

____

11. A bottle of lotion contains 20 fluid ounces and costs \$3.96. Which of the following best represents the cost per fluid ounce?

a. \$0.18
b. \$0.20
c. \$0.22
d. \$0.24

12. Solve the equation for x: $3^2 + 2x = 17$.

____

13. A cylinder has a diameter of 12 m and a height of 9 m. What is the cylinder's surface area?

a. $5.65x10^7$ cm²
b. $1.58x10^9$ mm²
c. $1.58x10^{-3}$ km²
d. $5.65x10^2$ m²

14. Given the sequence represented in the table below, where n represents the position of the term and a_n represents the value of the term, which of the following describes the relationship between the position number and the value of the term?

n	1	2	3	4	5	6
a_n	5	2	−1	−4	−7	−10

a. Multiply n by 2 and subtract 4
b. Multiply n by 2 and subtract 3
c. Multiply n by −3 and add 8
d. Multiply n by −4 and add 1

15. What statement is true about the rectangles below?

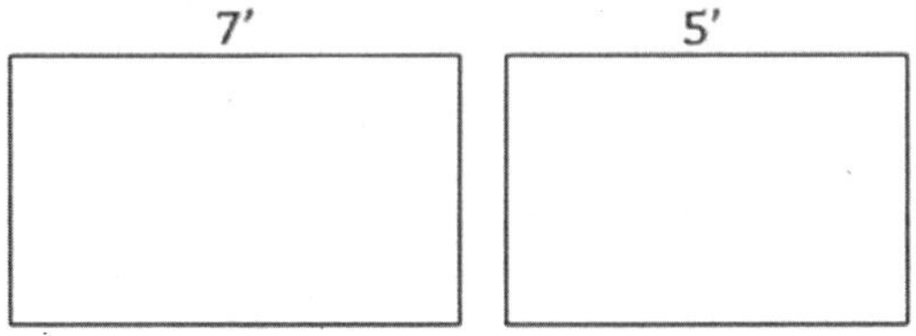

a. They are congruent.
b. They are similar.
c. They are both congruent and similar.
d. They are neither congruent nor similar.

16. Kevin pays \$12.95 for a text messaging service plus \$0.07 for each text message he sends. Which of the following equations could be used to represent the total cost, y, when x represents the number of text messages sent?

a. $y = \$12.95x + \$0.07$
b. $y = \$13.02x$
c. $y = \frac{\$12.95}{\$0.07}x$
d. $y = \$0.07x + \$12.95$

17. Hannah draws quadrilateral *ABCD*. Hannah uses a protractor to measure out three angles: 95°, 97°, 67°. What is the measure of the fourth angle?

a. 11°
b. 79°
c. 101°
d. 259°

18. A box has a length of 22 centimeters, a height of 5 centimeters, and a width of 8 centimeters. How many square centimeters of plastic are needed to shrink wrap the box?

a. 560
b. 652
c. 748
d. 880

19. In the figure below, *ABCD* is a parallelogram. The angles are m∠$A = (5x)°$ and m∠$B = (2x - 9)°$. Find m∠C.

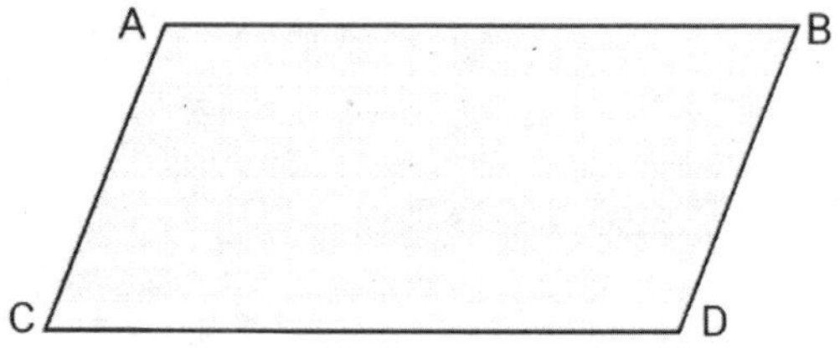

a. m∠$C = 135°$
b. m∠$C = 54°$
c. m∠$C = 45°$
d. m∠$C = 27°$

Refer to the following for question 20-21:

Jordan has a bag full of red and blue marbles. There are 16 red marbles and 24 blue marbles.

20. What is the probability of him drawing a red marble?

____

21. Jordan has continued to draw marbles and has now taken out 4 red and 6 blue. What is the probability of him drawing a red marble now?

____

22. Plot the two ordered pairs on the graph below: A(x-3, 5) and B(7-x, -2) where x = 2.

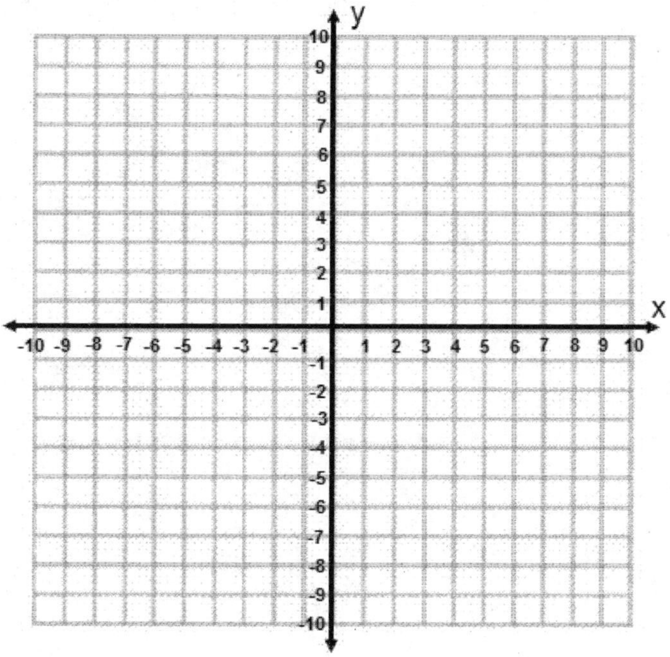

23. Bookstore A sells a particular book for \$15.25, but they have it on sale for 20% off. Bookstore B sells it for \$12.45. How much more does it cost at Bookstore B?

____

24. How are the following quadrilaterals related?

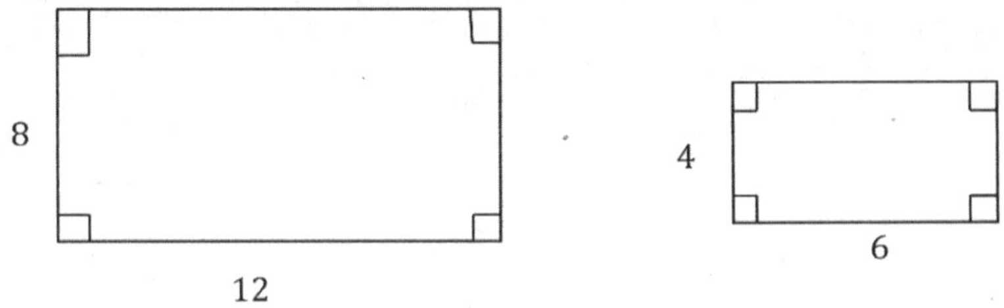

a. They are congruent.
b. They are acute.
c. They are similar.
d. They are adjacent.

25. Which of the following is the best representation of 30,490 in scientific notation?

a. 3.049×10^{-4}
b. 3.049×10^{3}
c. 30.490×10^{3}
d. 3.049×10^{34}

26. Which figure has two circular bases and a lateral face?

a. Cone
b. Prism
c. Cylinder
d. Sphere

27. Sally is driving to the store. It takes her $\frac{1}{12}$ of an hour to go 3.4 miles. How many miles an hour is Sally driving?

a. 36 mph
b. 17 mph
c. 40.8 mph
d. 42.4 mph

28. If n=4, which of the following is also equal to $4n^2 + (3n + 5)^2$?.

a. 353
b. 985
c. 545
d. 793

29. Which of the following correctly compares the given rational numbers?

a. $0.2 > 0.0499 > 0.007$
b. $0 < -2 < 7$
c. $\frac{1}{5} > \frac{1}{4} > \frac{1}{3}$
d. $-1 < -4 < -10$

30. Solve the inequality: $|x + 6| < 9$

a. (-15,-3)
b. (-15,3)
c. (3,-3)
d. (6,-9)

31. A rectangular prism has a length of 14.3 cm, a width of 8.9 cm, and a height of 11.7 cm. Which of the following is the best estimate for the volume of the rectangular prism?

a. 1,512 cm^3
b. 1,287 cm^3
c. 1,386 cm^3
d. 1,620 cm^3

32. A can has a radius of 3.5 cm and a height of 8 cm. Which of the following best represents the volume of the can?

a. 294.86 cm^3
b. 298.48 cm^3
c. 307.72 cm^3
d. 309.24 cm^3

33. Solve for x:

$$4x + 4 = 36$$

a. 5
b. -8
c. 8
d. 11

34. Solve for x:

$$5x + 12 = 72$$

a. 2.4
b. 26.4
c. 60
d. 12

35. A hat contains 6 red dice, 4 green dice, and 2 blue dice. What is the probability that Sarah pulls out a blue die, replaces it, and then pulls out a green die?

a. $\frac{1}{18}$
b. $\frac{1}{3}$
c. $\frac{1}{2}$
d. $\frac{1}{16}$

36. The histogram below represents the overall GRE scores for a sample of college students. Which of the following is a true statement?

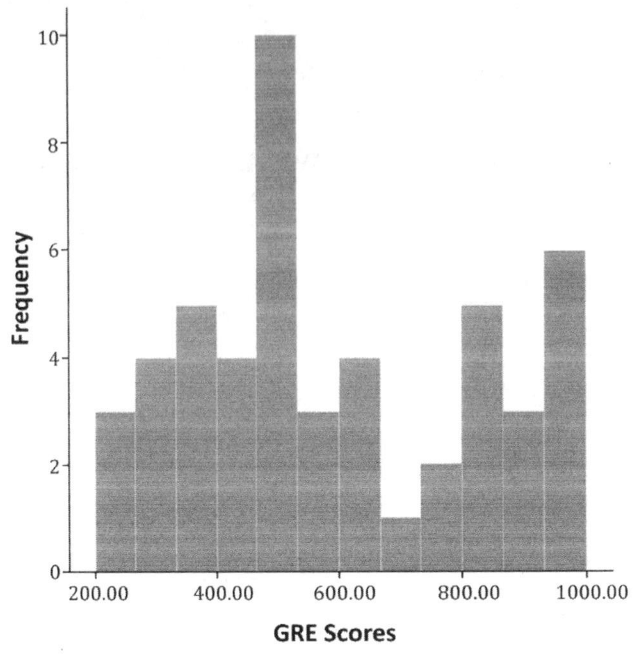

a. The range of GRE scores is approximately 600.
b. The average GRE score is 750.
c. The median GRE score is approximately 500.
d. The fewest number of college students had an approximate score of 800.

37. In the following inequality, solve for x.

$$-4x + 8 \geq 48$$

a. $x \geq 10$
b. $x \geq -10$
c. $x \leq 10$
d. $x \leq -10$

38. For two points (4,2) and (3,5), what is the slope of a line going through both?

a. -1
b. 4
c. -3
d. 5

39. Gabriel went to a taco shop for lunch. He ordered 3 tacos and paid $4.14. The next day he decided to try a different taco shop and ordered 4 tacos and paid $4.80. How much more expensive was the first taco shop per taco? Express your answer as a percent.

____

40. Amy rolled a die and flipped a coin and spun a spinner with four equal sections numbered 1-4. What is the probability that she rolled an even number, got heads, and then spun an even number?

a. $\frac{1}{4}$
b. $\frac{1}{2}$
c. $\frac{3}{4}$
d. $\frac{1}{8}$

Refer to the following for question 41-42:

Edward spins the spinner below three times.

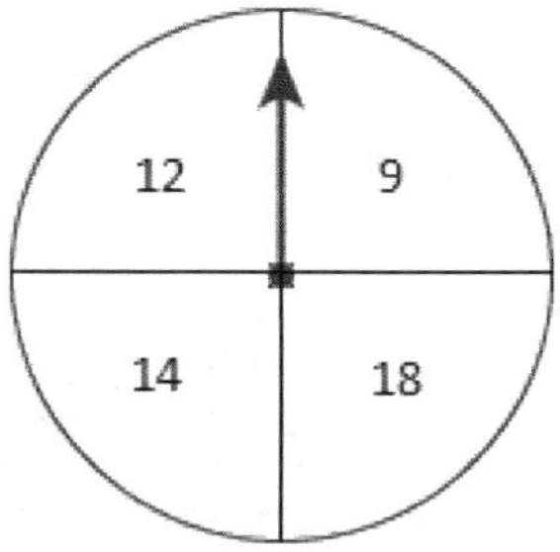

41. If the spinner lands on a different number each time what is the highest total he could get?

____

42. He decides to spin it one more time. What is the probability that he will land on a number that he has already landed on?

____

43. Solve for x:

$$25x - 12x + 6x - 27 = 35$$

a. 0.42
b. 1.44
c. 3.26
d. 5.23

44. What is the slope of the line described by the equation $5 - 3y = 2x + 8$?

a. $-\frac{2}{3}$
b. -1
c. $\frac{2}{3}$
d. 2

45. Solve for *x* in the following inequality.

$$\frac{1}{4}x - 25 \geq 75$$

a. $x \geq 400$
b. $x \leq 400$
c. $x \geq 25$
d. $x \leq 25$

46. Which of the following is the graph of the equation $y = 3x - 2$?

a.

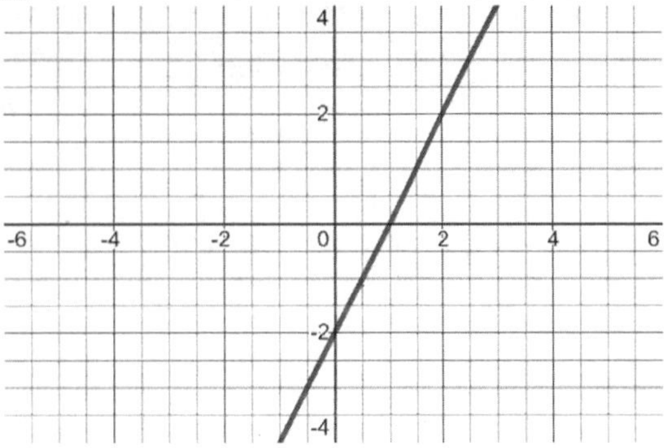

b.

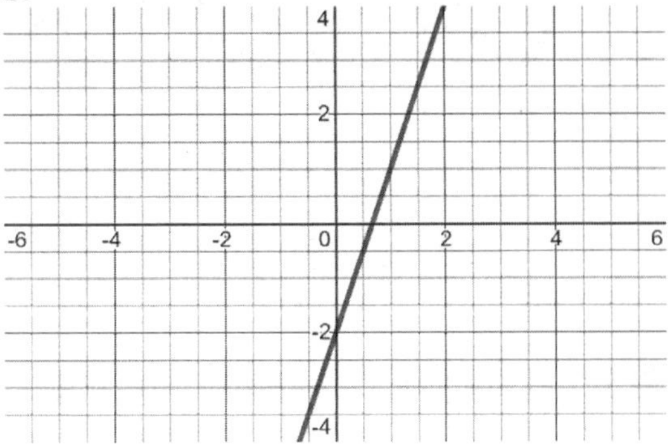

c.

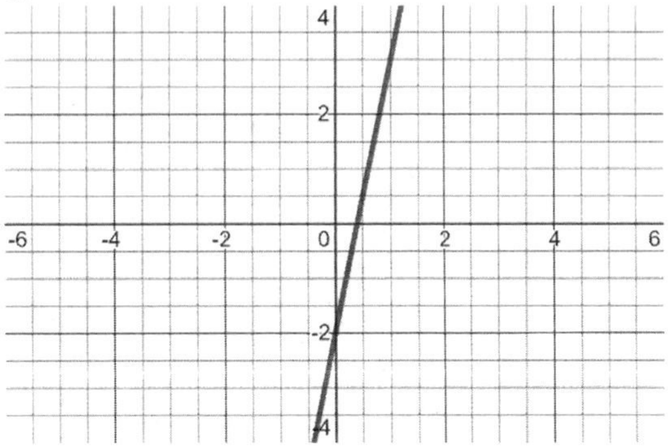

d.

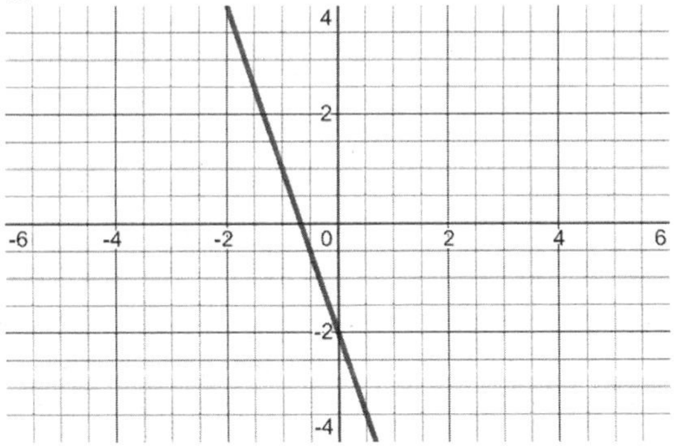

47. A right circular cylinder with a radius of 5 centimeters has a volume of 25π cubic centimeters.

Quantity A	Quantity B
The height of the cylinder	1 centimeter

a. Quantity A is greater.
b. Quantity B is greater.
c. The two quantities are equal.
d. The relationship cannot be determined from the information given.

48. The graph of a line has a slope of $-\frac{2}{3}$ and intersects with a different line at (3,0). What is the y-intercept of the first line?

a. $y = -2$
b. $y = 0$
c. $y = 2$
d. $y = 8$

Refer to the following for question 49-50:

The original price of a jacket is $36.95. The jacket is discounted by 25%.

49. Before tax, which of the following best represents the cost of the jacket?

a. $27.34
b. $27.71
c. $28.82
d. $29.56

50. If tax is 8% how much does it cost?

____

51. Based on the histogram below, how many students scored 75 points or fewer on the math test?

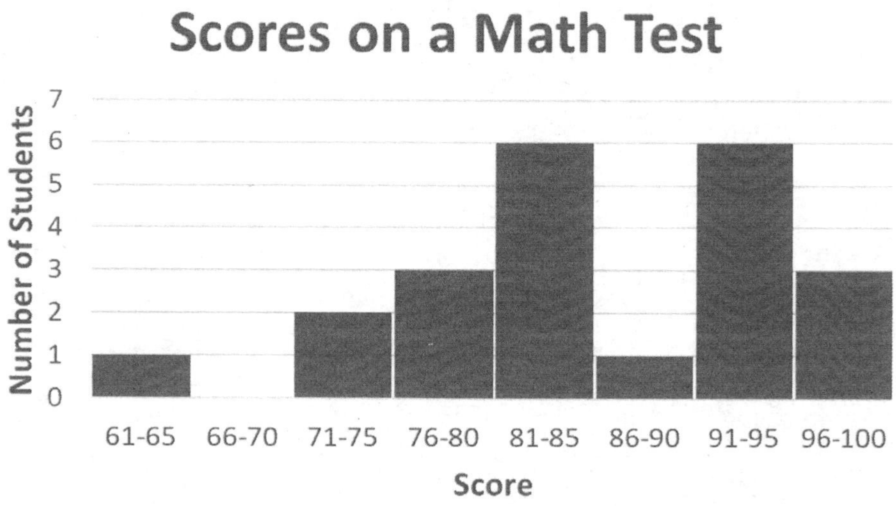

a. 2
b. 3
c. 6
d. 19

52. The variables *x* and *y* have a linear relationship. The table below shows a few sample values. Which of the following graphs correctly represents the linear equation relating *x* and *y*.

x	y
−2	−11
−1	−8
0	−5
1	−2
2	1

a.

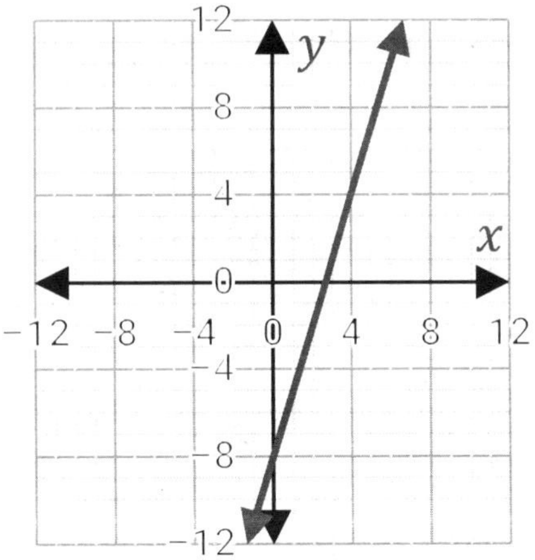

b.

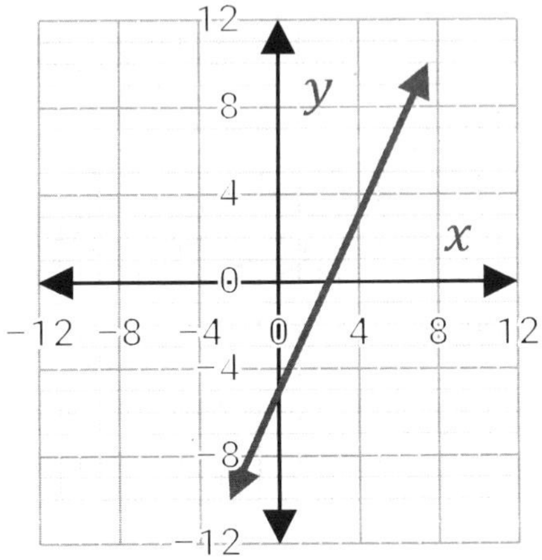

c.

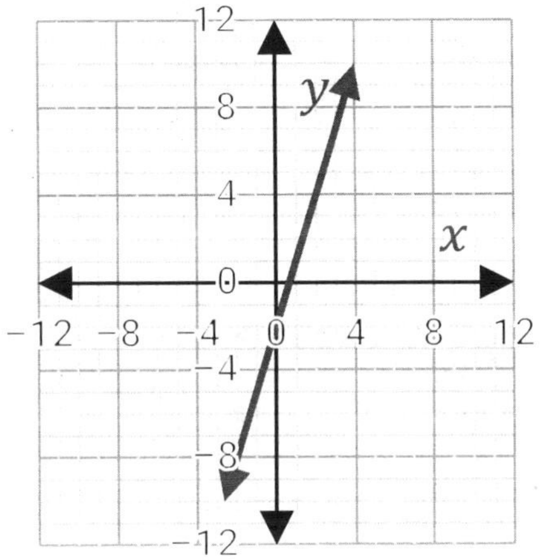

d.

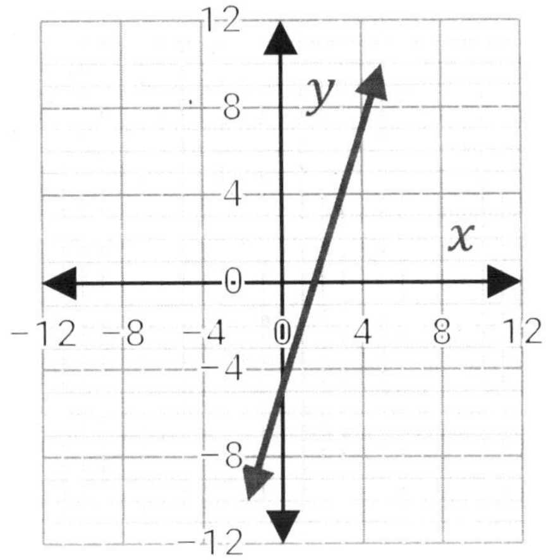

53. Which number is equivalent to 2^{-3}?

a. $\frac{1}{2}$
b. $\frac{1}{4}$
c. $\frac{1}{8}$
d. $\frac{1}{12}$

Answers and Explanations for the Mathematics Test

1. D: In order to convert the given fraction to a percentage, divide 2 by 7. Doing so gives a decimal of approximately 0.29. The decimal can be converted to a percentage by multiplying by 100, which moves the decimal point two places to the right and gives 29%.

2. $2n + (3n - 2)^2 = 2n + 9n^2 - 6n - 6n + 4 = 9n^2 - 10n + 4$

3. D: In order to determine the amount available to each guest, the total amount of prepared lemonade should be divided by 25 guests. Thus, the expression $2\frac{1}{2} \div 25$ represents the amount that each guest has available for consumption. The mixed fraction can be rewritten as $\frac{5}{2}$. The expression can be simplified by writing $\frac{5}{2} \div 25 = \frac{5}{2} \times \frac{1}{25}$, which equals $\frac{5}{50}$, or $\frac{1}{10}$.

4. M=$\frac{1}{2}$, N=$1\frac{3}{4}$, and O=$2\frac{1}{4}$, so N-M+O=$3\frac{1}{2}$. The number line is shown below.

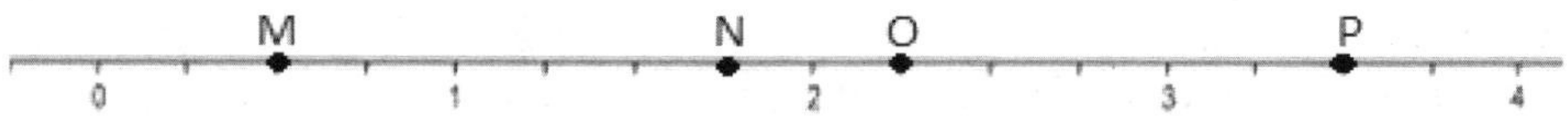

5. C: A reflection is a transformation producing a mirror image. A figure reflected over the x-axis will have its vertices in the form (x, y) transformed to $(x, -y)$. The point W at $(1, -7)$ reflects to W' at $(1,7)$. Only choice C shows $WXYZ$ being carried onto its image $W'X'Y'Z'$ by a reflection across the x-axis. Choice A shows a reflection across the line $y = x$. Choice B shows a 90° counterclockwise rotation about the origin. Choice D shows a reflection across the y-axis.

6. D: The cost per ounce can be calculated by dividing the cost of the bag by the number of ounces the bag contains. Thus, the cost per ounce can be calculated by writing $9.85 ÷ 16, which equals approximately $0.62 per ounce.

7. D: The order of operations states that numbers with exponents must be evaluated first. Thus, the expression can be rewritten as $64 + 12 \div 4 + 64 \times 3$. Next, multiplication and division must be computed as they appear from left to right in the expression. Thus, the expression can be further simplified as $64 + 3 + 192$, which equals 259.

8. C: Both flour and butter are given in cups so they are easy to compare. First find a like denominator. $\frac{1}{2}$ is equal to $\frac{2}{4}$, and $1\frac{3}{4}$ is equal to $\frac{7}{4}$. So the ratio is 2:7.

9. C: The triangle A, when translated parallel to the y-axis by 5 units, produces the triangle B. Adding 5 to the coordinates would raise the y-coordinates the proper amount, but would also translate the triangle parallel to the x-axis by 5 units. Rotation and reflection of the figure would change the relative orientations of the apices, producing non-congruent triangles.

10. 1479 miles: The first day they went 69 miles per hour for 11 hours, so they went $11 \times 69 = 759\ miles$. The second day they went 72 miles per hour for 10 hours, so they went $10 \times 72 = 720\ miles$. Total they went 1479 miles.

11. B: In order to find the unit rate, the cost of the bottle should be divided by the number of fluid ounces contained in the bottle: $\frac{\$3.96}{20} \approx 0.20$. Thus, the cost per fluid ounce is approximately \$0.20.

12. x=4: $3^2 + 2x = 17, 9 + 2x = 17, 2x = 8, x = 4$

13. D: The formula for the surface area of a cylinder is $SA = 2\pi r^2 + 2\pi rh$, where r is the radius and h is the height. Since the cylinder has a diameter of 12 m, the radius is half of the diameter, or 6 m. The height is 9 m. Therefore, $SA = 2\pi(6\ m)^2 + 2\pi(6m)(9\ m)$= 565.2 m² or $5.65x10^2$ m². This can be converted to other units. To convert to centimeters (Answer A), multiply by 100^2 to obtain $5.65x10^6$ cm³. To convert to millimeters (Answer B), multiply by $1{,}000^2$ to obtain $5.65x10^8$ mm³. To convert to kilometers, divide by $1{,}000^2$ to obtain $5.65x10^{-4}$ km³. Answer A does not have the correct number of decimal places. Answers B and C used the diameter in place of the radius.

14. C: The equation that represents the relationship between the position number, n, and the value of the term, a_n, is $a_n = -3n + 8$. Notice each n is multiplied by -3, with 8 added to that value. Substituting position number 1 for n gives $a_n = -3(1) + 8$, which equals 5. Substitution of the remaining position numbers does not provide a counterexample to this procedure.

15. D: Similar figures have a proportional shape but not necessarily the same size, and congruent figures are exactly the same size and shapes. These two figures are neither similar nor congruent.

16. D: The constant amount Kevin pays is \$12.95; this amount represents the y-intercept. The variable amount is represented by the expression $\$0.07x$, where x represents the number of text messages sent and \$0.07 represents the constant rate of change or slope. Thus, his total cost can be represented by the equation $y = \$0.07x + \$12.95$.

17. C: All angles in a quadrilateral add to 360 degrees. Therefore, the other angle is equal to the difference between 360 degrees and the sum of the other three interior angles: $360 - (95 + 97 + 67) = 101$. Thus, the other angle measures 101°.

18. B: The surface area of a rectangular prism may be calculated using the formula $SA = 2lw + 2wh + 2hl$. Substituting the dimensions of 22 centimeters, 5 centimeters, and 8 centimeters gives $SA = 2(22)(8) + 2(8)(5) + 2(5)(22)$. Thus, the surface area is 652 square inches.

19. C: In a parallelogram, consecutive angles are supplementary; that is, the sum of their measures is 180°. Use this to write an equation and then solve for x.

$$\begin{aligned} m\angle A + m\angle B &= 180^\circ \\ (5x) + (2x - 9) &= 180 \\ 7x - 9 &= 180 \\ 7x &= 189 \\ x &= 27 \end{aligned}$$

In a parallelogram, opposite angles are congruent. Thus, $m\angle B = m\angle C$, so find the value of $m\angle B$.

$$\begin{aligned} m\angle B &= 2x - 9 \\ &= 2(27) - 9 \\ &= 45^\circ \end{aligned}$$

Therefore, $m\angle C = 45^\circ$.

20. $\frac{2}{5}$: There are a total of 40 marbles in the bag. The probability of him drawing a red one is $\frac{16}{40}$ or $\frac{2}{5}$.

21. $\frac{2}{3}$**:** If 4 red and 6 blue are missing then there are only 12 red and 18 blue remaining. The probability of drawing a red one then is $\frac{12}{18}$ or $\frac{2}{3}$.

22. The point A(x-3, 5) is (2-3, 5) or (-1, 5). The point B(7-x, -2) is (7-2, -2) or (5, -2). Both are graphed below.

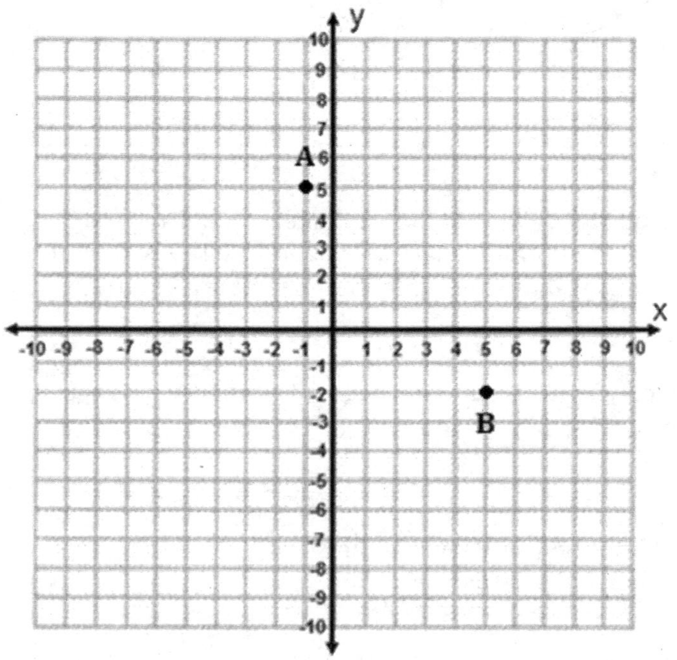

23. $.25: First find the cost of the book at Bookstore A. The price would be $15.25(.8) = $12.20. The cost at Bookstore B is $12.45 so it is $.25 more.

24. C: Similar polygons are polygons for which all corresponding angles are congruent and all corresponding sides are proportional.

25. D: In scientific notation, only one digit should remain to the left of the decimal. In the original number, the decimal point is 4 places to the right of the first digit, 3. Therefore, $30{,}490 = 3.049 \times 10^4$ is the correct answer. Choice C, 30.490×10^3 is equal to the correct value, but incorrectly places two digits to the left of the decimal point.

26. C: A cylinder has two circular bases and a rectangular lateral face.

27. C: If she goes 3.4 miles in $\frac{1}{12}$ of an hour then just multiply by 12 to see how far she will go in one hour. Then that is her miles per hour.

28. A: Start by substituting 4 into the expression. Then evaluate using order of operations.

$$4n^2 + (3n + 5)^2$$
$$4(4)^2 + (3(4) + 5)^2$$
$$4(4)^2 + (12 + 5)^2$$
$$4(4)^2 + (17)^2$$
$$4(16) + (17)^2$$
$$4(16) + (289)$$
$$64 + 289$$
$$353$$

29. A: In choice A, a comparison of the digits in the tenths place shows that 0.2 is greater than both 0.0499 and 0.007. Then, a comparison of the hundredths place shows that 0.0499 is greater than 0.007. Choice B should read $-2 < 0 < 7$. Choice C should read $\frac{1}{3} > \frac{1}{4} > \frac{1}{5}$. Choice D should read $-10 < -4 < -1$. Therefore, the correct answer is choice A.

30. B: The inequality is solved by writing a double inequality equivalent to the given inequality but without the absolute value bars.

$$-9 < x + 6 < 9$$

Solve the double inequality by subtracting 6 from all three parts.

$$-15 < x < 3$$

The solution set can be written using interval notation.

$$(-15,3)$$

31. A: The dimensions of the rectangular prism can be rounded to 14 cm, 9 cm, and 12 cm. The volume of a rectangular prism can be determined by finding the product of the length, width, and height. Therefore, the volume is approximately equal to $14 \times 9 \times 12$, or 1,512 cm^3.

32. C: The volume of a cylindrical can be found using the formula $V = \pi r^2 h$, where r represents the radius and h represents the height. Substitution of the given radius and height gives $V = \pi(3.5)^2 \cdot 8$, which is approximately 307.72. Thus, the volume of the can is approximately 307.72 cm^3.

33. C: To solve, isolate the x on one side of the equation.

$$4x = 36 - 4$$
$$4x = 32$$
$$x = 8$$

34. D: When isolating the variable of a two-step equation, we must first apply the inverse operation for any addition or subtraction. Here, we must apply the inverse of addition, which is subtraction, to both sides of the equation. When we subtract 12 from both sides of the equation, we are left with $5x = 60$. Finally, we must apply the inverse operation of any multiplication or division. In this case, we must apply the inverse of multiplication, which is division. When we divide both sides of the equation by 5 we're left with $x = 12$. We can check our answer by inserting 12 into the original equation. Because $5(12) + 12 = 72$, we know that we have correctly solved for x.

35. A: The events are independent since Sarah replaces the first die. The probability of two independent events can be found using the formula $P(A\ and\ B) = P(A) \cdot P(B)$. The probability of pulling out a blue die is $\frac{2}{12}$. The probability of pulling out a green die is $\frac{4}{12}$. The probability of pulling out a blue die and a green die is $\frac{2}{12} \cdot \frac{4}{12}$, which simplifies to $\frac{1}{18}$.

36. C: The median is the value that splits the data in half. Thus, approximately 50% of the scores are above it and 50% are below it. From the histogram, there are a total of 50 data points, so the median would be located between the 25th and 26th scores when the data are ordered from least to greatest. Counting the frequencies from left to right, the halfway point lies in the interval around 500. Therefore, the median GRE score is approximately 500.

37. D: To solve for x, first isolate the variable by subtracting 8 from both sides.

$$-4x + 8 \geq 48$$
$$-4x \geq 40$$

Then, divide both sides by –4 to solve for x. When an inequality is divided by a negative number, the sign must change directions.

$$\frac{-4x}{-4} \geq \frac{40}{-4}$$
$$x \leq -10$$

38. C: The equation for finding the slope is $\frac{y_2-y_1}{x_2-x_1}$. With the points provided, the equation becomes $\frac{5-2}{3-4}$, or $\frac{3}{-1} = -3$.

39. 15%: First find the cost of the first taco shop by dividing $4.14 by 3, which comes out to $1.38 per taco. Then find the price at the second shop by dividing $4.80 by 4 to get $1.20 per taco. The difference is .$18. To get a percentage divide $.18 by $1.20 and multiply by 100. The first shop cost 15% more than the second.

40. D: The probability of getting an even number is $\frac{3}{6}$. The probability of getting heads is $\frac{1}{2}$. The probability of spinning an even number is $\frac{2}{4}$. The probability of all three occurring can be calculated by multiplying the probabilities of the individual events: $\frac{3}{6} \cdot \frac{1}{2} \cdot \frac{2}{4}$ equals $\frac{1}{8}$.

41. 44: I the spinner must land on a different number each time then the highest three numbers are 12,14, and 18. Added together they equal 44.

42. $\frac{3}{4}$: He has already landed on three of the four numbers so the probability is $\frac{3}{4}$.

43. C: To make solving easier, combine like terms.

$$19x = 35 + 27$$
$$19x = 62$$
$$x = 62 \div 19$$
$$x = 3.26$$

44. A: The slope is the variable in front of the x when the equation is in the following form: $y = mx + b$. We rewrite the equation $5 - 3y = 2x + 8$ by first subtracting 5 from both sides.

$$-3y = 2x + 8$$

Then, divide both sides by –3.

$$y = -\frac{2}{3}x - 1$$

The slope is the number in front of the x, which is $-\frac{2}{3}$.

45. A: First, add 25 to both sides to isolate x.

$$\frac{1}{4}x - 25 \geq 75$$

$$\frac{1}{4}x - 25 + 25 \geq 75 + 25$$

$$\frac{1}{4}x \geq 100$$

Then, multiply both sides by 4 to solve for x.

$$4 \times \frac{1}{4}x \geq 4 \times 100$$

$$x \geq 400$$

46. B: Each of the graphs shows the correct y-intercept of –2, but only graph B shows the correct slope. Using the points $(0, -2)$ and $(1,1)$, the slope of graph B may be written as $m = \frac{1-(-2)}{1-0}$, which simplifies to $m = 3$.

47. C: The volume of a right circular cylinder is $V = \pi r^2 h$. In this case, $25\pi = \pi(5^2)h$, so $h = 1$ cm. The height of the cylinder is equal to 1 centimeter.

48. C: The problem gives the slope of a line and a point it goes through, so it is possible to find the y-intercept with no other information. First, find the equation of the line, using the formula $y = mx + b$. The slope is m, and the values from the point for x and y get substituted in the equation: $0 = \left(-\frac{2}{3}\right)(3) + b$. Solve for b, which is the y-intercept. It can be determined that $b = 2$, so the y-intercept is $y = 2$.

49. B: The discounted price is 25% less than the original price. Therefore, the discounted price can be written as 36.95 – ((0.25)(36.95)), which equals approximately 27.71. Thus, the discounted price of the jacket is $27.71.

50. $29.93: If sales tax is 8% then that can be written as ($27.71)(1.08), which is approximately $29.93.

51. B: The question asks us how many students scored "75 points or fewer" on the math test. This means we are looking for all the data contained in the intervals 61–65, 66–70, and 71–75. From the histogram we may not know the exact scores of these students, but we do know that all the scores contained in these intervals must be 75 points or less. Only 1 student scored between 61 and 65 points, 0 students scored between 66 and 70 points, and 2 students scored between 71 and 75 points. Because $1 + 0 + 2 = 3$, we can conclude that 3 students scored 75 points or fewer on the math test.

52. D: We can use the table to find the linear equation in slope-intercept form, $y = mx + b$, where m is the slope and b is the y-intercept. The table shows the y-intercept (the y-value at $x = 0$) to be –5. The slope is the ratio of the change in y-values to the corresponding change in x-values. As the x-value increases by 1, the y-value increases by 3. Thus, the slope is $\frac{3}{1}$, or 3. So the equation is $y = 3x - 5$.

Only the graphs in choices B and D have a y-intercept at –5. Of these two graphs, only choice D has a y-value increase of 3 for each x-value increase of 1, indicating a slope of 3.

53. C: According to the exponent rule $a^{-n} = \frac{1}{a^n}$, the expression 2^{-3} is equivalent to $\frac{1}{2^3}$. Since $2^3 = 2 \times 2 \times 2 = 8$, this expression is equivalent to $\frac{1}{8}$.

Reading Practice Test

Refer to the following for questions 1–10:

ADVENTURE LAND CHASE

(1) I had been waiting for Saturday afternoon for what seemed forever. I had the date circled on the calendar in the kitchen, and my mom even let me cross off the days leading up to it. Every day when I would walk into the kitchen, I would see the date circled in a bright green marker and get even more excited.

(2) Saturday was the day that Adventure Land was opening. It is the largest theme park in three states, has massive rollercoaster's that travel at super speed and loop three times, and has a full water park. But it wasn't just the grand opening of Adventure Land about which I was excited. Saturday was also my best friend Riley's birthday, and to celebrate, she was having her birthday party at Adventure Land.

(3) I woke up very early Saturday morning because I could not sleep. I kept thinking about all the rides that we would go on, the games we were going to play, but more than anything, spending time with all of my friends. While I was eating my cereal, my mom packed us a large bag filled with things she said we were going to need at the theme park all day. She packed sunscreen, sunglasses, and water bottles. I didn't pay attention, because I was still too excited about the biggest rollercoaster, the Slithering Cobra. It was the one that shot up really high and had three loops. It was going to be so much fun!

(4) When we first got to the park, my first thought was that it was a lot bigger than I thought it was going to be. It was huge! I could see the tops of the rollercoasters from the car in the parking lot. Inside, everything was made to look like a jungle. There were lots of different kinds of trees, both real and fake, there were long green vines draped across the park like telephone lines, and the workers were dressed up as if they were going on safari. The park was so big, and there was so much to do, but then I noticed one huge problem. There were so many people in the park. Everywhere I looked, there were more people. I was even bumped a few times while we stood at the entrance.

(5) Riley's mom gave all of us wristbands and said that we had to stay with one of our friends at all times.

(6) "Have a buddy," she said. "If anyone gets lost, come to the food court. We will meet at Lickin' Fried Chicken at one o'clock."

(7) Riley was my buddy, and we immediately ran off to go ride the Slithering Cobra.

(8) "Wait up," Charlotte and Ryan called. "We want to come too!"

(9) We stood in line for the ride for over half an hour. There were so many people, and more people kept coming.

(10) "I'm hot," Riley said.

(11) "This is boring," Ryan complained.

(12) When we finally were at the front of the line, the gates opened, and we were allowed to take our seats. Since it was Riley's birthday, they let us ride in the front seats. The rollercoaster took off really fast and went straight into the air. It stopped at the top of the tracks, and it felt

as if we were going to fall out of our seats! The rollercoaster tipped over the edge, and soon we were rushing toward the ground. Riley put her arms up, and we both started screaming. The coaster then went straight up and into the three loops. Before we knew it, we were back at the platform, and the ride was over.

(13) "That was awesome!" Charlotte yelled.

(14) "I want to go again!" Ryan added.

(15) We looked at the line, and it had doubled since we had gotten there.

(16) "Maybe later," I said.

(17) When we got off the ride and were walking toward the arcade, our friend Natalie came running up to us. She looked really worried.

(18) "I've lost him," she said. "I lost George! I wasn't supposed to leave him, but I went to the bathroom and now I can't find him!"

(19) "Did you go to the food court?" Ryan asked.

(20) "Yes, and he wasn't there!" she said.

(21) I didn't know what to do. The park was so big, and there were so many people.

(22) "We will have to retrace your steps," Charlotte said. "Where were you the last time you saw him?"

(23) "In the arcade. Playing skee ball."

(24) We all started running toward the arcade, which was shaped like a giant tiger.

(25) "Make sure we all stay together!" Ryan called.

(26) It was really hot, and the sun was beating down right on our faces. I probably should have thought about putting on my sunglasses, but all I could think of was George.

(27) "Who is George?" Riley asked me while we were running.

(28) "I thought you knew!" I said. "I have no idea. Maybe her brother?"

(29) It felt really nice to be inside of the arcade. It looked just like a jungle, too. I kept thinking there was no way we were going to find him, but we had to try. We ran up a flight of stairs and across the room to the skee ball games.

(30) "There he is!" Natalie pointed forward. We didn't see anything. She ran to one of the alleys and picked up a large stuffed monkey. It was George, the stuffed animal from our homeroom that one student has to take home every weekend and write a story about their adventures. We were bewildered.

(31) "That's the George you were talking about?" Riley whined.

(32) "Of course. Mrs. Miller would have killed me if I lost him! But now I have a great adventure to write about!" she said.

(33) We looked at Natalie and laughed.

(34) "Let's go on another ride," I said, and we all started walking back into the jungle.

1. What is the first reason the narrator gives to explain why she was excited about Saturday?

a. It was her best friend's birthday
b. She was going to the beach
c. Adventure Land was opening
d. She was going to have the class's stuffed animal

2. In paragraph 3, the author creates a mood of:

a. Anger
b. Frustration
c. Unease
d. Excitement

3. Paragraphs 1-3 are mainly about:

a. Why the narrator is looking forward to Saturday
b. The fun attractions in the narrator's state
c. Why Adventure Land is fun
d. Who is coming to the party

4. The narrator uses the words "vines" and "safari" to explain that:

a. It is hot outside
b. The theme of the park is the jungle
c. The park is decorated nicely
d. The children are not at home

5. Why were the children allowed to ride in the front seat of the rollercoaster?

a. They had been waiting a really long time
b. They were in the line for the front seat
c. They ran and reached the seat the quickest
d. It was their friend's birthday

6. Why does the narrator discuss the number of people at the park?

a. To explain why it was important to not get lost
b. To explain the popularity of the park
c. To justify her complaints about waiting in line
d. To explain that it was hot

7. What is the children's main conflict in this selection?

a. Beating the crowds to get in line for the best ride
b. Wearing sunscreen
c. Trying to find a friend they think is lost
d. Meeting their parents for lunch

8. Why does Ryan ask Natalie if she has been to the food court?

a. He is hungry and wants to know if the food is good
b. It is where they were supposed to go if they were lost
c. It is time to meet up for lunch
d. He thinks she should talk to one of the parents

9. In paragraph 30, what does the word bewildered mean?

a. Happy
b. Upset
c. Confused
d. Numb

10. How is the conflict of the story resolved?

a. The children find George
b. The lines on the rides become shorter
c. The children don't care about a stuffed animal
d. The children leave the park

Refer to the following for questions 11–16:

Happily Never After

(1) The tragic story of two star-crossed lovers was first brought to attention in William Shakespeare's play, Romeo and Juliet.

(2) The entire plot of the play is explained in the prologue. It is stated that there are two households of equal status in Verona, Italy. There is an ancient feud between the two families that has progressed into the younger generations, meaning the fight between the parents has now become the fight between the parents' children. The narrator continues, saying, "A pair of star-crossed lovers take their life" and in doing so, end their parents' feud. Romeo and Juliet, a child of each household, fall in love, but cannot live happily together because of the feud. The feud is ended, but it is an act that only the death of these children could make happen.

(3) The majority of stories that audiences enjoy have a happy ending. From childhood, people have grown up with the expectation of an ending that comes with the phrase, "And they lived happily ever after." It is interesting that the story of Romeo and Juliet, a famous tragedy, has extreme popularity and interest among both storytellers and audiences. This raises the question of fascination with tragedy.

(4) In the last act of the play, Juliet has faked her death to escape marriage to another man. A message is supposed to be sent to Romeo explaining that she is alive with a plan for their escape. The message, however, does not reach Romeo. In his despair that he has lost his love, he comes to Juliet's side, drinks poison, and dies. Moments later, Juliet wakes up to find Romeo dead. In her grief, she takes his dagger and kills herself.

(5) Within the prologue, the first moments of the play, the audience is told that the main characters die. It is an interesting way of storytelling. The plot has been ruined, and there is no suspense. The audience is told that Romeo and Juliet die, and in doing so, end their parents' feud. The audience, however, remains, and watches the events take place, even though they know the ending and that it will not be happy.

(6) It is therefore logical to assume that audiences want to believe that a story will end happily, even though they are given evidence that it will not. Audiences will watch the entire play, hoping that something will be done so that the lovers can be saved. And yet, as the prologue stated, the message is not delivered, and the only way that Romeo and Juliet can be together is in death. Their deaths had to take place before the ancient feud would end.

(7) The theme of tragic love has been repeated throughout literary history, although perhaps not brought to the extreme of Romeo and Juliet. Although audiences enjoy stories with a happy ending, the popularity of tragic themes proves that audiences also enjoy stories that do not end happily. It is the hope for happiness that gives tragedies strength, and the hope that things will end differently.

11. Paragraph 2 helps the reader to understand:

a. The characters in Romeo and Juliet
b. The conflict and plot in Romeo and Juliet
c. The mood and tone in Romeo and Juliet
d. The theme of Romeo and Juliet

12. What does the word feud mean in paragraph 5?

a. Fight
b. Happiness
c. Sadness
d. Wealth

13. What is the author's main argument?

a. Romeo and Juliet is a great play
b. Audiences will still hope a tragic story will end happily
c. Tragedies are not as good as stories that have a happy ending
d. Prologues should not ruin the story

14. The author explains that Romeo believes Juliet to be dead because:

a. He watched her take his dagger
b. She drank poison
c. She was ill on her wedding day
d. He never received the message explaining that she faked her death

15. Why does the author think that the prologue in Romeo and Juliet is "an interesting way of storytelling"?

a. The prologue explains that the play is a tragedy
b. The prologue explains how the story will end
c. The prologue is very long
d. The prologue asks the audience a question

16. Why, according to the prologue and author, are Romeo and Juliet's deaths necessary?

a. To make the play a tragedy
b. To show the dangers of poison
c. To end their parents' feud
d. To earn more money and power

Refer to the following for questions 17–24:

THE RESPONSIBILITIES OF BEES

(1) While some people see bees as a nuisance or just another insect, they are a crucial part of the global ecosystem and survival. They support human and animal life through their role in food production and help maintain healthy habitats in a variety of ecosystems. Their ability to pollinate plants, provide resources for animals, and support biodiversity are their most important roles.

(2) Bats, birds, and a variety of insects pollinate plants, but bees are responsible for around 80% of global pollination. Pollinators transfer pollen from the male organs of one plant to the female organs of another. Pollination occurs when plants become fertilized and develop seeds. Fruits and vegetables then develop around the seed and grow into the produce that we find at grocery stores and farmer's markets. Bees are one of the most important pollinators. They move from flower to flower transferring pollen while they search for nectar. Without bees, food as we know it would change. Many of the fruits and vegetables we enjoy rely on bees to grow, so without bees the amount of food grown would significantly decrease.

(3) Not only would this impact us by reducing the amount of available food, but it would also hurt farmers economically. If the amount of food a farmer was able to grow decreased because of a decline in the bee population, they would not make enough money to support their farm. Even though there are other animals and insects that help with pollination, they aren't as effective as bees. If there were no more bees, most plants would have to be pollinated by hand to compensate for all of the work they do. The pollen would need to be manually transferred from one plant to another. This would take a lot of time, manpower, and money. The low supply of food would drive up the cost, hurting the consumers as well.

(4) We aren't the only ones who enjoy the fruits and vegetables bees help grow! Many animals eat fruits and vegetables just like us, so they need bees to keep pollinating too. Bees also play a direct role in supporting animal life and habitats. While we need an abundance of bees for our crops to thrive, it is necessary that some are eaten by birds, small mammals, and other insects as part of the food web. If the bee population were to disappear, an important food source for these animals would too. This could cause animals that rely on the bees to begin starving to death or consuming other insects and animals, further disrupting the ecosystem. Changes in food webs are capable of decimating entire species and ecosystems.

(5) Biodiversity is the variety of life found on Earth. This doesn't just include people and animals, but plants, insects, and all living organisms. Bees' role in supporting biodiversity is

highlighted in the foods they help produce and the animals they help support, but it also goes beyond that. The seeds produced by the fertilized plants that were mentioned earlier continue to spread and grow new plants, allowing plant life cycles to continue. Sometimes bees help with spreading these seeds in a process known as seed dispersal. The seeds become attached to the bees while they collect nectar and fall off as they fly to another plant. This helps the seeds spread to new places. Not only does this create food for animals, but also habitats. The plants that grow as a result of seed dispersal create grassy, plant-filled homes for animals in a variety of ecosystems like meadows, forests, and grasslands.

(6) Even though bees are not the only pollinators, they're the most important ones. Bees keep our food sources and ecosystems stable! We need to maintain the bee population in order to keep the Earth and its inhabitants safe, healthy, and happy.

17. Based on the information in the passage, what can the reader infer about bees?

a. The total loss of bees is not preventable.
b. Pollinators can be completely replaced by people.
c. Bees are capable of destroying crops.
d. Protecting bees is beneficial to everyone.

18. Which sentence from the passage best supports the idea that bees support biodiversity?

a. They move from flower to flower transferring pollen while they search for nectar.
b. The plants that grow as a result of seed dispersal create grassy, plant-filled homes for animals in a variety of ecosystems like meadows, forests, and grasslands.
c. Many animals eat fruits and vegetables just like us, so they need bees to keep pollinating too.
d. Many of the fruits and vegetables we enjoy rely on bees to grow, so without bees the amount of food grown would significantly decrease.

19. What is the most likely reason that the author uses a cause-and-effect structure in paragraph 3?

a. To illustrate the financial impact that the loss of bees can have
b. To reveal the importance of bees in many food webs
c. To outline the process for manual pollination
d. To suggest solutions for increasing the bee population

20. What is the most likely reason the author wrote "The Responsibilities of Bees"?

a. To highlight the ways that bees are harmful
b. To describe the importance of bee movement
c. To highlight the worldwide impact of bees
d. To show why so many people appreciate bees

21. What is the controlling idea of this passage?

a. Pollination by bees is required for crops to grow on their own.
b. How diverse a habitat is depends on how many bees are present.
c. Bees support the survival of plants and animals worldwide.
d. Bees are the most efficient pollinators in most ecosystems.

22. Which detail from the selection supports the key idea that bees are an essential part of Earth's global ecosystem?

a. If the amount of food a farmer was able to grow decreased because of a decline in the bee population, they would not make enough money to support their farm.
b. Bats, birds, and a variety of insects pollinate plants, but bees are responsible for around 80% of global pollination.
c. Bees' role in supporting biodiversity is highlighted in the foods they help produce and the animals they help support, but it also goes beyond that.
d. Sometimes bees help with spreading these seeds in a process known as seed dispersal.

23. What is the best summary of this passage?

a. Bees are the most important pollinator. They pollinate the majority of the Earth's plant life. Without them, the cost of producing food would increase. This would harm the economy.
b. Bees are an important part of the global ecosystem. They support animal and human life and maintain a balance in a variety of habitats. Without them, the world as we know it would be very different.
c. Bees help seeds from plants spread across large areas. They then grow and develop into habitats that support biodiversity. Without bees, many organisms would not have homes or food.
d. Bees are a part of the food web in several different habitats. This means that animals and other insects eat them as a source of energy. If bees went extinct, the food web would not be complete.

24. Why did the author most likely use a cause-and-effect structure in this passage?

a. To show the connections between humans and animals
b. To highlight the possible effect of a decline in the bee population
c. To present bees as solutions to pollination problems
d. To demonstrate how animals and humans rely on bees differently

Refer to the following for questions 25–31:

Musically Inclined

(1) Gibson thought, at least, that it could have been worse. His parents could have named him Fender, given him the middle name Les Paul, or worse yet, Stratocaster. This was a small comfort to him as he reminded himself that he really never had a chance. It was not he who chose the music. He was born into it, and even named after one of the most famous guitars. It was like the music had found him.

(2) Gibson could not remember a time when he did not know how to play music. His mother was a singer when she was younger, and his father played the lead guitar in the band Mookie Harper. Growing up, he learned to read music at the same time he learned to read words. Music felt as natural to him as walking and was a big part of his life.

(3) There were many instruments in Gibson's house, and over the years, he had learned how to play most of them. He started with a piano when he was very young, moved to the harmonica and drums when he was a bit older, and had just begun learning how to play the violin. But Gibson's favorite instrument was the one he had been playing the longest: his father's Gibson Les Paul guitar.

(4) At school, Gibson felt lonely most days. His family had just moved from Seattle, and the other kids at school thought it was weird that he carried a violin case to school for his fourth period music class. At his old school, he was in the school band, and had a lot of friends who enjoyed playing music with him.

(5) "Why would you play the violin?" Joe asked as he snickered in his chair. "Only girls play that. I bet it was the only thing you could learn," he laughed. The rest of the class laughed behind him.

(6) Gibson sat in his chair and rolled his eyes. He thought that this kid obviously didn't know anything about music, because the violin was one of the most challenging instruments to learn. He left the case on the floor by his chair and waited for his second period history class to begin.

(7) The teacher walked into the classroom pushing a cart. Gibson immediately sat up in his chair. He knew exactly what was in the cases and smiled.

(8) "I was able to borrow these from the music section of the museum to show you today," Ms. Conway said. "Can anyone tell me what these are?" she asked.

(9) "They are guitars, Ms. Conway. Duh," Joe, a boy in the back of the room, said. The class laughed.

(10) Ms. Conway squinted her eyes at Joe. "He is half right," she said. "These are in fact guitars. But can anyone tell me what kind of guitars they are?" She looked around the room. Everyone sat still.

(11) "The one on the right is a 1958 Gibson Les Paul," Gibson said out of the silence. "And the one of the left is a vintage Fender Stratocaster from 1954. Oh, and they are electric guitars," he said.

(12) The class looked at Gibson and stared in silence. Ms. Conway clapped her hands together. "Wow! You're right, Gibson. Great job!"

(13) "How'd you know that?" a girl asked behind him.

(14) "My dad has both of them," he said. "And I've been playing them since I was little."

(15) "You can play the guitar?" Joe laughed. "Yeah right! You play the violin!" He looked around, but no one else was laughing.

(16) "Would you like to play something?" Ms. Conway asked. Gibson looked down at his feet. He didn't know what to say. He just wanted to stay in his seat and have no one look at him.

(17) But then he thought of his dad and smiled. "I'll play the Les Paul," he said. "It's my favorite."

(18) He walked toward the front of the class and picked up the guitar. He played the opening notes of "Gone into the Sun." It was his favorite Mookie Harper song. All of the children sat in awe as they watched him play, and when he was done, they all started clapping and cheering.

(19) "Maybe I'll start playing the violin," the boy next to him said. "If it will get me to play a guitar like that!"

25. Paragraphs 1 through 3 are mainly about:

a. How music has inspired Gibson's family and his life
b. How Gibson will be in a band one day
c. How Gibson wanted to be named after a Fender guitar
d. Why Gibson is moving schools

26. This story is told in what point of view?

a. First-person limited
b. First-person omniscient
c. Third-person omniscient
d. Third-person limited

27. Why did the narrator include the detail that the family was from Seattle?

a. To show why the family loves music
b. To show that Gibson was a new student
c. To show that the family moves a lot because of the father's band
d. To show that the family is on vacation

28. What does Gibson mean when he assumes that he "never really had a chance?"

a. That he was destined to play music because of his family and his name
b. That he was never going to be good at playing the violin
c. That he was never going to be popular at school
d. That he is going to be in a band one day like his father

29. In paragraph 16, why did Gibson want to sit in his seat?

a. He did not like the guitar and did not want to play it
b. He did not want the attention of the other children to be on him
c. He wanted to play the violin instead
d. He thought the guitar was too old to play

30. The author arranges this selection by:

a. Explaining how Gibson grew to like to play the violin
b. Showing how Gibson taught his classmates how to play guitar
c. Listing why the children laughed at Gibson
d. Describing how his love for music helped Gibson be himself at school

31. How is the internal conflict in the story resolved?

a. Gibson is himself and is liked by his classmates
b. Gibson decides not to play in front of everyone
c. Gibson decides to start a band with people in his class
d. Gibson plays a song for his dad

Refer to the following for questions 32–39:

This is an essay that Timmy has written on why he feels books will soon be a thing of the past:

The Inventions of Technology

(1) Stories have been a part of the world since the beginning of recorded time. For centuries before the invention of the printing press, stories of the world were passed down to generations through oral tradition. With the invention of the printing press, which made written material available to wide ranges of audiences, books were mass-produced and introduced into greater society.

(2) For the last several centuries, books have been at the forefront of education and entertainment. With the invention of the Internet, reliance on books for information quickly changed. Soon, almost everything that anyone needed to know could be accessed through the Internet. Large printed volumes of encyclopedias became unnecessary as all of the information was easily available on the Internet.

(3) Despite the progression of the Internet, printed media was still very popular in the forms of both fiction and non-fiction books. While waiting for an appointment, enduring a several-hour flight, or relaxing before sleep, books have been a reliable and convenient source of entertainment, and one that society has not been willing to give up.

(4) With the progression and extreme convenience of technology, printed books are going to soon become a thing of the past. Inventions such as the iPad from Macintosh and the Kindle have made the need for any kind of printed media unnecessary. With a rechargeable battery, a large screen, and the ability to have several books saved on file, electronic options will soon take over and society will no longer see printed books.

(5) Although some people may say that the act of reading is not complete without turning a page, sliding a finger across the screen or pressing a button to read more onto the next page is just as satisfying to the reader. The iPad and Kindle are devices that have qualities similar to a computer and can be used for so much more than just reading. These devices are therefore better than books because they have multiple uses.

(6) In a cultural society that is part of the world and due to a longstanding tradition, stories will always be an important way to communicate ideas and provide information and entertainment. Centuries ago, stories could only be remembered and retold through speech. Printed media changed the way the world communicated and was connected, and now, as we move forward with technology, it is only a matter of time before we must say goodbye to the printed past and welcome the digital and electronic future.

32. What is the main argument of this essay?

a. iPad and Kindles are easier to read than books
b. The printing press was a great invention
c. The Internet is how people receive information
d. Technology will soon replace printed material

33. What is the main purpose of paragraph 1?

a. To explain oral tradition
b. To explain the importance of the printing press
c. To explain the progression of stories within society
d. To introduce the essay

34. What does the word enduring mean in paragraph 3?

a. Quitting
b. Undergo
c. Sleeping
d. Thriving

35. According to the essay, what was the first way that stories were communicated and passed down?

a. Oral tradition
b. Printed books
c. Technology
d. Hand writing

36. According to the essay, what changed the reliance on books?

a. Inventions such as the iPad
b. The printing press
c. The Internet
d. Volumes of encyclopedias

37. Which of the following statements is an opinion?

a. Despite the progression of the Internet, printed media was still very popular in the forms of both fiction and non-fiction books
b. Although some people may say that the act of reading is not complete without turning a page, sliding a finger across the screen or pressing a button to read more onto the next page is just as satisfying to the reader
c. With the invention of the Internet, reliance on books for information quickly changed
d. Stories have been a part of the world since the beginning of recorded time

38. How is the essay organized?

a. The author explains details as to why he wants to have an iPad
b. The author explains how stories eventually let into oral tradition
c. The author explains technology to explain why books are not needed
d. The author explains the history of stories within society and the ways they progress with time

39. Which of the following statements is not an example of a categorical claim?

a. With a rechargeable battery, a large screen, and the ability to have several books saved on file, electronic options will soon take over and society will no longer see printed books.
b. Soon, almost everything that anyone needed to know could be accessed through the Internet.
c. The iPad and Kindle are devices that have qualities similar to a computer and can be used for so much more than just reading.
d. With the progression and extreme convenience of technology, printed books are going to soon become a thing of the past.

Refer to the following for questions 40–45:

The Educational Market Town

(1) Aberystwyth is a market town on the West Coast of Wales within the United Kingdom. A market town refers to European areas that have the right to have markets, which differentiates it from a city or village. The town is located where two rivers meet, the River Ystwyth and River Rheidol and is the best known as an educational center, housing an established university since 1872.

(2) The town is situated between North Wales and South Wales, and is a large vacation destination as well as tourist attraction. Constitution Hill is a hill on the north end of Aberystwyth, which provides excellent views of Cardigan Bay and which is supported by the Aberystwyth Electric Cliff Railway. Although Aberystwyth is known as a modern Welsh town, it is home to several historic buildings, such as the remnants of a castle.

(3) Although there are several grocery, clothing, sporting goods, and various other miscellaneous shops, Aberystwyth is best known for its educational services. Aberystwyth University, formerly known as University College Wales, as well as the National Library of Wales, which is the legal deposit library for Wales and which houses all Welsh publications, are both located within Aberystwyth. The two main languages traditionally spoken in Aberystwyth are English and Welsh. With local live music, arts center, and educational opportunities in gorgeous scenery, Aberystwyth is a hidden luxury within the United Kingdom.

40. What is the purpose of this essay?

a. To explain that the university was established in 1872
b. To explain the legal deposit library in Wales
c. To provide a portrait of a town
d. To explain the views in Aberystwyth

41. What does the word situated mean in paragraph 2?

a. located
b. fighting
c. luxurious
d. hidden

42. Which of the following statements is an opinion?

a. Although Aberystwyth is known as a modern Welsh town, it is home to several historic buildings, such as the remnants of a castle
b. With local live music, arts center, and educational opportunities in gorgeous scenery, Aberystwyth is a hidden luxury within the United Kingdom
c. The two main languages traditionally spoken in Aberystwyth are English and Welsh
d. Aberystwyth is a market town on the West Coast of Wales within the United Kingdom

43. How many languages are traditionally spoken in Aberystwyth?

a. One
b. Two
c. Three
d. More than three

44. What makes Aberystwyth a market town?

a. It is a city
b. It is a village
c. It has the right to have a market
d. There are markets in town every day

45. What is Constitution Hill supported by?

a. Cardigan Bay
b. The ocean
c. North Wales
d. Aberystwyth Electric Cliff Railway

Answer Key and Explanations for the Reading Test

1. C: In the first sentence in paragraph 2, it is stated that "Saturday was the day Adventure Land was opening." In paragraph 1, the narrator explains that she is excited and later states that Saturday is her friend's birthday, but the first reason given is that Adventure Land is opening.

2. D: The narrator provides many examples of her excitement throughout paragraph 3, such as that she could not sleep and was not listening to her mom because she was thinking about all of the fun things she was going to do.

3. A: The narrator begins the essay by stating that she was looking forward to Saturday, and the following paragraphs explain why. Although other elements are explained, the main focus is why Saturday is exciting.

4. B: Words like "vines" and "safari" bring about images that reflect the jungle. The narrator explained that the amusement park was decorated in the theme of the jungle and used these words to help create the image.

5. D: In paragraph 12, the narrator states that since it was her friend's birthday, they were allowed to ride in the front seats.

6. A: The narrator mentions being lost several times throughout the essay, and the central conflict is when the children think someone is lost. The narrator explains that there are many people in the park to create an image that it would be easy to get lost, which would be bad.

7. C: Paragraphs 17-26 explain the conflict the children have when they think someone is lost. They become very worried and try to find George. The narrator mentions earlier that Riley's mother did not want anyone lost, and so the conflict is to find the lost friend.

8. B: Natalie was with George and the children assume that she was his buddy. In paragraph 6, Riley's mother states that if anyone gets lost, they should go to the food court. Since George is lost, the children assume he must have gone to the food court.

9. C: Bewildered means to become confused. Since the children were expecting George to be a person, they were confused to find a stuffed animal.

10. A: The conflict of the story is trying to find George, who is lost. The conflict is resolved when George is found.

11. B: Paragraph 2 explains all of the information that is in the prologue, and the author says that the prologue provides the plot of the play. The conflict is also explained in discussing the feud between the families.

12. A: Feud means disagreement, argument, or fight.

13. B: Paragraphs 6 and 7 explain that the author believes that even though they watch a play with the understanding that it will be tragic, they continue to watch it because they hope it will end happily.

14. D: In paragraph 4, the author explains that Juliet faked her death and that Romeo does not receive the message.

15. B: In paragraph 5, the author explains that it is interesting to explain at the beginning of the play that Romeo and Juliet die and that their deaths end their parents' feud.

16. C: In paragraph 2, the narrator explains that the prologue states that Romeo and Juliet take their lives and in doing so, end their parents' feud.

17. D: This passage describes the roles that bees play and explains how they benefit the Earth's inhabitants. The passage shows that bees keep the systems that provide people with food stable, and that bees help flowers and animals get the things they need. Therefore, the reader can infer that protecting bees benefits everyone, so choice D is correct. Choice A is incorrect because the statements in the passage do not suggest that losing all bees is unpreventable. Choice B is also incorrect. The passage mentions that plants would have to be hand pollinated by humans if bees went extinct. However, the passage describes other roles that pollinators play, so it cannot be assumed that they can be replaced by people. Bees support crops by pollinating the plants and assisting in reproduction. The passage does not suggest that their behavior can destroy or harm crops, so choice C is incorrect.

18. B: The passage defines biodiversity as "the variety of life found on Earth" and explains that this refers to all living organisms. Bees' ability to help create supportive homes for a variety of living organisms through seed dispersal best demonstrates their role in supporting biodiversity. This makes choice B correct. Choice A defines the process of pollination. It does not show that bees support a wide variety of organisms, so it is incorrect. Choices C and D are incorrect as they only focus on bees' role in food production. These statements do not show that bees make it possible for a wide variety of organisms to live as clearly as choice B does, so choices C and D are incorrect.

19. A: The third paragraph uses a cause-and-effect structure to explain what would happen to farmers and the economy if the bee population declined. The loss of bees would cause fewer plants to grow, causing food prices to rise. It would also require farms to pay for plants to be manually pollinated. Choice B is incorrect. The importance of bees in food webs is explained in paragraph 4. Choice C is incorrect. While manual pollination is mentioned in paragraph 3, the structure of the paragraph does not outline the process. Paragraph 3 does not contain solutions for increasing the bee population, making choice D incorrect.

20. C: The author most likely wrote this passage to highlight the worldwide impact of bees. The passage explains how bees can support all forms of life, so choice C is correct. Choice A is incorrect. This passage does not explain any harmful, or otherwise negative, effects of bees. The movement of bees is discussed and explained as important in both pollinating and seed dispersal. However, this is not the main message of the passage. This makes choice B incorrect. The author does not discuss people's appreciation of bees in the passage. In fact, the author suggests that some people find them to be a nuisance, making choice D incorrect.

21. C: The passage explains why plants and animals are dependent on bees for survival. The introduction also states that bees support animal and plant life, so C is the best answer. Choice A comes from the third paragraph and does not show the purpose of the entire passage. Choice B refers to the biodiversity explained in paragraph five, which is also a detail and not the point of the whole passage. Choice D is incorrect. The efficiency of bees is referenced in the passage, but it is not what the passage is about.

22. B: The idea that bees are an essential part of the ecosystem is supported by the statement that bees are responsible for 80% of global pollination. This shows the widespread need for bees. Choice A shows that the loss of bees could have a financial impact on farmers, not the ecosystem. This makes choice A incorrect. Choice C shows that bees can support biodiversity, but it does not show that biodiversity and bees' role in it are essential to preserving the ecosystem. Choice C is incorrect. Choice D describes another important role bees play, but it is incorrect because it does not explain the global impact of seed dispersal.

23. B: Choice B best summarizes the passage. It covers the main ideas from the passage, including the fact that bees support human life, animal life, and habitats. It also explains that the world would be different without bees. Choice A is incorrect because it only focuses on the economic issues associated with the loss of bees. Choice C is incorrect because it is only focused on how bees support biodiversity. Choice D discusses the food web and the roles bees play, but doesn't mention any other ways bees support the environment, so it is incorrect. Choices A, C, and D only discuss one idea from the passage, while choice B summarizes all of these ideas.

24. B: The cause-and-effect structure shows the reader what effects a decline in the bee population may have. This allows the reader to understand what the world would be like without bees, so choice B is correct. While the passage describes connections between humans and animals, this is not the purpose of the passage. It is also not made clear by the cause-and-effect structure, so choice A is incorrect. Choice C is incorrect because the passage does not present bees as a solution to pollination problems. Instead, it describes changes in bee populations as the problem. Though the passage explains why bees are important to both humans and animals, this is not explained through causes and effects, so choice D incorrect.

25. A: Paragraph 1 discusses how Gibson was named and that he was born into music. Paragraph 2 discusses music within his parent's lives. Paragraph 3 discusses how he came to play instruments.

26. D: The story is third-person limited as it is not told in the first-person, by Gibson or any other character, and the narrator only knows the thoughts and feelings of one character, Gibson.

27. B: Paragraph 4 states that Gibson's family had just moved from Seattle, which explains that he is a new student in the school.

28. A: Paragraph 1 discusses music in Gibson's life and the fact that he was born into music through his family and even his name. He thinks that it was the music that chose him, and because of this, he "never really had a chance" to not have music be very involved in his life.

29. B: The narrator explains that Gibson wanted to stay in his seat and have no one look at him. He did not want the attention of the other children.

30. D: From the beginning of the essay, the narrator states that music was always a part of Gibson's life and helped shaped his interests. The essay moves into discussing Gibson at a new school, and eventually how his love of music helps him to be himself at school.

31. A: The conflict in the story is that as a new student, Gibson is teased by his fellow classmates. By showing his love of music as well as his talent, Gibson is himself and is liked by his classmates.

32. D: The main argument is stated in paragraph 4: "With the progression and extreme convenience of technology, printed books are going to soon become a thing of the past."

33. C: Paragraph 1 explains how stories have progressed, beginning with oral tradition and past the invention of the printing press. In context with the rest of the essay, this paragraph is important in explaining how stories progress and are provided within society.

34. B: Enduring means to put up with something unpleasant. Within the sentence, the phrase, "enduring a several hour flight," the word enduring, means to undergo.

35. A: In paragraph 1, it is stated that oral tradition was the main medium for storytelling before the invention of the printing press.

36. C: In paragraph 2, it is stated that reliance on books for information was changed with the invention of the Internet.

37. B: It is not a fact that "sliding a finger across the screen or pressing a button to move onto the next page is just as satisfying to the reader." Satisfaction is not something universal that can be proven for every reader. This statement is an opinion.

38. D: In the beginning of the essay, the author explains how stories were passed through oral tradition. This was changed by the printing press, which is becoming less important with technology and the invention of the Internet and devices such as the iPad and Kindle.

39. C: A categorical claim is an arguable understanding of facts, rather than an absolute fact. The statement regarding the qualities of the iPad and Kindle is the only statement that is a fact.

40. C: The essay provides information on various aspects of the town of Aberystwyth, providing a portrait of the town as a whole.

41. A: Situated means to be placed in a certain location.

42. B: In an essay that is factual, proclaiming that the scenery is "gorgeous" or that a town is a "hidden luxury" is an opinion.

43. B: Paragraph 3 states that two main languages are traditionally spoken in Aberystwyth.

44. C: Paragraph 1 states, "A market town refers to European areas that have the right to have markets, which differentiates it from a city or village."

45. D: Paragraph 2 states, "Constitution Hill is a hill on the north end of Aberystwyth, which provides excellent views of Cardigan Bay and which is supported by the Aberystwyth Electric Cliff Railway."

Online Resources

Due to our efforts to try to keep this book to a manageable length, we've created a link that will give you access to all of your online resources:

mometrix.com/resources719/vsolg7

It's Your Moment, Let's Celebrate It!

Share your story @mometrixtestpreparation